Electricity Market Reform in Norway

Also by Eivind Magnus

ECONOMIC INCENTIVES AND PUBLIC FIRM BEHAVIOR (*with Eimar Hope and Richard Matland*)

AN INTERNATIONAL REVIEW OF INSTITUTIONAL REFORM IN THE ELECTRICITY SECTOR (*with Mark Davis*)

MANAGING SOCIAL AND ENVIRONMENTAL OBLIGATIONS IN LIBERALIZED MARKETS (*with Mark Davis*)

Also by Atle Midttun

APPROACHES TO AND DILEMMAS IN REGULATION (*editor with Eirik Svindland*)

EUROPEAN ELECTRICITY SYSTEMS IN TRANSITION: A Comparative Analysis of Energy Forecasting in Western Europe and North America (*editor*)

THE POLITICS OF ELECTRICITY FORECASTING: A Comparative Study of Energy Forecasting in Western Europe and North America (*editor with Thomas Baumgartner*)

Electricity Market Reform in Norway

Edited by

Eivind Magnus
Partner and Director
ECON Centre for Economic Analysis
Oslo
Norway

and

Atle Midttun
Professor
Norwegian School of Management
Sandvika
Norway

palgrave
macmillan

Softcover reprint of the hardcover 1st edition 2000 978-0-333-77772-5

Published by
PALGRAVE MACMILLAN
Houndmills, Basingstoke, Hampshire RG21 6XS and
175 Fifth Avenue, New York, N. Y. 10010
Companies and representatives throughout the world

PALGRAVE MACMILLAN is the global academic imprint of the Palgrave Macmillan division of St. Martin's Press, LLC and of Palgrave Macmillan Ltd. Macmillan® is a registered trademark in the United States, United Kingdom and other countries. Palgrave is a registered trademark in the European Union and other countries.

ISBN 978-1-349-41752-0 ISBN 978-0-333-98274-7 (eBook)
DOI 10.1057/9780333982747

This book is printed on paper suitable for recycling and made from fully managed and sustained forest sources.

A catalogue record for this book is available from the British Library.

Transferred to digital printing 1999.

Contents

Preface

This book brings together research on the Norwegian electricity market reform, one of the pioneering reforms in this sector in Europe. It pools economic and organisational analysis undertaken on this sector at the Norwegian School of Management and ECON Centre for Economic Analysis under several research programmes sponsored by the Norwegian Research Council and the Federation of Norwegian Energy Utilities. Together, these studies shed light on most aspects of the Norwegian reform.

We are grateful to the Norwegian Research Council for supporting the publication of the book, which we hope will contribute towards shedding light on the options available for the present de-regulation in Europe.

Oslo

EIVIND MAGNUS
ATLE MIDTTUN

Acknowledgements

The editors and publishers wish to thank the following for permission to reproduce copyright material: Elsevier Science, for model simulations; and Figures 4.1–4.3, from A. Halseth, 'Market Power in the Nordic Electricity Market', *Utilities Policy* (1998).

Notes on the Contributors

Jan Bråten is senior economist at the ECON Centre for Economic Analysis, a Norwegian research and consulting group. He has a Cand. Oecon. degree from the Department of Economics (1994) and a BA in Mathematics, Sociology and Philosophy (1981), both from the University of Oslo. Since 1994 Bråten has worked as an economist the ECON, with electricity economics and market analysis. His main field of work is monopoly regulations, regulatory reforms and efficiency studies. His most recent publications are 'Transmission Pricing in Norway', *Utilities Policy*, 3 (1997) and 'OPEC's Response to International Climate Agreements', *Environmental and Resource Economics*, 12 (1998) (with R. Eolombek).

Arve Halseth is senior economist and partner in the ECON Centre for Economic Analysis. He has a Cand. Oecon. degree (Economics) from the University of Oslo. Halseth started in ECON in 1991, primarily working with analysis of the Nordic electricity market. His main field of work has been market modelling and analysis, with special emphasis on how the hydro and thermal electricity systems interact through the Nordic power exchange. Halseth has more recently been involved in studies of intermodal freight transportation and the Norwegian food processing industry. His most recent publication is 'Market Power in the Nordic Electricity Market', *Utilities Policy*, 7 (1998).

Anders Houmöller is Market Manager with Nord Pool in Denmark. He has also worked in the airline and shipping industries.

Eivind Magnus is director and partner in ECON, Centre for Economic Analysis, a Norwegian research and consulting group. His main publications include *Upstream Profitability in Vietnam* and *Upstream Profitability in Malaysia*, both commissioned by the Norwegian Research Council.

Atle Midttun is Professor at the Norwegian School of Management and Co-Director of the Centre for Energy and Environment. His publications include *Approaches to, and Dilemmas in Regulation* (with Eirik Svindland), *European Electricity Systems in Transition, Norway the Energy Nation: Societal Interests and Company Strategies in Energy Intensive Industry* (1995) and *The Politics of Energy Forecasting* (1987).

Per Ingvar Olsen is Assistant Professor at Norwegian School of Management, Institute for Innovation and Economic Organization, Center for electricity studies. He holds a Master of Science degree in economics (1994), and has been a doctoral student since 1995. His main research areas are energy economies, electricity market reforms and public regulations, other infrastructure sectors, agriculture and food industry.

Jan Arild Snoen is an analyst in the ECON Centre for Economic Analysis and formerly director of the policy unit of major political party. His main field at ECON is electricity market analysis and environmental and climate policy. He is the editor of a monthly report on the Nordic electricity market – *Nordisk Kraft*.

1
The Norwegian Model: Competitive Public Economy

Eivind Magnus and Atle Midttun

Introduction

In 1990 the Norwegian Parliament approved a new Energy Act. This legislation was to mean radical reforms within the Norwegian Electricity Supply Industry (ESI): it introduced competition in production and trade with electricity, while at the same time strengthening central governmental control over transmission and distribution activities. The new act entered into force on 1 January 1991.

With this electricity reform, Norway has gone further in opening the door to competition in power generation and in end-use markets than any other country in the world. Today all electricity consumers in Norway can choose among more than 100 suppliers of hydro-electric power. This is made possible through a set of regulatory measures characterised by open access to the network; explicit, distance-neutral and cost-based net tariffs; the development of institutions for advanced market trade; and the right for small customers to avoid metering costs by buying on so-called pre-determined profiles.

Unlike the case in Britain, the Norwegian reform has aimed primarily at introducing competition, rather than privatisation. The Norwegian electricity industry has thus remained in public hands, but the largely municipally and intermunicipally owned electricity industry no longer enjoys a monopoly on local and regional supply.

Compared with classical ideal-types in economic literature such as capitalist free trade and the socialist planned economy (Table 1.1), the Norwegian model seems somewhat of an anomaly. It combines the market competition of capitalism with the public ownership traditionally associated with planned economies.

Table 1.1 Politico–economic configurations

	Private ownership	**Public ownership**
Competition	Capitalist competitive market economy	Socialist competitive market economy
Monopoly/oligopoly	Private/capitalist Monopoly/oligopoly	Socialist planned economy

This chapter gives an overview of the Norwegian reform and the main lines of its development. We shall start out with a brief recapitulation of its historical roots, followed by a description of the reform process and essential features of the Norwegian reform. We then go on to discuss the technical and organisational characteristics and structural and institutional preconditions, before presenting some major outcomes for different market segments and consumer groups. The final section places the Norwegian reform within the context of the larger Nordic and North European market.

The historical roots of the Norwegian model

The current structure of Norwegian electricity industry has emerged as the product of three formative forces in the supply of electricity in Norway. First, the country's widely dispersed hydro-resources; secondly, the strong tradition of municipal and regional autonomy; and thirdly, a nationalistic orientation that has emphasised public ownership and exploitation of national resources.

The wide natural dispersion of hydro-resources made it possible for a number of municipalities and inter-municipal consortia to engage in local development hydropower projects. From the late 1920s the state became involved in hydropower production through the Norwegian State Power Board – initially mostly to supplement the efforts of local authorities. After the Second World War, the Board also became an important supplier of cheap electricity for energy-intensive industry. Even as technological advantages made larger projects attractive, and the state became more heavily involved in hydropower construction, the right to tap local resources often meant that the state had to negotiate joint ventures with local and regional companies, which served to uphold the decentralised industrial structure.

Norway's system of extensive decentralised municipal and county ownership of its hydropower resources must be seen as a product of these institutional conditions. Local banks, municipal electricity companies and local enterprises characterised by relatively small units were integrated in local politico–economic systems where financial resources, electrical power and political decisions supported each other (Thue 1995).

In a Nordic perspective, Norway stands out as having the most decentralised electricity system, although all of the Nordic systems are characterised by extensive local ownership. Natural conditions were important here: the decentralised Norwegian resource base in the form of numerous small waterfalls, as contrasted with the larger Swedish river systems, required less central co-ordination. Moreover, the shift to nuclear technology in Sweden and Finland in the 1970s and 1980s set these countries onto a more centralistic track than hydro-based Norway. More recently, however, combined heat and power systems have again started to allow a scaling down of industry.

However, also the Norwegian model had strong centralistic elements, and may in fact be described as a dual regime (Thue 1995). On the one hand, as noted above, local authorities won hegemony over production for general consumption. Small industry, households and agriculture were given priority as consumers of electricity. On the other hand, the important power-demanding industry generated its own power, delivering only small quantities to other customers. Furthermore, the above-mentioned involvement of the state also contributed to centralisation.

The reform process[1]

When the Norwegian electricity market reform was introduced this was in a pragmatic vein, in sharp contrast to the highly politicised British reform process. Norway's reform was very much administratively driven. (Central officials within the Ministry of Finance, for example, had for some time been dissatisfied with the investments and pricing decision within the existing electricity regime.) In 1988, inspired by the British reform as well as by EEC initiatives to liberalise European electricity markets, the Ministry of Finance in collaboration with the Ministry of Industry and Energy ordered an investigation into the possibility of market reform for Norway. This investigation concluded with a recommendation for a decentralised competitive electricity market, later adopted as part of the actual reform.

What was the rationale for introducing market reform into the Norwegian electricity supply system? This can be explained in relation to some perceived deficiencies of the old system, including the following concerns:

- There were significant price differences at the regional level. Companies with low-cost power stations were selling power at prices considerably lower than those of companies with high-cost power.

- The sequence of developing new projects was not optimal. In some areas, projects with obviously too high costs were developed before other, more economically sound, projects.
- Producers were local or regional monopolies, and thus did not have to carry the economic risk in investment decisions.
- The utilities lacked incentives for cutting costs.
- In the absence of an efficiently functioning market, consumers did not receive correct signals about the marginal costs of production.
- The high degree of vertical integration between production and transmission/distribution meant that there was no clear distinction between production and natural monopoly activities within the individual entities.

Paradoxically, and illustrative of Norway's pragmatic attitude, the first attempt to handle these deficiencies was through the introduction of a centralistic planned economy reform, proposed in a 1985 Government Green Paper (*NOU* 1985, 9). Here, the intention was to integrate the more than 130 suppliers and 100 producers into 20 regional vertically integrated companies with exclusive service areas. Influenced by paradigm shifts in economic regulation, however, the same arguments that supported the centralistic planned economy approach in 1985 were adduced to motivate the competitive market reform three or four years later.

The proceedings in Parliament confirmed the Norwegian pragmatic/administrative strategy. Political proponents of the planned economy reform accepted the liberal turnabout without too much dissent, and the Centre (Agrarian) Party minister responsible for the reform under the Conservative/Centre/Christian Democrat coalition government took care not to provoke his colleagues. Political involvement was therefore characterised by the building of strategic political alliances with a low ideological profile. Verbal skirmishes during the parliamentary debate were unavoidable, but they did not result in fundamental objections to the reform, which was passed by an overwhelming majority vote.

The avoidance of a drastic structural reform, as had been the case in Britain, and the reliance mainly on procedural measures, probably helped to win acceptance for reforms within the ESI and prevented any sharp left/right politicisation. Some of the largest electricity companies, in fact, saw the reforms as opportunities for greater autonomy and for freer commercial expansion. The reform in Norway also gained support from energy-intensive industry, which expected to be able to derive benefits from price cuts. The influential Norwegian Confederation of Industries therefore lobbied actively for reform.

The mode of liberalisation in Norway was thus much more a compromise between government policy and traditional ESI values than in Britain. The negotiated character, along with the fact that the reforms did not interfere overly with the industrial structure and the largely public ownership, obviously served to make a compromise with the ESI possible. This reform could at the same time meet demands within major companies, especially the larger state companies, for greater autonomy and freedom from political interference.

Essential features of the Norwegian reform

The results of the reform process were embodied in the new Energy Act, but the exposure of the electricity industry to market competition has also subsumed it under the regulatory domain of the competition law. The Energy Act governs matters specifically related to the ESI, whereas competition legislation provides the legislative framework for the sector of the electricity market that is exposed to competition, and applies in addition to the Energy Act.

In fact, the Energy Act was only a starting point for the larger reform process in the Norwegian energy sector. It indicated the direction: more detailed regulations, regulatory institutions and industry structure are still under development. The liberal elements that were implicitly and explicitly embodied in the Energy Act and that facilitated free trade were as follows:

- The principle of open access was introduced for all networks, national as well as regional and local. Suppliers thereby lost their exclusive right to supply their franchise area, and were instead subjected to price competition.
- Consumer participation in the spot market for occasional power was made possible. After the reform, this spot market has been further differentiated; a set of markets has been established or is now emerging. Nord Pool ASA, a subsidiary of Statnett SF and Svenska Kraftnät that acts as a clearing institution, now operates these markets.
- A distance-neutral point tariff system was introduced for energy transportation.
- Consumer segments were allowed to trade in the liberalised electricity market for their own consumption, without further restriction.

- Utilities were forced to de-bundle, or ring-fence, network activities from production and sale through separate divisions with separate accounts.

In line with classical theory of natural monopoly, the basic idea behind the Norwegian reform was to split up different functions of the electricity system, according to the expected consequences of exposing them to competition. Functions with the characteristics of a natural monopoly were to be organised as regulated monopolies, while other activities were to be open to competition.

Production and trading were seen as activities that could be regulated by competition, whereas transport functions of transmission and distribution were seen as natural monopolies and were hence regulated by administrative control (Figure 1.1).

For the production function, securing of efficient competition was therefore seen as the essential task of regulation. Here the assumption was that effective competition would force the actors to allocate resources productively and to develop efficient organisational behaviour.

For the transmission and distribution functions, the essential task was to secure open access and to control the efficiency of the natural monopolies.

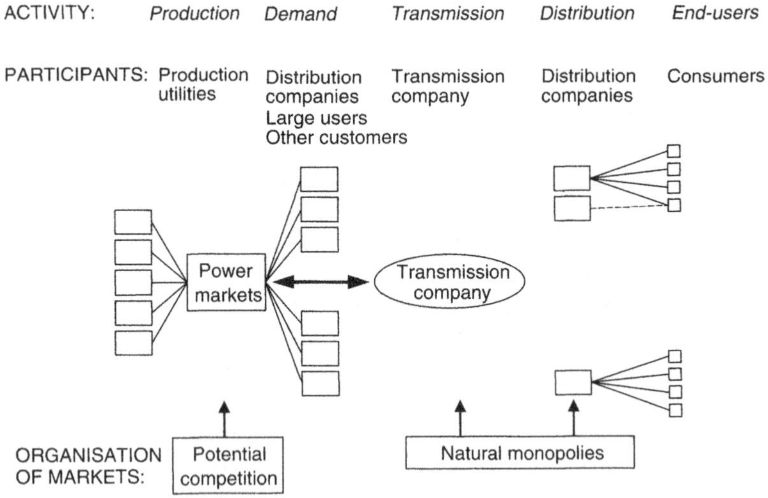

Figure 1.1 Principal sketch of the electricity system, 1992
Source: From Hope and Strøm (1992).

The main legislative instrument in the Norwegian reform was the introduction of *trading licences*. According to the new Act, any public or private company or person involved in electricity generation, trade or distribution of electricity must hold a trading licence. Such a licence is granted subject to the following conditions:

- Licensees must keep separate accounts of grid operations and operations exposed to competition.
- Licensees are required to give other suppliers and users of electricity access to their transmission and distribution network.
- Licensees with network operations are required to stipulate network tariffs in accordance with the price regulation principles formed by the Norwegian Water Resources and Energy Administration (NVE), the regulator.
- Formal arrangements tying distribution companies to producers are not allowed.
- Licensees are required to inform NVE about prices and other aspects of their operations considered necessary in regulating monopoly activity or in monitoring the electricity market.

The basic organisational structure from the 'old' regime, however, remains, and many of the traditional contractual and collaborative ties between companies are still active. Thus we need to see what the reform did *not* change:

- It did not affect ownership structure, so the main part of the electricity system remains public.
- It did not alter concession rules that strongly disfavour transfer of power generation from public to private ownership.
- It did not require organisational separation of network activities from production and trade functions at the regional and municipal levels.
- It retained a foreign trade regime for electricity based on licences for long-term agreements.
- It did not open up the special contract market for power to energy-intensive industry.

In sum, the reform did not fully implement a free trade model: what it did was to introduce competitive elements into a cost-based supply-oriented infrastructure. Both the system of public ownership as well as the political and contractual embeddedness of large portions of the electricity trade served to limit the effects of competition, particularly in the first years. On the other hand, the increasing participation of new commercially-oriented traders and brokers, together with a strong commercial reorientation of some leading companies, is gradually exerting a general 'commercialising' effect on Norway's electricity industry. A 1995 ruling from the regulatory authorities, allowing small customers to buy on so-called pre-determined curves, also increased competitive pressure on the Norwegian electricity system.

Technical and organisational characteristics

Norway ranks as Europe's most electricity-intensive country, alongside Finland and Sweden. Norway tops European statistics with 25 000 kWh electricity consumption *per capita,* as against the EU average of 8000. The reason behind this exceptionally high figure is the attraction that Norway's cheap hydropower resources has exerted on the energy-intensive multinational electro–metallurgical and electrochemical industry.

Norway's electricity industry today is fairly decentralised and predominantly publicly owned. It consists of 56 generators, 34 industrial generators, 24 wholesale and 206 distribution and supply companies.[2] A review of the 20 largest distributors/suppliers and generators (Midttun 1996) shows that distribution/supply is almost completely in public hands, whereas public ownership in production stands at 82 per cent. The state company Statkraft alone controls around one-third of total production, but has no role in distribution/supply. Here it should also be noted that Statkraft is formally obliged to provide a large part of the electricity supply to energy-intensive industry on contracts with no direct reference to the new competitive market. This means that the effective role of the state power company in the competitive market is in fact far smaller than its total generation figures would suggest.

The Norwegian electricity system is almost 100 per cent based on hydropower. Generation takes place in some 850 power stations, with a total capacity of about 27 000 MW. Although it includes a number of large dams and plants, the Norwegian generation system is fairly decentralised; only 76 stations have more than 100 MW of installed capacity. Mean energy production capacity in a year with normal precipitation is 113 TWh.

Being based on hydropower, generation varies considerably, depending on hydrological conditions over the year and between years. Water inflow to the generation system in a single year may vary by as much as one-third, relative to a normal year. Storage capacity – currently

81 TWh – enables Norwegian generators to manage these variations, within certain limits. Short-term electricity trade with neighbouring countries has traditionally been used to even out large variations.

Norwegian hydropower resources are, as mentioned, attractive to energy-intensive industry. This is reflected in the structure of the Norwegian electricity consumption (see Table 1.2). Consumption in the residential and commercial sector accounts for some 65 per cent of Norwegian electricity supply, while 25 per cent goes to energy-intensive industry, such as aluminium production. In 1996, around 8 per cent were consumed in flexible boilers, which can switch between fuel oil and electricity.

Like most electricity systems, the grid in Norway is divided into three levels. The high-tension central grid (usually 300–420 kV) links together generation and use in various parts of the country. It is also connected to the transmission lines to other countries. The central grid company, Statnett SF, is owned by the Norwegian state. The company owns 75 per cent of the transmission facilities, and rents the balance from other wholesale and vertically integrated utilities.

The regional grids comprise the next level. They are connected to the central grid, and form the links between generating companies, the central grid and distribution grids. These regional grids are owned by 30 utilities, which are also involved in other parts of the electricity sector. Some of these are primarily generation utilities, but many are also vertically integrated.

The third level is constituted by the distribution grids – the low-tension local networks that distribute electricity to the end-users. The supply utilities own the local distribution grid, trading power in the market and selling it to end-users in their geographical area. There are around 135 distribution/supply utilities in Norway, most of them owned

Table 1.2 Electricity consumption in Norway, 1996

	TWh	(%)
Residential and commercial sector	73.6	64.6
Energy-intensive industry	28.0	24.6
Flexi-boilers	3.2	2.8
Electricity consumption in pumped storage	0.4	0.4
Losses	8.7	7.6
Total	113.5	100

Source: ECON, NORDEL.

by one or more municipalities. Together with the vertically integrated utilities, some 200 units are involved in the distribution of electricity to end-users.

The crucial role of the market for occasional power

The market for so-called occasional power was of central importance to the Norwegian reform and deserves special discussion as a major institutional precondition for the swift implementation of the reform. As opposed to other trading in the pre-reform Norwegian system, the market for occasional power was organised on an idealised free trade basis, with an industry-owned organisation, 'Samkjøringen', acting as a clearing house. The need for such a market, even within a system based on institutional monopoly, stems from the fact noted above: the Norwegian electricity system is nearly 100 per cent hydropower-based, with production varying extensively with hydrological conditions in the course of the year and from year to year.

These variable hydrological conditions motivated the decentralised production units to engage in internal trade, to permit optimal use of their water reservoirs. The exchange prices signalled to each reservoir owner whether to sell or buy, as well as indicating whether to use electricity or oil for heating the large industrial boilers that were usually linked to electricity companies on special flexible contracts. The Norwegian market for occasional power also had a Nordic extension, as it was indirectly accessible for Swedish and Danish producers as well, with the Norwegian State Power Company acting as intermediary. Prior to the reform there were over 60 Norwegian production companies trading on this market.

The essence of the Norwegian reform was that it opened up this market to end-users, thereby supposedly also making it a reference market for the bilateral forward market. If the actors in the bilateral forward market had the alternative of moving into the spot market, then the expected spot price would become a reference price for bilateral trading. The existence of a fully developed pre-reform spot market helps to explain how Norway was able to develop a reform so quickly.

The evolving Nordic power market

The reforms that ensued in Finland (1995) and Sweden (1996) subsequently placed the Norwegian electricity industry within the context of a larger Nordic market. Integration of the Norwegian and Swedish markets was particularly strong, as it included the development of common spot market institutions and harmonisation of pricing and regulation policies for the two national grids. This integration has come about through close collaboration between the two national grid companies. The traditionally decentralised electricity industrial structure in Norway and in Sweden proved fairly conducive to free trade competition.

The Nordic power pool

In 1996 the Norwegian Pool system was extended to Sweden and gradually to Finland and Denmark, and organised into a new company, Nord Pool, owned jointly by the Norwegian and Swedish grid companies. Nord Pool has continued to operate the same market structure previously available in Norway, basically including three markets: the spot market; the regulation market; and the futures market. The first two are markets for physical power exchange, while the futures market is a financial market for hedging and risk management.

The *spot market* is a physical electricity market where contracts are bought and sold on a day-to-day basis for delivery the next day. The basic time-unit for market clearing and settlement is the hour. In principle, there can be 24 so-called 'price sections' per day/night, but normally only six price sections are issued per day and only four price sections during the weekend. These price sections are determined by Nord Pool in advance. Market participants state their supply and demand in the form of a number of price–quantity combinations for each price section. This information is then aggregated by Nord Pool, which derives supply and demand schedules and determines the equilibrium price for each section. Since the el-spot market is settled on an hourly basis, the agents have to have necessary equipment to measure hourly power exchange.

Deviation from contracted volumes is settled over the *regulation market*. This market has developed in response to the need to adjust system production at very short notice – mainly because deviations may arise between the production plan determined in advance on the basis of the price formation in the spot market, and the production schedule when the power is actually delivered. The regulation market is operated by Statnett which is responsible for balancing production and transition in the electricity system. Generation capacity is made available for regulation through an auction process, which provides the regulator with a list of participants who can significantly regulate their power take-offs or deliveries on very short notice. All other actors are passive participants in the market and merely register their deviations in generation and consumption from contractual rights or obligations.

The *futures market* offers participants an organised power market for price hedging and risk management. The market utilises the spot market price as the underlying reference price. In the futures market there are also market-makers who are obliged to post buying and selling prices. This enables participants to make quick alterations in their strategy and portfolio arrangements.

As of late 1997, there were more than 140 participants trading contracts at the Nord Pool power exchange, including generators, suppliers, private industry, large-scale customers, brokers and traders. It is reasonable to say that the Nordic power market is very close to a perfect competitive market. Prices are transparent, and the number of actors secures sufficient liquidity, at least in the spot market. As opposed to the UK pool, Nord Pool is based on bids from both producers and consumers – not only the producers, as is the case in the UK. The number of participants is also much larger in the Nordic Power Pool, which again diminishes the risk of one or a few companies manipulating the market, compared to the British Pool. For further discussion of the Nordic Pool, see Chapter 3.

Structural integration

The liberalisation of three Nordic markets has also set in motion a process of structural transformation including integration of Nordic companies. This transformation has been most extensive in Finland and Sweden, but there are also examples of mergers and networks affecting Norwegian actors.

On the generation side, Statkraft, the Norwegian state power company, has recently become involved in the large Swedish company Sydkraft, buying 17.1 per cent of the shares and 20.8 per cent of the votes, as well as in Oslo Energy generation, with 20 per cent of the shares. Both these engagements may be harbingers of larger strategic blocks in the Nordic market.

In Sweden, the Finnish state power company Imatran Voima, IVO, has acquired 90 per cent of the Sweden distribution and production company Gullspång, after having fought off Vattenfall and Graningeverken, which each owned 23 per cent in the company. As a part of the settlement with Vattenfall, IVO had to offer hydropower generation rights in Finland. For Vattenfall, having generation rights is important in their strategy to increase their current 7 per cent market share of Finnish supply.

Across the border, Vattenfall of Sweden have acquired the Finnish supply companies Hämeen Sähkö Oy and Lapuan Sähkö Oy, as well as trying to acquire the local supplier Savon Voima at a very high price. So far the local authorities controlling Savon Voima have refused to sell, but this battle is not yet settled.

Developing new channels for North European trade

Despite the asymmetric pace between the slow Continental and the quick Nordic reform processes, there has been an opening up for commercial orientation, which has created incentives and possibilities for Nordic–Continental trade across the old NORDEL–UCPTE boundaries. This trade has emerged as company-to-company business between Nordic and continental firms, accompanied by parallel cable investments to be financed in conjunction with the trade. At present there are four trade agreements and parallel cable agreements between Norway and the continent: the Denmark Connection, the Viking Cable and the Euro Cable to Germany, and the Nor-Ned Cable to the Netherlands. Between Sweden and the continent there are at present three trade agreements: The Jutland and Zealand Connections to Denmark, and the Baltic Cable to Germany. One of the main motives for this trade lies in the complementarity of resources, between Nordic hydropower and continental heat-based electricity generation, where the former can deliver peak load and the latter may provide base load, thereby safeguarding the hydro-based system against dry-year supply. These resource complementarities mean considerable business profits and welfare gains to be made from co-ordinated operation of the Nordic and Continental systems.

Normally, integration of national markets will mean that firms will have to move towards a single, common pricing policy with regional price differences in transportation cost only. With the integration of a larger resource base and extended competition as result of a larger market with more players, the integration of two markets should normally also lead to increased efficiency and lower consumer prices.

However, integration may take many forms. Depending on the institutional structuring of the markets and of the linking trade agreements as well, integration may have widely different implications for the parties involved. At present, the Norwegian authorities seem to be aiming for a model with continental oligopoly and asymmetric cable agreements (Midttun, Svindland and Andreassen 1997). By this, they seem to have attempted to stabilise domestic prices at a low level, at the same time as the leading Norwegian electricity companies are making money on peak-load sales. However, this model will be threatened by multinational clustering strategies from the electricity companies, and may also be vulnerable to pressure in response to changes in EU regulation.

Retail competition

The electricity reform in Norway immediately opened the way to retail competition. Large consumers, especially industrial customers, were quick to use the new market opportunity and started to shop around for more favourable contracts. Two years later, the industry segment of the end-user market had become highly competitive, with decreasing margins for the suppliers. Small consumers, however, found themselves locked in with their local suppliers owing to high metering and transaction costs.

In the old system with only one supplier within the network area, it was sufficient to meter exchange data with adjacent networks. With more than one supplier in a network area, data had to be collected at the end-user level in order to determine the exchange with each individual supplier. This data collection had to be based on hourly data, which necessitated individual metering equipment and imposed costs 10 times what a small consumer could gain by changing suppliers. Hence small customers were effectively excluded from being an active part of the competitive retail market.

In the first phase, from 1991 and up to and including 1994, suppliers were responsible for obtaining settlement data for their customers and sending it to the clearing house (Nord Pool 1997). In practice, however, it was often the new supplier who had to provide for the installation of metering equipment and cover the cost of providing metering data. Annual costs per metering point for the new supplier were in the magnitude of 5000 NOK. The dominant local supplier avoided these costs, because only new suppliers had to meter end-user consumption on an hourly basis. In order to determine his exchange volume, the local supplier simply used the network company's exchange data with other networks, and then deduced the hourly values from the new suppliers in the network. Thus, by virtue of his integration with the network company, the local supplier got access to the hourly values paid by the competitors.

This system was clearly unfair, and represented major barriers to the entry of new suppliers. In order to stimulate competition, the regulator wanted a method which could give all the suppliers the same competitive conditions and a reasonable degree of market access for all end-user groups. To improve market access for small consumers, the practice of forcing anyone who switched suppliers to install equipment for hourly metering had to be discontinued. The challenge was to find a method that could provide an approximately correct estimate of the end-user's consumption profile without exposing the network companies to the risk of significant losses from covering inaccuracies. In addition, all suppliers would have to be treated equally.

The solution was to establish standard load curves, which avoided installation of new costly metering equipment. With a standard load curve, it is sufficient to meter consumption once a year.

Different types of standard curves were considered. One was so-called pre-defined curves for different consumer groups; another was pre-defined network profiles calculated on the basis of the system load profile of each individual network company, based on historical data. The first option proved very complicated to implement, while the other was considered to be inaccurate, since large consumers with hourly metering could have great impact on network's system load curves. The regulator ended up with so-called network company's *adjusted system load profile:* this was to reflect the average consumption profile for those end-users that were not metered on an hourly basis. The adjusted system load curve is established by taking the total system load curve and deducting the network loss and the accumulated load curve for end-users that are metered hourly. Since it is based on the actual hourly power input, it is not a pre-defined curve, but a function of the actual input to the network.

For any consumer whose annual consumption exceeds 500 000 kWh, hourly metering is obligatory. The argument here is that consumers with such high consumption tend to be factories using electricity in industrial processes with load curves that deviate from those of households and service companies. If these major power consumers are included in the adjusted load profile, then the profile would not be representative of considerable segments of the electricity consumers, including households. This system of adjusted load curves for consumers whose annual consumption is less than 500 000 kWh was introduced on 1 January 1996.

Up to 1997 network companies were permitted, in order to cover costs incurred, to charge a fee of maximum 246 NOK each time an end-user changed suppliers. In addition, they were allowed to charge a fee of maximum 4000 NOK per year for each individual supplier within their network area. In 1997 the regulator eliminated both fees, mainly because marginal costs have dropped owing to considerable economies of scale. After 1997 any cost incurred by customers changing suppliers is to be covered by the network companies through the general transportation tariff.

Tariff regulation under a competitive regime

Traditionally, public ownership in itself has been considered a sufficient mechanism for regulating natural monopolies like ESI grid activities. The pre-reform Norwegian power sector had a regulation system based upon this tradition. Local public ownership was assumed to protect consumer interests; it was not considered necessary to have a formal monopoly regulation similar to what has been the tradition in countries with private utilities.

The Energy Act introduced competition in generation and supply of electricity. At the time of deregulation, these were owned and operated by a mixture of municipal, state-owned and private companies, which also had grid operations as an integrated part of their business. The government actively motivated local authorities to develop commercial entities through corporatisation of the local utilities even when their main activity was electricity supply, which was considered to be a natural monopoly.

Facing new challenges in a power sector that was now market-based, many municipalities followed the government's recommendations and were reorganised as limited companies, still owned by the same authority. Normally, they also restated their objectives from public service to modified profit maximisation. However, this step was often taken with considerable hesitation, and many public service values still lingered on. The government assumed that the reorientation and corporatisation of former municipal utilities necessitated the development of monopoly regulation similar to that applying to private monopolies in countries like the USA and the UK. The new policy was also motivated by the government's claim that the utilities had been performing poorly in running the grid.

The Norwegian Water Resources and Energy Administration (NVE) was tasked with regulating and controlling grid activities. Two years after the reform, in 1993, the NVE introduced rate-of-return regulation. Based on a cost of service principle, the new regulation model was criticised for not giving companies economic incentives to reduce costs. The regulator was aware of this weakness, and began assessing various options for introducing an incentive-based regulation model. This process culminated on 1 January 1997, when a new regulation model based on individual income caps was introduced. This new regime could be considered as a variant of the British RPI–X system. Each company is given a maximum income according to its own cost and production conditions; this will be adjusted every year to compensate for general inflation (RPI) and the productivity growth (RPI–X) required by the regulator. The maximum income will also be adjusted following an increase in the energy transmission, in general a 0.5 per cent rise in allowed income for every 1 per cent increase in annual transmission. The regulator has also promised that in the next regulation period (2002–6), utilities will be compensated for growth that demands new investments, and that their maximum income will also be influenced by the quality of the services they supply. It is not yet clear according to what criteria this compensation will be decided.

The background for the new regulatory regime, which also includes the central grid, is the belief that grid companies have had unnecessarily high operating costs and that they have tended to over-invest. Under the previous regulatory regime, the grid owners were economically more or less indifferent to investment costs, since they could simply pass on all costs to the customers. The new regime gives the grid companies incentives to reduce their capital costs, and is therefore expected to result in efficiency improvement.

The information problem facing the regulator in carrying out regulation with individual company caps was reduced by the development of an efficiency measurement model that took into consideration cost variations due to differences in climate, topography and population density. To support the regulator, a reporting system for tariffs and accounting data was established. Results from measurements are today considered a crucial input to the regulator in defining individual income caps.

The impacts of reform

The ups and downs of electricity prices

As already mentioned, the Norwegian reform has set market-based price formation at the centre of the electricity trade, thereby creating greater volatility and risks in the electricity business. Pre-reform transactions at the wholesale level were basically made in two separate segments, one for long-term delivery contracts at stable and cost-related prices, the other for spot deliveries in the so-called market for occasional power. There were no trading opportunities between the two segments, which in turn meant that price changes in one segment did not influence price formation in the other. The introduction of wholesale competition which opened up for arbitrage between previously separated market segments removed the preconditions for price discrimination between the two segments.

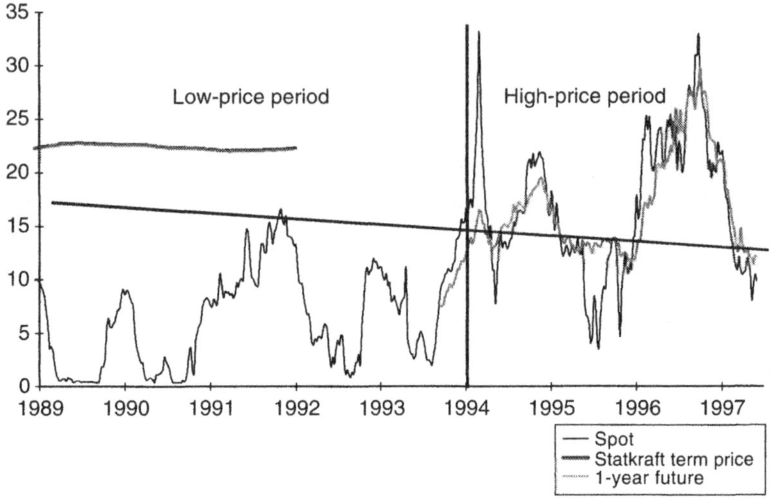

Figure 1.2 Prices in the Norwegian electricity market, 1989–97
Source: Statnett Marked (1996); Nord Pool (1997).

In the course of the eight years that have now passed since the market reform, prices to end-users have been reduced in most market segments, and have basically changed the strategic positions of the electricity generation industry in Norway.

Figure 1.2 shows price developments in the Norwegian electricity sector for the period 1989–97. The 'Statkraft price', which was stipulated by the Norwegian government as a reference price for long-term contracts between Statkraft and other power companies, is included to illustrate the price level for cost-based contracts in the pre-reform wholesale market.

In the first years after the reform, which also coincided with high precipitation and ensuing water abundance in the hydropower-based generation system, there were considerable arbitrage profits to be made by buying from the spot market and selling to industrial end-users and distribution companies. New trading companies with competence in spot trading emerged in this period, under-cutting the traditional cost-based contracts. Such trading companies flourished during this period, and triggered market competition. Producers were forced to re-negotiate price terms, and price levels in the different market segments gradually converged. From 1994 the golden opportunities for large risk-free profits diminished. As a consequence, some traders went bankrupt or shifted to brokerage; the traditional electricity industry regained an upper hand.

In order to understand movements in the Norwegian power market we must recognise the impact of short-term power trade with neighbouring countries on price formation. In 1991, the pre-reform power trade organised by the Nordic despatch cooperation, NORDEL, was replaced by a new mechanism, where both Danish and Swedish producers were allowed to trade at prices related to the Norwegian spot market. From 1996, the Norwegian and Swedish markets were fully integrated, while the Danish producers remained participants in spot market transactions. Consequently, the price level in the spot market has been increasingly influenced by the marginal costs of generation throughout the entire Nordic electricity market. Price movements are gradually becoming independent of demand and supply conditions in Norway, and are more and more a result of the market balance in the whole region.

Another significant effect of the reform with market implications was the shelving of most expansion plans for new generation capacity, resulting in significant reductions in investment activity. As the investors found themselves faced with market risk and falling electricity prices, many observers saw reduced investment as a positive result of the reform. The view is that excess investment was an inherent property of the old system, partly because generators did not take risk into consideration in making investment decisions.

Lower electricity prices and higher economic activity in Norway have stimulated consumption in parallel with fading investments. Today there is no excess capacity in the Norwegian electricity market – in fact, for the first time in recent decades, Norway is becoming a net electricity importer in years with normal precipitation and temperature values.

The *de facto* ban on new investments and an upswing in the economy in the Nordic countries towards the mid-1990s were clearly important elements in the upward price development (Figure 1.3). In addition, 1996 was a very dry year, so water scarcity also helped to push prices upwards. More normal hydrological conditions have since forced a new downward trend for market prices, but prices have remained considerably higher than during the 1991–4 period.

The Norwegian electricity reform also seems to have affected transport costs. In the first years after the reform was introduced, there was a significant decrease in the transportation tariffs paid by households, especially between 1993 and 1995. During this period, the nominal reduction in tariffs paid by Norwegian households was 6.5 per cent.

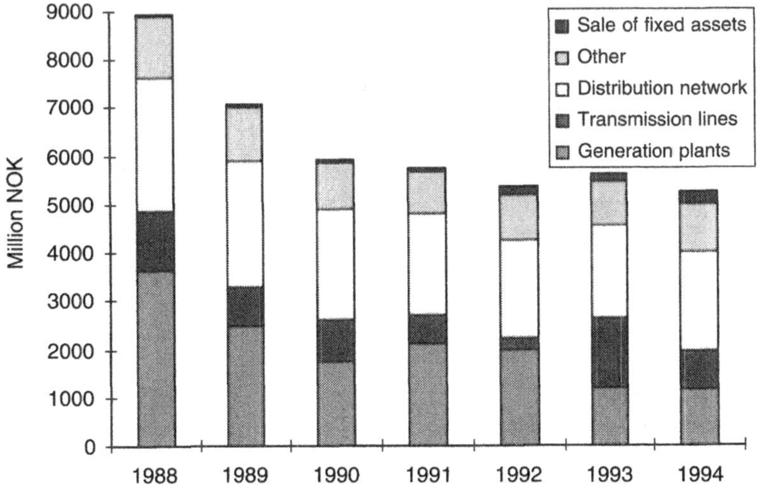

Figure 1.3 Capital investments in the Norwegian power sector, 1985–95
Source: ECON.

With annual inflation standing at 4 per cent, the reduction in real terms was as large as 11 per cent. However, of this 6.5 per cent reduction in the nominal tariffs, 3.7 per cent was due to factors not related to higher cost efficiency, such as a lower interest rate, a higher valuation of net loss and higher transportation volumes. Since 1995, the decrease in transportation costs has levelled out. Nevertheless, many Norwegian economists and regulators still hold that there is a large potential for efficiency improvements in transportation, which the reform has not yet succeeded in bringing about properly.

The Norwegian Energy Act of 1990 was radical insofar as it opened the door to free sale of electricity to end-users. It has, however, taken several years before framework conditions could be established that allow real market access for all consumers of electricity. The establishment of rights for small consumers to trade freely without metering costs in 1995 marked a bold step to put their formal rights into practice. However, large price differences have remained, indicating that old customer loyalties and traditional public service strategies from companies still play important roles.

Figure 1.4 shows the development of prices on the household market from 1995 to October 1996. That the greater part of the prices for energy sold to household customers were in the range of 14–21 øre/kWh

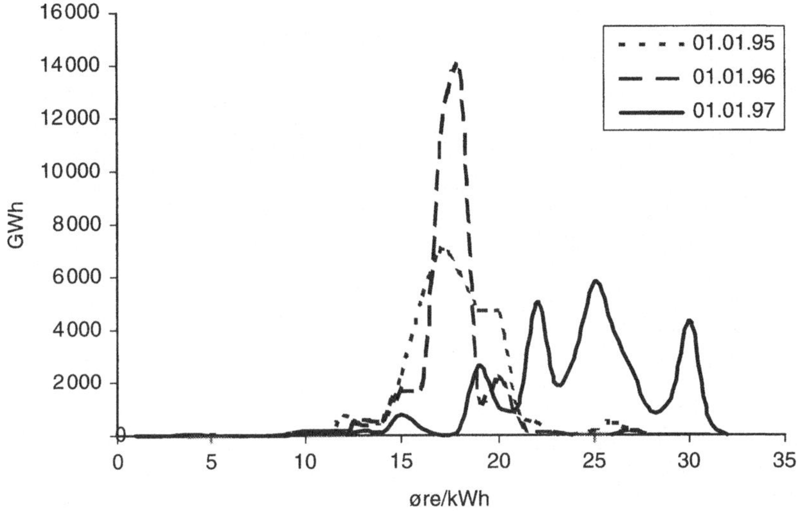

Figure 1.4 Electricity prices for household customers, 1995–6 (excl. transmission price, electricity tax and VAT)
Source: NVE and ECON.

in January 1995. In January 1996 the range of prices was reduced, and most prices were in the range from 16–19 øre/kWh. However, this picture changed in the course of 1996. A survey of household prices undertaken in October 1996 shows a significant increase in the range of prices. Prices are now divided into four distinct groups and range from 16 to 31 øre/kWh.

As far as company liquidity is concerned, lower prices in both the spot and contract segments reduced income from generation activities in the first years after the reform, and some producers encountered severe financial problems. However, the financial trouble caused by falling prices was limited, owing to the relatively strong financial basis of most generators. Increased prices in 1994 and 1995 boosted the financial performance of Norwegian producers, as illustrated by the steady improvement in Statkraft's net result. This state company, which overnight lost all its general supply contracts in the initial low-price market, was immediately heavily exposed to spot prices and suffered extensive losses in 1992 and 1993. Thereafter, the state-owned producer came to profit from the rise in market prices. Statkraft achieved a positive result in 1994 (Figure 1.5); by 1996 its net result after taxes was an impressive 450 million NOK.

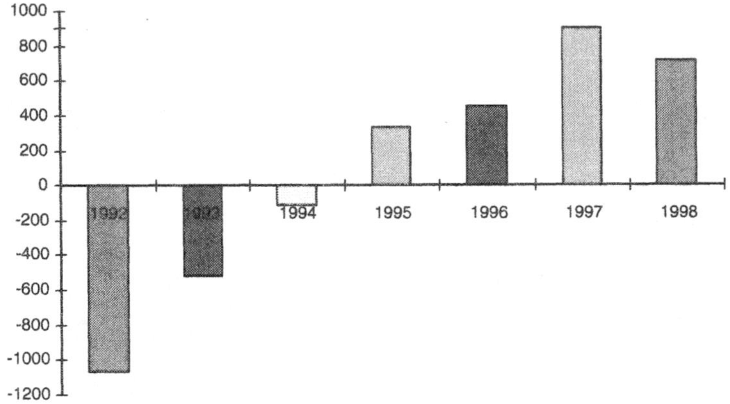

Figure 1.5 Net income, Statkraft SF, 1992–6
Source: Statkraft SF.

By contrast, distribution and supply utilities which had little or no generation capacity and which were able to terminate old long-term contracts, profited from the reduced prices of the first few years after the reform. They could benefit from the low prices at the same time as their sales prices to large consumer groups were not subject to competition. Although all consumers were in principle free to trade against the spot market, from the very start of the reform metering costs set an effective barrier to household consumers.

Concluding remarks

The Norwegian reform has largely been successful with respect to short-term efficiency in electricity generation. However, the effect on transportation, and the long-term benefits of the reform, still remain to be proven. The production of electricity is highly capital-intensive, and investment decisions will always be subject to political attention and interference.

The Norwegian experience has shown that it is possible to achieve efficiency improvements in electricity trade and production without privatisation. Facing the well developed and transparent Nordic market, the public owners have to a large extent reorganised their utilities and reoriented their contractual and investment strategies. Greater focus on trading and marketing activities has changed the way of thinking among management and staff in general.

It is in grid management that the largest efficiency potential lies. Here, the problem of promoting improved efficiency is greater, but is rather similar for publicly and privately owned companies alike. In neither case does the natural monopoly allow direct competition, so it is up to the regulator to design quasi-competition regimes that can motivate efficiency. The wide variety of topographic and demographic conditions in Norway, however, makes this a very difficult task.

The structure of the book

The following chapters of this book discuss various aspects of the Norwegian reform in three main parts: Electricity Trade in Competitive Markets, Grid Management Under a Competitive Regime and the Norwegian Model in a Nordic and a European Context.

Part I deals with the competitively exposed parts of the de-regulated electricity business. Chapter 2 – the first in this part – looks into the process of transition from public service to market competition in electricity companies, focusing specifically on the impacts of political, contractual and ownership networks in this process.

Chapter 3 describes the Nordic Pool, perhaps the most important institution in the Nordic electricity market system. The chapter provides a fairly detailed description of the various markets and trading instruments, and how trading on the Nordic Pool is done.

Chapter 4 deals with the incentives and abilities of generators to exercise market power in the Norwegian and Nordic electricity markets. The analysis is based on standard game-theoretical models, augmented by some extensions aimed at dealing with the specificity of the hydropower system.

Chapter 5 focuses on the problems of risk management in the deregulated electricity trade.

Part II of the book is concerned with grid management, the natural monopoly element in the electricity system.

Chapter 6 – the first chapter in this part – looks at incentives for efficiency in grid operations. It presents the principles for regulation of the Norwegian grid companies and discusses limitations of the cost-based model which was used until 1997, and also the new income regulation model introduced in 1997.

Chapter 7 – on efficiency and cost in distribution companies – highlights the measurement problems involved in determining cost levels in transmission networks. The Regulator's model is here compared against a value chain model (VCM), and the chapter discusses how the outcomes of these two approaches may be reconciled.

Chapter 8 – on local grid management – focuses on local grid management from the perspective of the utilities. This chapter discusses how the Norwegian market reform has altered attitudes to economic objectives among owners and top management, and to what extent the public owners are motivated to promote higher productivity under the prospect of higher profitability.

Part III deals with the Norwegian model in a Nordic and European context. Chapter 9 looks into trade and competition in the Nordic context and discusses the economic rationale for trade. It shows how the benefits related to foreign trade in electricity vary with different regulatory assumptions.

The final chapter in this part, Chapter 10, deals with structure and strategy in the Nordic power market. It presents an overview of ownership and structural patterns for Nordic electricity industry and discusses the strategic evolution of the Nordic markets.

Notes

1 Some of the main official documents spelling out the legal and political basis for the Norwegian reform are listed under Norwegian Parliamentary documents in the References (p. 235).

2 *Source*: NVE.

Part I

Electricity Trade in Competitive Markets

2

From Public Service to Market Competition: Norwegian Utilities' Adaptation to Market Reform

Atle Midttun

Trading under competitive public ownership

The competitive public ownership mode of liberalisation that characterises the Norwegian model has left Norwegian utilities with rather complex premises in their adaptation to market reform. Faced with market demands for efficiency and competitive prices, yet with political stakeholders still in an ownership position, many utilities have experienced strong tensions between commercial and political forces. These tensions have not been lessened by the fact that the electricity market is one of the most volatile commodity markets – especially in the Norwegian–Swedish pool, so vulnerable to precipitation variations in a hydro-based system.

Political ties have been a source of considerable tension – but they have also represented strategic opportunities. In its first phase of adapting to the new market order, the Norwegian electricity companies relied heavily on old political ownership and contractual ties, hereafter referred to as 'network ties'. The result was a development characterised by a remoulding of old networks to suit the new market order, rather than any shift from political planning to atomistic competition.

The first part of this chapter presents an empirical overview and discussion of company strategies in this phase, focusing on the interplay between political and economic forces. The empirical basis consists of case studies of the strategic transformation of producer–distributors in selected clusters that represent the major organisational varieties in Norway's electricity system at the outset of the market reform.[1]

Gradually, the old political ties have become supplemented by or transformed into more genuinely commercially-based alliances. However, the large share of political ownership and the concession laws in Norway that enable the state to take over electricity resources in the case of privatisation, have tended to give political networks a stronger hold on the Norwegian market than elsewhere in the other liberalising Nordic countries. The Norwegian state has the right to a first offer in cases of privatisation, and also to reclaim the production facilities owned by private companies without cost at the end of the concession period, which is usually 60 years.

The present Norwegian scene is therefore a mixed one, with political and commercial elements intertwined. The second part of this chapter discusses recent strategic developments. Here, the focus will be on larger companies, on the basis of systematic studies of the 20 largest Norwegian producers and distributors. The discussion will also be illustrated with relevant material from secondary sources.

Remoulding networks in an early transition phase

Opening the Norwegian wholesale market for free trade both between electricity companies and with end-users meant that the regional production/wholesale companies lost their traditional position as exclusive suppliers of electricity to the distribution companies in their region, and that the distribution companies became exposed to competition within their traditional supply areas. Nevertheless, old network ties remained for several years, exercising considerable influence in the forward market for bilateral contracts. This has traditionally been the dominant market for power in Norway and has remained so under the new market regime. Therefore, a long transitional period was necessary, together with effective end-use competition, before spot market price reference gained prominence in bilateral trade contracts.

The old network of ties between electricity generation and supply in Norwegian electricity industry involved complex patterns of agreements, ownership relations and implicit obligations. These may be grouped into three models: organised vertical integration, ownership-based integration and contractually-based integration.

The first group consisted of large city works and some regional companies with integrated generation and supply, where the 'network' was basically integrated within one organisation. This put the companies in a position to operate a self-supply economy largely outside the market with internal transactions between production and distribution functions, at least until metering costs to end-users were lowered in 1995. About 45 per cent of electricity to end-users were traditionally provided through this model (Midttun, Garsjø and Joa 1993).

The second group, ownership-based networks, typically consisted of a number of municipal suppliers with ownership shares in a commonly-owned generator. It delivered about 25 per cent of electricity supply to end-users (Midttun, Garsjø and Joa 1993). These clusters generally had long-term supply contracts running parallel to the ownership; ownership shares were adjusted to match electricity demand from each supplier. Sometimes county electricity companies also participated in the cluster.

The third group, contractually-based networks, typically consisted of a central generator or wholesale company, usually county-owned, with various distribution companies attached to them through long-term delivery contracts. These clusters traditionally provided about 15 per cent (Midttun, Garsjø and Joa 1993) of the electricity supply to end-users.

Vertical integration was, however, not universal: there was also a group of independent actors that provided about 14 per cent of the supply. These were typically municipalities with excess production that traded their surplus to clusters or individual companies. Their customers were not necessarily located in their region. Furthermore, even integrated groups needed transactions in the spot market to balance out variations in water inflow.

Multi-level exchange

Both the ownership-integrated and the contractually-integrated clusters were usually embedded in extensive political ties. Within the three types of vertically integrated networks, formal contractual relations were thus supported by a larger generalised political exchange. Sometimes, in fact, the contractual parties were the political entities, the municipalities, and not the distribution companies. Typically, both the ownership and contractual clusters were characterised by geographical proximity. We may speak of institutionalised exchange relations at three levels within the vertically integrated clusters: (1) immediate commercial exchange: power against payment was thus internalised in a more extensive strategic exchange; (2) long-term resource access against stable market accesses. Both these exchange levels were then again co-ordinated through (3) an over-arching political–societal exchange. This exchange was directed at ensuring a reliable infrastructure service, certain allocation of resources to the municipalities, contributions to local and/or regional industrial development and continuation of a decentralised production structure in return for monopoly privileges in the

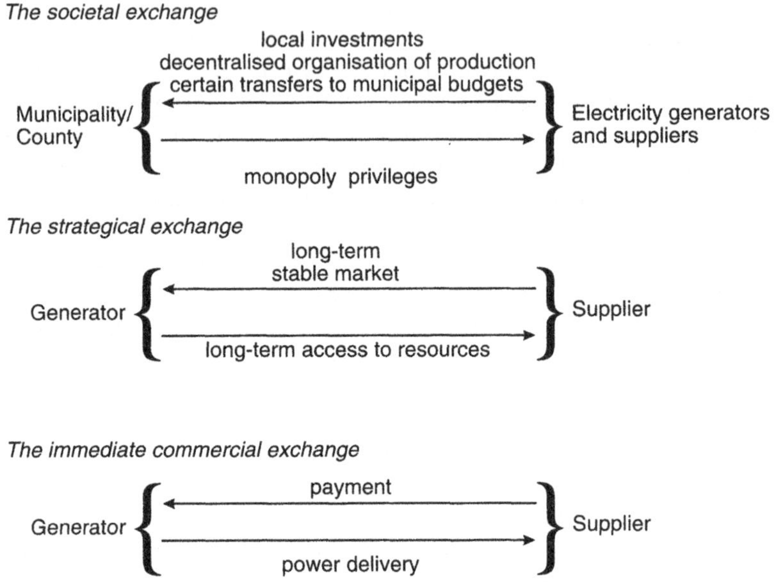

Figure 2.1 Exchange relations in the power sector before the market reform
Source: Midttun (1995).

form of exclusive rights to serve customers within a given geographical area (see Figure 2.1).

Because of the existence of these formal ties and informal networks between many of the actors in the electricity system, a seemingly decentralised structure with over 60 generators and about 200 suppliers functioned in what was in practice a far more centralised way. Political and strategic networks, agreements, ownership relations – all contributed a potential for collective co-ordination in Norwegian electricity supply during the transition to a market economy.

Under the new market regime, these networks have continued to function as governance and co-ordination systems between the main actors in the power market – generators and suppliers – and their environment. The three types of networks all had basically the same functions: they continued to ensure the suppliers long-term access to electricity at stable prices, while also continuing to ensure the generators a stable long-term market outlet and thereby security for large up-front investments. These networks also continued to include political actors at municipal and regional levels, thereby serving to embed even the new market-exposed power sector into a broader political exchange.

Thus, when Norwegian electricity suppliers set about adapting to the new market order, this did not generally involve a shift from political planning to atomistic competition: it was more a remoulding of networks to suit the new market order. Both political and organisational ties from the old public-service oriented regime exercised an active shaping role on the strategic positioning of large segments of Norway's electricity industry (Midttun, Garsjø and Joa 1993). As mentioned, the situation in Norway is characterised by a greater share of public ownership, as well as concession laws entitling the state to a first offer in the case of sale of electricity resources to private take-over, and the right to reclaim production facilities without cost after the concession period. All this has tended to give political networks a stronger hold on the Norwegian market than in the other liberalising Nordic countries.

Exit, voice and loyalty

Faced with new trade opportunities opened up by the liberal market reform, suppliers and generators were invited to re-evaluate their network relationships. This situation resembles the strategic choices of customers in case of dissatisfactory performance of a deliverer, as described by Hirschmann (1970). Hirschmann claims that two basic customer strategies are available, in terms of exit or voice/loyalty. The *exit option* means that customers stop buying the firm's products and shop around for other suppliers instead. The *voice/loyalty option* means that customers express their dissatisfaction within the old commercial relationship, but remain loyal to old deliverers in the hope of improvement.

Expressed in Hirschmann's terms, the strategic choices faced by electricity distributors under market reform can be viewed essentially in terms of:

- an *exit* or competitive strategy, with the enterprise breaking out (or attempting to break out) from its traditional producer–distributor network and establishing a new competitive one
- a *voice and loyalty* strategy, with the enterprise choosing to remain within its pre-existing network, seeking instead to reform it to suit current needs.

Here we should note that the surrounding network context will affect both the exit and the voice/loyalty strategies.

At first sight, the market reform would seem to invite the electricity companies to break out of old political and administrative alliances (exit), and to develop competitive strategies on the basis of free access to the newly opened market systems. However, there might be various reasons for remaining loyal to the old networks and attempting voice restructuring from within: first, the network relations and long-term strategic collaboration, based on old network ties, could be seen as insurance against price risks in a volatile and unpredictable market. Motives for network participation will obviously vary with the market situation. When pool prices are low, generators/wholesalers may prefer collective cost-based trade agreements, where suppliers continue to buy from their traditional suppliers. When pool prices are high, the incentives would be inverse: suppliers would have the strongest incentives to remain 'loyal', whereas the generators might be tempted to choose an exit strategy. In the long run, both parties might be better served by collaborating.

Secondly, the old pre-reform networks might serve as an alternative to direct market participation for actors without the strength and competence to participate fully in the market game. Suppliers and smaller generators may prefer collective solutions where their 'allied' producer would trade on their behalf, so as to avoid the organisational, information or transaction costs involved in full participation in commercial trade in the spot market.

In addition, actors might see the old network ties as a good basis for future commercially-oriented strategic alliance building. Generators might wish to maintain good relations to their favoured distributors as a hedge against the possibility of low price markets in the future, or in order to reap the synergy benefits of integrated control over the whole value chain. In addition come expectations from the political owners for a stable and efficient electricity supply, which may be served by integration and network-based co-ordination. The following sections discuss the patterns of competitive adaptation for each of the three network types.

Adaptation in contractually integrated networks

In the Norwegian bilateral wholesale market, 12 out of the total of 23 clusters were contractually integrated without any ownership ties. The cluster around Akershus Energy Company (AEC) in the Oslo area may serve as an example of a contractually integrated network. At the introduction of the market reform, AEC constituted the central core of a cluster of distribution companies that were independently owned by municipalities, inter-municipal consortia and private owners. The Akershus county authorities owned AEC itself. In addition to its own generation, AEC bought supplementary power from external sources, traditionally largely from the State Power Company, Statkraft, for resale to the supply companies.

Given the political and institutional set-up under the old regulatory regime, this network was sufficient to secure stable long-term relations between the actors. With the new market reform, however, the cluster was exposed to competition as the institutional monopolies of both generators and suppliers were abolished, and low spot prices indicated attractive options for power supply outside the network. In this situation, most actors chose voice/loyalty, but the exit strategy has also been employed.

Loyalty strategy with market space – Romerike Energy Company

Within the county of Akershus, Romerike Energy Company (REC) may serve as an example of a loyalty strategy by a supplier. Formed in 1993, REC includes three former municipal companies in the Romerike area: Blaker, Rælingen and Skedsmo electricity companies. At the introduction of the market reform, these three companies all had five-year contracts for electricity supply from AEC. In 1991, AEC invited REC to re-negotiate new contracts along with other supply companies in the county. In this renegotiating process, Rælingen and Skedsmo distribution companies re-signed new five-year contracts, whereas Blaker signed up for a two-year contract only. Although these contracts were signed with the old network, they also to some extent reflected spot market prices. On the other hand, the political ties surely also committed the parties towards more cost-based solutions.

When REC was created, the company entered into new negotiations with AEC, following AEC's own re-negotiating of its supply contract with Statkraft. REC then entered into a long-term fixed-price agreement for 50 per cent of its supply, and a short-term one- to two-year agreement based on market price for 10 per cent. The remaining 40 per cent were to be purchased on the spot market.

To date, REC has concentrated on deliveries to its 'own' traditional supply area, where little happened to sales to household consumers in the first three years after the market reform. For industrial consumers, which represent 20 per cent of the company's sales, there has been a massive transfer from standard tariffs to individual company contracts, and REC has lost several large customers to other suppliers. REC has also faced steep competition in the market for electric boilers.

REC has subsequently attempted to provide competitive offers to industrial consumers by combining the close customer relations of a traditional supplier with the resources and scale advantages of a large producer like AEC. The preconditions for this collaboration are that REC must loyally channel its buying within the traditional network, and the AEC must not attempt to capture REC's industrial customers directly.

Competitive exit strategy – Gjermå Energy Company

Loyalty strategies with a basis in traditional networks have been the major pattern in Akershus, but we can also find examples where both producers and distributors have chosen competitive answers to the challenge of the market reform.

Competitively-oriented companies have typically aimed at taking market shares from other distributors through offensive commercial means targeted at customers outside their 'own' distribution system. To the extent that they entered into strategic alliances, they typically sought partners outside the old networks, and on commercial terms.

Gjermå Energy Company in Akershus may serve as an example. Gjermå is an inter-municipal limited company with Ullensaker, Nannestad and Gjerdrum municipalities plus seven private shareholders as owners. At the outset of the market reform, Gjermå conducted tough negotiations with AEC to be released from old contractual ties for its electricity supply. These negotiations ended with Gjermå reducing its obligations to buy from AEC to 60 per cent of its demand, shifting the rest to spot- and market-based forward contracts. Gjermå's managing director claimed to have had considerable marketing success and to have doubled the company's sales from 400 to 800 GWh by 1993–4.

Gjermå has left its traditional network and oriented itself towards new strategic alliances on a commercial basis. Characteristically, the company participated in several alliances with different partners oriented towards specific commercial targets. Thus, it entered into a strategic alliance with Asker and Bærum electricity companies to achieve scale advantages when negotiating new electricity supply contracts. It made attempts to start a broker company with private electricity suppliers and a consultancy firm. Gjermå has also worked actively to secure deliveries to the new central airport at Gardermoen, which falls within the company's distribution area; in order to present a competitive offer, Gjermå planned to create a new electricity trading company together with Oslo Energy Company.

Conclusions

From these cases in Akershus county, we can see that although some actors chose competitive solutions, the contractual clusters from the pre-market regime were still, three years after the market reform, available as a basis for loyalty solutions. The motivation for such strategies among distributors seems to lie in the perceived lack of competence to operate directly on the wholesale markets, in the perceived risks of such operations and in the perceived trust that collaboration with AEC represents a good alternative to direct market involvement.

In the Gjermå case, however, the basic priorities on the supply side were clearly different. Here, competitive orientation dominated over loyalty orientation. The traditional network was not held together by through communication and trust, but would have to be reinstated by competitive offers or coercion.

Adaptation in ownership integrated networks

Suppliers in ownership integrated clusters were in principle faced with the same alternatives as in the contractual networks: a choice between actions of solidarity within the traditional network, and individual commercial orientation.

At the outset of the market reform, there were in Norway 16 clusters integrated by ownership. As with the contractual networks, these ownership clusters were built up around a central generator and with a supply-oriented periphery.

The ownership cluster around Lyse Kraft in the county of Rogaland on Norway's southwest coast is as an example (Midttun 1995). At the start of the market reform, there were four suppliers and one wholesale company linked to the cluster. Behind these companies were 16 municipalities. Electricity trade largely followed ownership relations, so that the suppliers' ownership shares in the Lyse production company basically corresponded to their purchase of electricity from Lyse. In addition, Lyse had extensive deliveries to other parts of the country.

Loyalty Strategies – Lyse Kraft cluster

In the cluster around Lyse Kraft, most of the supply companies chose to orient themselves towards loyalty strategies in the early phase of liberalisation. One distributor opted for a more competitive orientation.

Typical of the loyalty strategy is the fact that both suppliers and generators sought to find exchange models that could give a reasonable balance between the interests of both parties in the new electricity market. For the contractual networks this meant that the suppliers had to consider the generator's need for long-term delivery contracts. The generators, on their side, had to understand that the supplier was being exposed to competition for certain customer segments.

The collective strategy in the Lyse cluster was formally contractually anchored in 25-year contracts between the distributors and Lyse Kraft just before the market reform. These contracts were, however, criticised by the state energy authorities and the Confederation of Industry as undermining the new Energy Law. The contracts were therefore annulled the following year.

The new contractual regime that replaced it included long-term, 8-year contracts between Lyse Kraft and the suppliers, varying from 30 per cent of their sales (for Stavanger) to 50 per cent of their sales (Dalane), with Sandnes in a middle position with 40 per cent. Beyond this, the suppliers bought spot power, provided by Lyse Kraft on a one-year contract, as well as buying some power from other suppliers.

The new contractual regime from 1992–3 did not, however, cover Lyse Kraft's generation expenses. In 1993 the company incurred a significant debt, and the network was again mobilised to achieve agreement on new 25-year contracts with the suppliers for about 60 per cent of consumption in the region. These contracts were intended to have a price profile that would make them profitable to the distributors in the long run.

As for the contractually integrated clusters, the co-operation between Lyse Kraft and the distributors also includes collaboration *vis-à-vis* industrial customers, where the suppliers could utilise Lyse's resources in negotiations with large customers.

The ownership relations provided a formal basis for political orchestration of collective strategies. Politicians were often represented on the boards of both sides. The mayors of Stavanger and Sandnes, for instance, were represented both on the boards of the municipal supply companies and on Lyse's board of directors.

Competitive exit strategy – Midtre Ryfylke Energy Company (MRE)

Midtre Ryfylke Energy Company (MRE) is the only supplier in the Lyse cluster that came close to a purely competitive strategy. In negotiations prior to the market reform, MRE entered into only a single one-year contract with Lyse, and bought from others on a long-term basis. In the traditional network, this was clearly seen as demonstrating a lack of solidarity, and led to pressure via the MRE board of directors to have the company show 'ownership' responsibility. MRE, however, developed a trader competence of its own, and also participated in the spot market. The company also collaborated with external brokers.

Starting in the autumn of 1993, however, MRE reoriented itself towards loyalty solutions after political pressure through its board of directors. In this case, the policy network seems to have carried enough weight to push the company back in line.

Competitive exit strategy – Lyse Kraft

Although Lyse Kraft primarily promoted a loyalty strategy for the suppliers within its cluster, the company had also spelled out an individual competitive strategy as a fallback strategy in case of supplier exit. If the owner companies/municipalities did not wish to buy loyalty from Lyse, Lyse could solve its liquidity problem by selling out for instance, 20 per cent of its power resources in that way gaining new capital to get rid of much of its long-term debt. The management of Lyse Kraft considered such a sell-out operation as feasible since the liquidity problem was temporary and the investments could be expected to have high pay-off in the long run. On the other hand, implementation of such a strategy would probably be barred by the distributor owners.

With a capital expansion and eventually also an organisational shift to a limited company form, Lyse Kraft would be in a position to compete in a free power market. The company was already involved in strategic alliances on a commercial basis through Norsk Krafteksport and Eurokraft, as well as being involved in Sydkraft, three major collaborative generator blocs aimed at power export. If Lyse were to pursue such a strategy it would be natural to move the ownership from the distribution companies to the municipal level for those cases where the municipal ownership resided with the electricity company. The municipalities would then be in a position to harvest profits in a regular way as an investor. In fact, such ownership transfers have been undertaken, but within the context of loyalty strategy.

Conclusions

The conclusions for ownership networks are in many ways parallel to our conclusions for contractually integrated clusters. It seems that both generators and suppliers often preferred loyalty to competitive solutions. However, loyalty solutions were possible only through communication. In the ownership case, this type of communication is clearly institutionalised in the board meetings of the producer company.

As in the Gjermå case, there was also an individually oriented competitive strategy – that of MRE. But, unlike Gjermå, MRE has been forced into modified collective behaviour. The tighter and more direct couplings of the ownership network may have provided a more forceful and lasting integrative pressure than the political persuasion of the contractually integrated systems.

Adaptation in vertically integrated networks

When the market reform was introduced in 1991, up to 45 per cent of the end-use of electric power in Norway was supplied through vertically integrated companies that united both generation and supply in the same organisation. This represents a larger share of the electricity supply than both the contractual and ownership clusters taken together.

As in the contractual and ownership clusters, the market reform exposed the supply section to competitive pressure, especially for industrial customers. This again limited the price that the supply section could pay to the production section of the company in a low-priced power surplus market, although the high metering costs of shifting supplier meant that the distributors had a fairly large *de facto* customer base. Let us now take a look at two vertically integrated companies, Nord-Trøndelag Elektrisitetsverk and Drammen Energi. They have chosen different approaches, exemplifying the loyalty and competitive strategies respectively.

Loyalty strategy – Nord-Trøndelag Electricity Company (NTE)

Nord-Trøndelag Electricity Company (NTE) of north-central Norway was gradually developed as a vertically integrated county company through a slow and extensive integration process. The company took over small supply companies that did not manage to continue as separate units. NTE negotiated take-overs with the municipal electricity supply under explicit promises of upholding a decentralised organisational structure. In other words, this vertically integrated company represented centralised co-ordination within a decentralised structure.

The precondition for reaping the strategic advantages of vertical integration was thus all the time that this solution should be acceptable to the local communities. Organisation building within electricity supply has thereby run parallel to political co-ordination between the county and the local municipalities. As one of the largest employers in the county of Nord-Trøndelag, NTE played a central role in district policy in terms of employment. As of 1994 NTE had 35 divisions and subdivisions spread all over the county. Even supply areas with fewer than 2000 inhabitants may have a separate division of their own.

NTE's decentralised vertical integration and the political conditions surrounding this company strategy constitute the central precondition for the loyalty strategy of the distribution part of the company and its customers under the market reform. Continued maintenance of decentralised organisation and favourable el-supply to the heavy industry of Nord-Trøndelag presupposes continued customer loyalty from the households and from municipal and county users in a situation with low spot market prices. With a threat of centralisation to harvest efficiency gains, NTE has real sanction possibility *vis-à-vis* individual strategies from important municipal end-user segments. Because of the societal effects, the municipalities of Nord-Trøndelag wished NTE to continue to uphold a decentralised structure – but in order to achieve this, they also had to behave loyally as power vendors. NTE is today in a process of policy change but is still counted among the more conservative companies.

Competitive exit strategy – Drammen Electricity Company

Drammen Energy Company stands out as the strategic counter-example to NTE. In April 1993, the municipality of Drammen, located southwest of Oslo, decided that the Drammen Energy Company should be organised as two independent companies with separate management and boards of directors, one company for transport of energy, and one for generation and sales of energy. The generation and sales company was to be organised as a limited company, while the transport company was to be organised as a municipal enterprise.

Through the split-up of a vertically integrated company, the institutional preconditions were created for both the production and supply to trade freely on a commercial basis. This structure also left the participants free to enter into strategic alliances based on purely commercial considerations.

The rather unique fission undertaken by Drammen did not, however imply that the municipality wished to cultivate a purely commercial relationship to its inhabitants as far as electricity supply was concerned. Instead, the cultivation of separate producer and distributor roles meant moving co-ordination up to a higher political level. By demanding return on capital laid down in the generation unit, the municipal authority as an owner could harvest profits generated through the company's commercial strategies. The political and administrative leaders of the municipality could, however, let some of this profit be transferred to the electricity customers through cross-subsidising of the distribution company. Alternatively, they could use the surplus for general industrial and welfare policies.

Conclusions

Even though they chose very different strategies at the company level, both the Drammen and Nord-Trøndelag models managed to secure a mixture of collective and commercial concerns, but within different institutional frameworks. The Drammen model gives the politicians and the municipal central administration stronger and more direct governance of redistribution and industrial policies. In a way we might say that co-ordination has been replaced with competition at the company level, but retained at higher decision-levels in the municipalities. In Nord-Trøndelag these policies are internalised in the company in a more or less implicit treaty with its political environment.

Network loyalty as 'cushioned' competition

Taken together, the case studies from Akershus, Rogaland and Nord-Trøndelag clearly document the negotiated character of adaptation to the new market reform and the importance of traditional contractual, ownership and political ties in its first three-year phase. This picture was, however, not quite without exceptions. Gjermå, Midtre Ryfylke and Drammen point in the direction of a more competitive pattern of adaptation, but they were clearly a minority in the first transition phase.

The extensive input of negotiated transformation in the power sector would seem to have contributed to solving an important problem in the first phase of the market reform. Because of the large capital costs incurred by hydropower construction, variable unit costs are small relative to the fixed costs, which under free trade will be treated as sunk costs by the producers.

When the companies in the first phase of the market reform were faced with a significant power surplus at very low prices, they were threatened by ruinous competition. An increase in electricity consumption would presume investment in new equipment that would make possible switches between energy carriers. In this situation, the institutional lag from the 'negotiated' market could serve to alleviate the effect of the market imbalance for producers and thereby guide the power sector away from potentially ruinous competition.

Emerging strategic configurations in the new commercial context

Several factors have contributed to the shaping of a new situation in the power market in the second half of the 1990s and to establishing new premises for the negotiated relations between producers and distributors, as they appeared in the early 1990s. First, spot market prices seem to be heading for a higher level. If this level in the long run remains substantively higher than the internal 'negotiated prices', this will obviously give the producers stronger incentives to sell outside traditional networks.

New rules affecting the transaction costs for switching suppliers also brought household customers more actively into the power market. From 1 January 1995, the regulator, NVE, has ruled that customers may shift power supplier without costs, without having to install new meters. This de-coupling of accounting from regular metering has been made possible by distributing annual consumption over the year according to the network owner's system load profile.[2]

Both the price increase and the regulatory innovation have strengthened the 'exit' propensity, away from traditional network ties in the Nordic market. The exit option for consumers limits the political freedom to design 'un-competitive' price structures. In a high price market a distributor with 'old' network ties to 'in-house or benevolent' producers will be at an advantage. Under high-price assumptions, however, the producer will also have strong incentives to pursue an exit strategy.

Furthermore, with the opening up of the Swedish and Finnish markets in 1996 there has been greater commercial pressure from external actors not integrated into the old domestic pre-reform network ties. The opening up of the Nordic market has also given opportunities for major Norwegian companies to configure *vis-à-vis* larger Nordic and North European markets. Factors such as scale and scope synergies, strategic alliances, and to some extent mergers and acquisitions are beginning to characterise company behaviour in the Norwegian electricity industry.

Patterns of industrial transformation

Considering Norway's early deregulation in 1991, the restructuring of supply and generation came remarkably late. An early organisational move was, however, taken by generators who formed export cartels to face trading with monopolised continental markets. More recently and in parallel with Swedish and Finnish industrial restructuring, Norwegian suppliers started integrating into regional clusters, all over the country. These groups have various degrees of integration and mixes of political and commercial logic. On the other hand, all of them clearly represent attempts of scaling up to meet larger commercial pressures.

Given the 'soft' and flexible mode of integration, regional clustering has not implied dramatic ownership transfers. The Norwegian commercial restructuring has until recently, been characterised by a negotiated approach with extensive political overtones.

Clustering in the Norwegian electricity supply industry

Following an increasing pressure of the liberalised market, clustering of municipal suppliers increased, in many cases leading to consolidation of large regional groups. So far, the clusters have mainly involved sales operations and marketing, but we may expect further integration into common companies.

One of the major reasons for the 'soft' regional Norwegian clustering strategy is probably that it is hard to transfer ownership on a large scale in Norway, for both legal and political reasons. Structural transformation in the Norwegian case has therefore largely been a clustering process based on both commercial and political 'logic'.

In Western Norway, Bergenshalvøens Kommunale Kraftselskap (BKK) was merged with Bergen Lysverker in 1996 into one of the biggest vertically integrated companies in Norway (Figure 2.2). So far, the company has expanded to the north through acquisitions in exchange for shares in BKK. In the south BKK has bought 22 per cent of the local vertically integrated company Sunnhordland Kraftlag, but without luck in acquiring further shares. More recently, in the autumn of 1998, BKK bought two adjacent suppliers, Osterøy Energi and Sotra Energi, in the latter case challenging Swedish Vattenfall.

Also in the autumn of 1998, BKK bought 49 per cent of local supplier Hurum Kraft, which operates in the greater Oslo area.

To support its growth strategy and acquire capital, BKK has allowed Statkraft to buy into its sales and generation/grid daughter companies (Figure 2.2).

Further north in the Western county of Møre og Romsdal, a smaller regional consolidation has taken place as small, supply-based companies with limited generation resources have merged. It is expected that the electricity industry in most of this county will be merged into one or two regional companies.

In the Southwest, Lyse Energi has been formed in a merger of five local companies and their commonly owned generator. The new firm will be a regional giant and a possible national actor with a generation of 5 TWh and a supply of more than 3 TWh to 117 000 customers.

In the South, five owners have formed the regional group Interkraft, former Sørkraft. They are vertically integrated municipal companies.

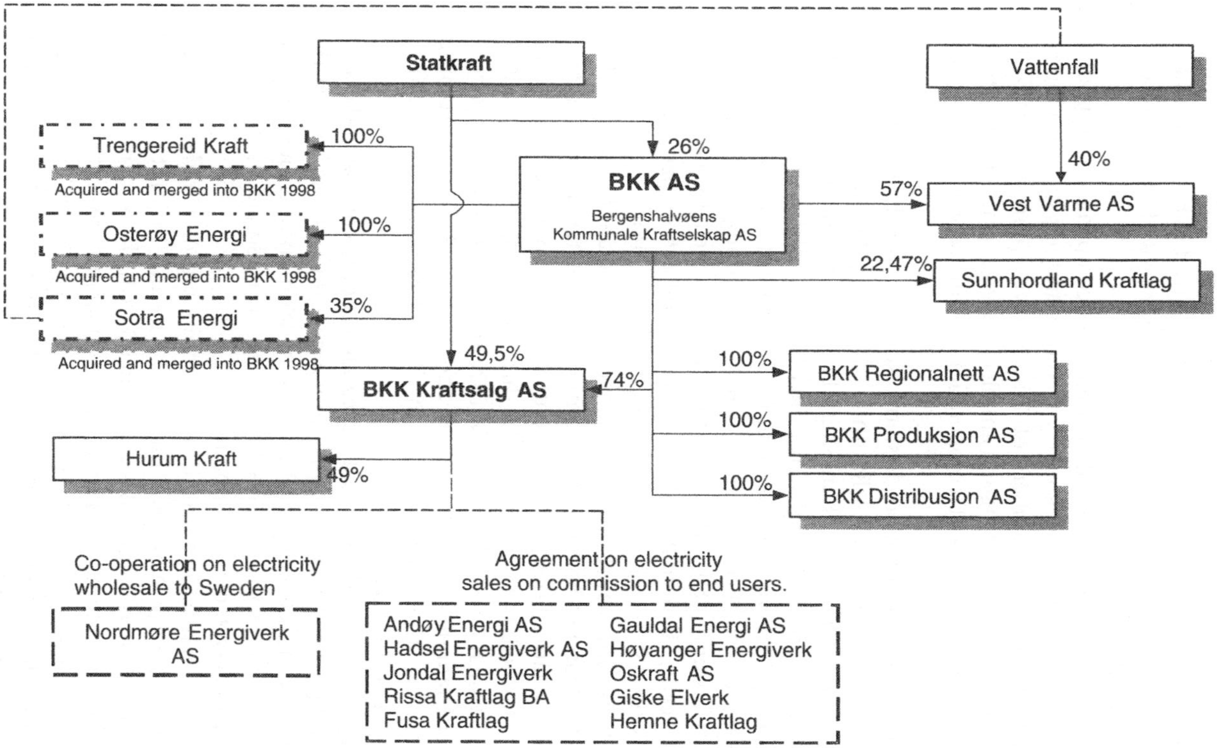

Figure 2.2 The strategic configuration of BKK AS
Source: Annual Reports from Norwegian electricity companies (1997), Press Briefings (TDN Power and Reuters Business Briefing, 1998).

Interkraft has so far concentrated its activities in trading and selling electricity outside its owners' concession area. Inside, the owners have so far purchased electricity on own behalf and sold electricity to customers under its own name.

In Northern Norway five local and regional companies have pooled resources on product development, marketing and logistics into a new company: Elinor. The members of Elinor have approximately 5700 GWh of supply and hold a significant electricity generation capacity. It is expected that the present co-operation is only a step towards full integration.

A second large cluster in Eastern Norway, Din Energi AS, was founded by a merger of the sales units of Asker og Bærum Energiverk, Drammen Kraft Omsetning Kongsberg Energi and Buskerud Energi AS. This new company will have a customer basis of 110 000, supply 3600 GWh of electricity/year and operate in the western suburbs and adjacent areas of Oslo. Part owner of Din Energi through a 12 per cent share is Hafslund ASA, which in turn is controlled by Oslo Energi (19.9 per cent), Vattenfall (20 per cent), Statoil (16.91 per cent) and Østfold Kraft AS (4.7 per cent), all potential competitors.

This cluster also has strong ties to a parallel generation-oriented cluster: In 1996 Statkraft bought 20 per cent of Oslo Energi Produksjon and, in 1997, the latter bought 33 per cent of Drammen Kraft Produksjon. A cluster formed as Oslo Energi also has a share of 19.9 per cent in Hafslund, which owns 12 per cent of DIN Energi, the result of a merger of former Drammen Kraft Omsetning and Asker og Bærum Omsetning. DIN Energi has three other owners in which Drammen Kraft Holding holds 36 per cent (Figure 2.3).

In Eastern Norway, the vertically integrated county company Akershus Energi bought several local supply companies and controls most of the supply to Akershus County, east of Oslo. In addition Akershus Energi is forming a cluster with suppliers in adjacent areas. So far, the company controls 2500 GWh of retail supplies.

Oslo Energi has been engaged in the formation of a trade and sales company, in Eastern Norway. This is to be formed in joint ownership with Østfold Energi and Akershus Energi, which is controlled by Østkraft. Supplies to end-customers have apparently been the first target and the three together supplied 11 200 GWh in 1997. The cluster links to the Din Energi cluster through the co-operation and possible merger with Hafslund grids and Østfold's regional and supply grids, respectively. A second link is Oslo Energi's 20 per cent ownership of Hafslund. That way, the whole Oslo area could be consolidated on the

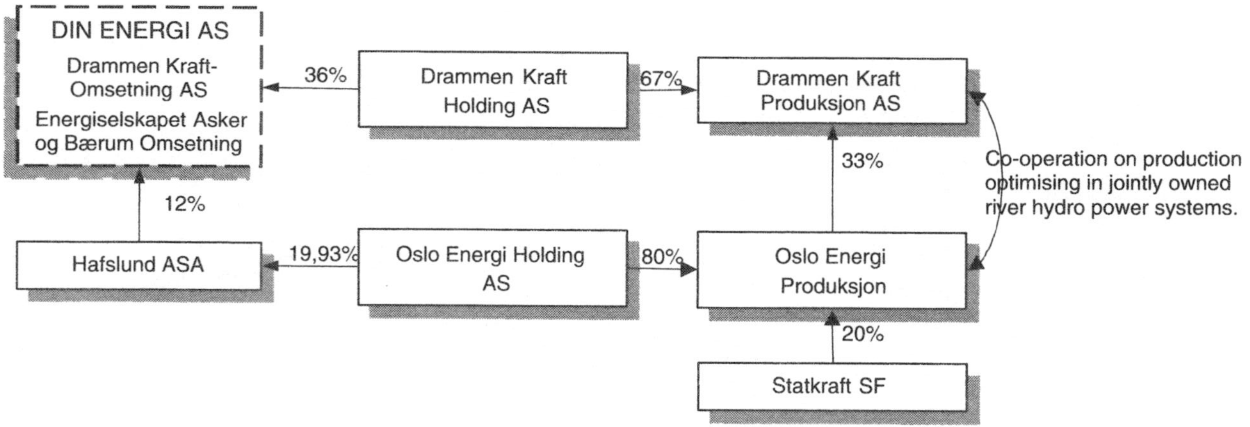

Figure 2.3 Clusters in Norwegian el-generation
Source: Annual Reports from Norwegian electricity companies (1997); Press Briefings (TDN Power and Reuters Business Briefing, 1998).

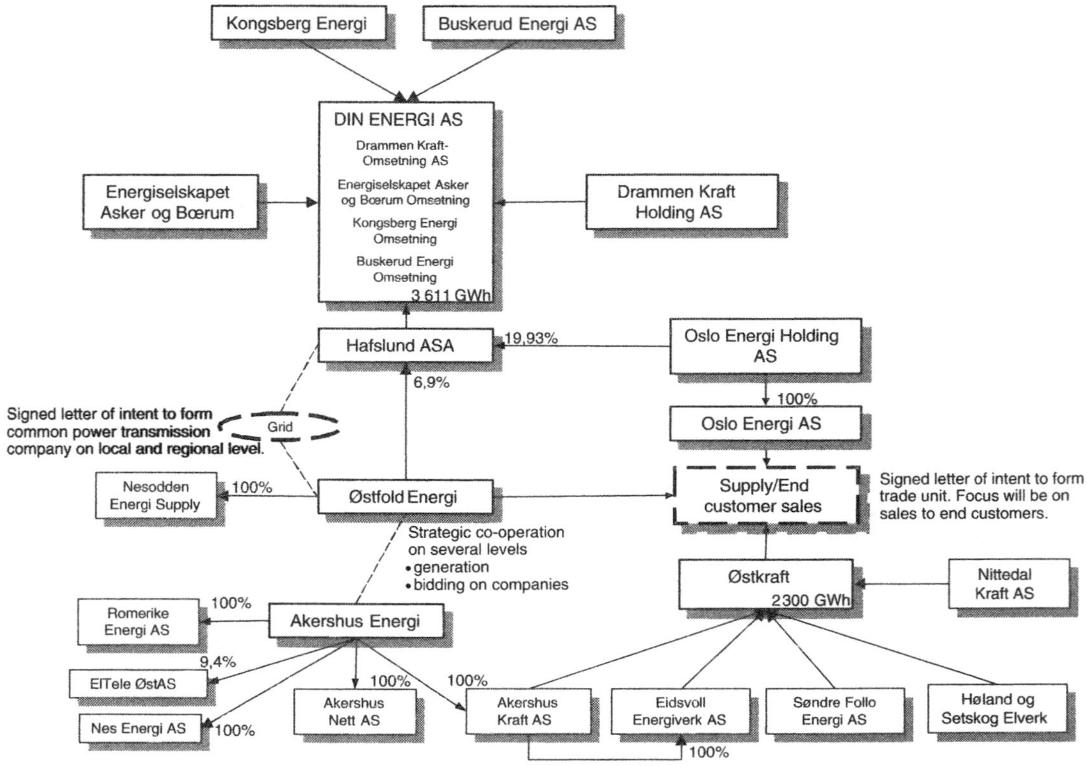

Figure 2.4 Clustering in the East-Norwegian el-supply industry
Source: Annual Reports from Norwegian electricity companies (1997); Press Briefings (TDN Power and Reuters Business Briefing, 1998).

supply side in a single company/cluster. Figure 2.4 is an overview of the biggest recent clusters in eastern Norway.

In 1999, the Swedish state company, Vattenfall bought 49 per cent of Oslo Energi and thereby acquired a strong foothold in the Norwegian supply market. Vattenfall will include its almost 40 000 Norwegian customers in Oslo Energi. This may enhance Oslo Energi's role in the regional context.

Like Sweden, Norway enjoys to some extend large rivers where several generators operate joint power plants or have generation capacity that needs co-ordination to ensure maximum output. However, the largest resources in the Norwegian system lie in the huge mountain reservoirs, many of which could be operated independently. Although some of the major dams were established as joint ventures between Statkraft and the regional generator, clusters of joint owners in common river systems play a smaller role than in Sweden.

Clustering in the Norwegian generation and export industry

The targeting of export markets is characterised by co-ordinated strategies in clusters. Two groups were formed in connection to two cable projects from Norway to the European continent: Norsk Krafteksport and Eurokraft. These groups gather companies across other clusters and are intended to export electricity (Figure 2.5).

The rationale behind this clustering has partly been the provision of access for many companies to a limited set of export licences. In addition, they also serve to co-ordinate Norwegian interests against Continental monopolists. Statkraft will soon operate a third cable connection.

Transformation in the Norwegian case

In conclusion, a compilation of the biggest Norwegian generators and suppliers in graphs (Figure 2.6) indicates extensive restructuring of the supply industry in a 'soft' form. However, none of the supply clusters includes transfer of the grids' ownership.

All three supply clusters make a heavy impact in Figure 2.6. Interkraft has the potential to be the larger supplier, but is weakened by internal conflict Din Energi is currently the real number two, after Oslo Energi. Østkraft, with 2300 GWh of supply, is currently the sixth largest. Since the plans for a co-operation between Oslo Energi, Østfold Energiverk and Østkraft are not yet known, and may be offset by Vattenfall's acquisition; they cannot be included in Figure 2.6.

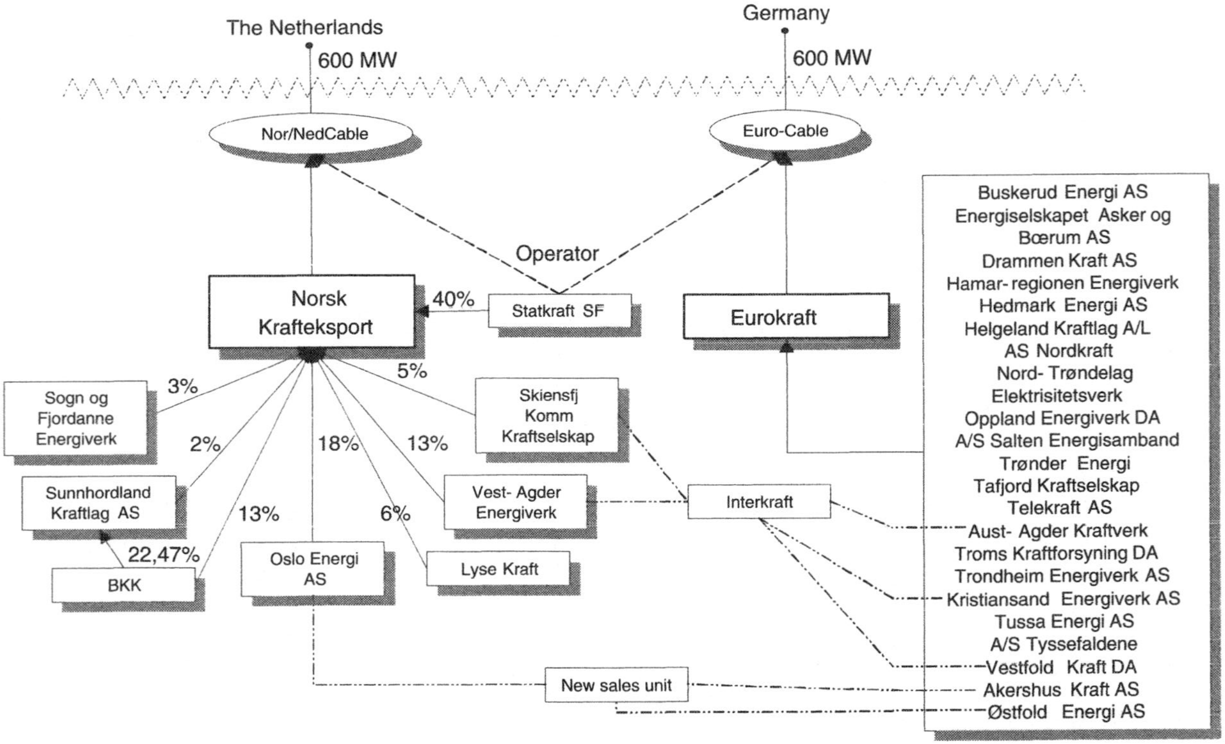

Figure 2.5 Export clusters among Norwegian generators
Source: Annual Reports from Norwegian electricity companies (1997); Press Briefings (TDN Power and Reuters Business Briefing, 1998).

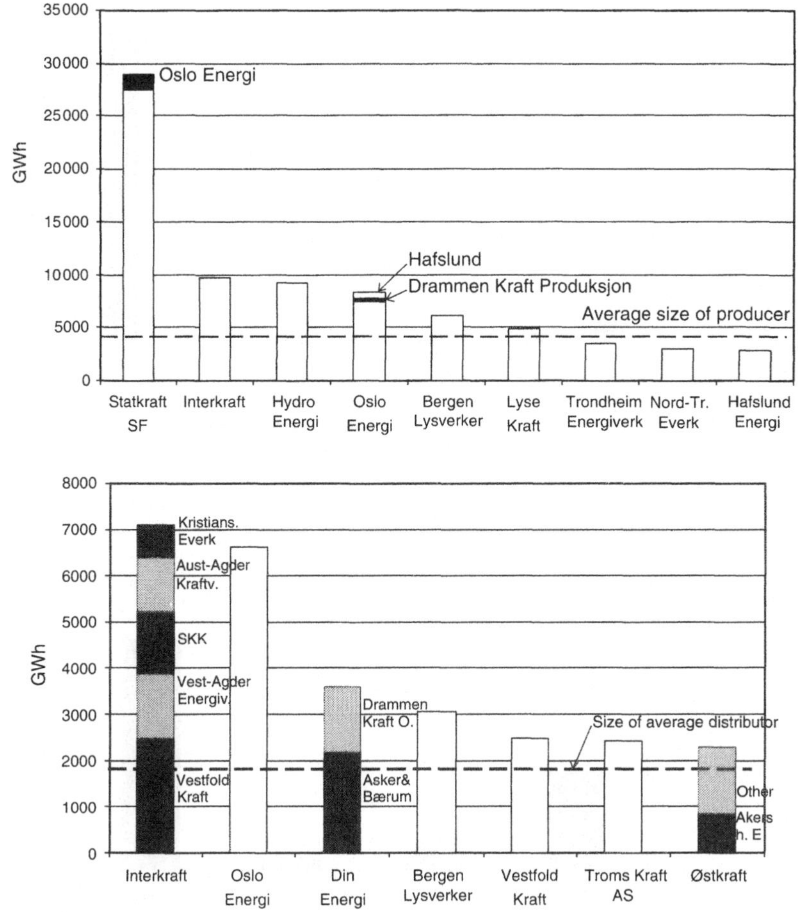

Figure 2.6 Structural change in large Norwegian el-industry companies
Source: *Annual Reports* from Norwegian electricity companies, 1991–7; Press Briefings (TDN Power and Reuters Business Briefing, 1991–8).

Concluding comments

Our discussion of new strategic organisation shows emergent patterns that seem headed away from traditional network ties into configurations with more explicitly commercial aims. However, the focus on the larger companies and most dynamic avant-garde should not mislead us

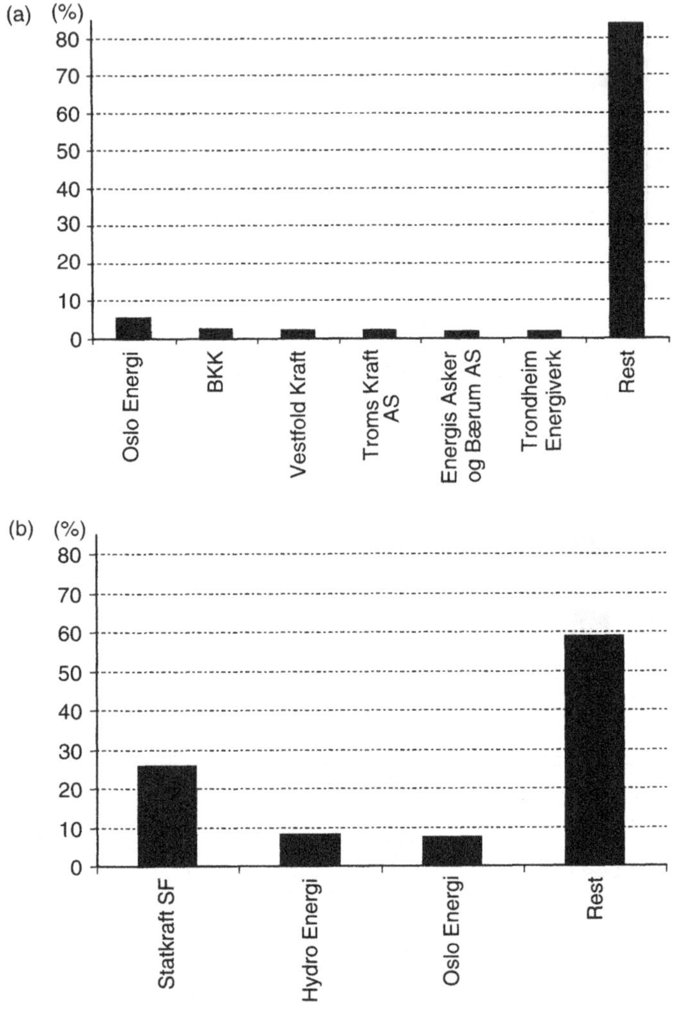

Figure 2.7 Market shares of large and small companies in the Norwegian electricity market, 1996; (a) Supply, (b) Generation
Source: *Annual Reports* from Norwegian Electricity producers.

into believing that these patterns are characteristic of the entire picture for all of Norway.

If we take the whole of the Norwegian electricity system into account, the pattern seems to be one of diversification and dual development, rather than any dramatic shift from the traditional network orientation to dynamic reconfiguration like that described above. Particularly on the supply side, development seems to be headed towards a tier of scale-oriented companies with dynamic Nordic and North European strategies on the one hand, and a small-scale company group of locally oriented 'followers' focused primarily on local customers and development possibilities on the other. This is illustrated in Figure 2.7(a,b) by the large proportion of small companies – i.e. those below 7 TWh production and distribution.

At the local level, in the dominant small-scale tier of the electricity system, old loyalties remain important, and political signals still matter in electricity sector management. Although the regulator has been stepping up efficiency pressure on local distributors, there is still considerable scope for political manoeuvring and traditional alliance structures in Norwegian electricity supply. The comfortable 'ground rent' to be harvested by mortgaged hydropower producers with hardly any production costs allows any actor with such resources a considerable degree of commercial freedom.

However, this freedom may also be invested in strategic alliances of the Sørkraft type. In this case, what we see is an emergent synthesis of the new and the old ties, where traditional networks and political alliance building, with a local anchoring, form the basis for forging new strategies directed towards the Nordic and North European markets.

Notes

1 For further discussion of the methodological basis, see (Midttun 1995).
2 See Chapter 5 below (p. 100) for a more detailed description.

3
The Nordic Power Exchange: Nord Pool

Anders Houmöller

Introduction

The market for so-called occasional power, which later developed into the Nordic Power exchange *Nord Pool* was of central importance to the Norwegian reform. This market was a major institutional precondition for the swift implementation of the reform and therefore merits a more detailed discussion.

The market for occasional power was organised on an idealised free trade basis, with an industry-owned organisation, *Samkjøringen*, acting as a clearing house. The need for such a market, even within a system based on institutional monopoly, stems from the fact that the Norwegian electricity system is nearly 100 per cent hydropower-based, with production varying extensively with hydrological conditions over the year and between years.

The subsequent reforms in Finland (1995) and Sweden (1996) included the development of common market institutions under the Nordic Power Exchange. In the Nordic framework of wholesale competition, the Nordic power pool is therefore an essential component, providing a framework for competition whilst performing the essential functions of dispatch and the balancing of supply and demand.

At the time of writing – March 1999 – the power exchange is owned 50/50 by the state-owned Norwegian power grid company Statnett and the state-owned Swedish power grid company Svenska Kraftnät and encompasses three countries: Norway, Sweden and Finland. Statnett and Svenska Kraftnät are also the Independent System Operators (the ISOs) in Norway and Sweden respectively.

From its beginning the power exchange operated in two markets:

- A spot market where power was traded for delivery the next day.
- A futures market in which trading took place only once a week, and where contracts with a time horizon of up to six months were traded. This was called the Weekly Market.

The Weekly Market converted from trading physical delivery of power to financial trading in 1995.

In January 1996 the Swedish power market was integrated into the power exchange. Thus the power exchange became a multinational exchange. By April 1996 Svenska Kraftnät had acquired 50 per cent ownership of the power exchange. At the same time the name was changed to *Nord Pool ASA*. The name the Weekly Market was also dropped in 1996. Since then the names of the two Nord Pool markets have been very simple:

- *Elspot* (the spot market)
- *Eltermin* (the futures market).

In 1996 a Finnish power exchange named *El-Ex* was started, and the two exchanges were merged through an alliance two years later. This alliance established a common Norwegian/Swedish/Finnish power exchange operated by Nord Pool. This common power exchange also opened the way for a common Norwegian/Swedish/Finnish power market. The tri-national power exchange began operating in June 1998.

In response to demands from a growing number of companies, Nord Pool in 1997 also developed a separate clearing service for bilateral contracts handled through brokers alongside the clearing of contracts traded at the pool.

Nord Pool today offers a whole range of trading and clearing possibilities throughout Norway, Sweden and Finland, ranging from physical to financial trading. The company's turnover and participation are already sizeable and also steadily increasing.

By 31 December 1998, Nord Pool had 258 participants from six countries, with 144 participants trading directly on the power exchange. The rest were participating as clearing customers (Table 3.1).

Out of a total physical power market in the Nordic countries around 360 TWh, 15 per cent is traded over the Elspot market (Table 3.2). The market share is increasing, however.

The purpose of this chapter is to present the main features of the two markets, Elspot and Eltermin. The chapter contains a description of

Table 3.1 Trading and clearing customers on Nord Pool, end-1998

	Norway	Sweden	Finland	Denmark	England	Germany	Total
Trading participants	88	28	21	3	3	1	144
Clearing customers	93	17	2	1	0	1	114

Table 3.2 Turnover and traded volumes on the Nordic Power Pool, Nord Pool, 1997 and 1998

	1997		1998	
Elspot	44 TWh	NOK 6.2 billions	56 TWh	NOK 6.8 billions
Eltermin	53 TWh	NOK 8.0 billions	89 TWh	NOK 12.5 billions
Clearing	147 TWh		352 TWh	

their trading mechanisms as well as an overview of the various contracts traded. Given the uniqueness of the Nordic Pool as the only international power exchange, and its central importance in the Nordic system, the description is fairly detailed.

Nord Pool's spot market, Elspot

The spot market is a Nordic contract market where electric power is traded on a daily basis for delivery the following day, with full obligation to pay. Bids for purchases and sales are placed for every hour of the day. Every contract concerns one load in MWh/h, one price (NOK/MWh) and a duration of one hour. A price is set for all 24 hours of the day. The prices are fixed on the basis of all participants' collected purchase and sale requests. The so-called *system price* is the balance price for the aggregated supply and demand graphs – i.e. the price is fixed at the *market equilibrium.* Spot is a price reference for Nord Pool's future market and the rest of the electricity market.

The system operator (i.e. the national grid companies) in Sweden, Norway and Finland are instructed to use the price mechanism in the spot market when adjusting the power flow at times of bottlenecks between bidding areas. This means that the price is reduced in surplus areas and increased in deficit areas until the transmission need has been reduced down to capacity level. The market participants are charged the costs through the so-called 'capacity fee', which will be explained later. Every day the grid companies set the maximum transmission capacities available for spot trade between countries/areas, and fix the price for the day.

When internal bottlenecks occur, either because of spot trade or other power flows, Sweden/Finland on the one hand and Norway on the other have different ways of dealing with such problems.

Sweden and Finland are always one bidding area each in the spot market. In these countries the counter-purchase principle is used to manage internal bottlenecks which therefore are not reflected in the spot prices. The costs for counter-purchases are financed through tariffs for power transmission. The principle of counter-purchasing is that Svenska Kraftnät (The Swedish National Grid Company) in Sweden and Fingrid in Finland pay for the downward regulation in the surplus area and the upward regulation in the deficit area.

In Norway all bottleneck problems are resolved through the price mechanism on the spot market according to the principle described above. In situations where capacity limitations may occur in the central grid, the system operator responsible in Norway, Statnett SF, divide the country into two or more geographical *bidding areas*. Statnett also stipulate the maximum transmission capacity between these bidding areas. The area division is based on Statnett's prognosis on the areas/sections where the power flow can be expected to exceed the capacity limitations. The prognosis includes the expected transmission capacity, revision plans and other conditions that may influence the flow. In every area the participants must bid in balance between sale obligations and contractual purchase rights, including their own production and consumption.

Placing bids for sales or purchases on Elspot

Each week Nord Pool informs all participants what bidding areas apply for the following week, based on data from the system operator in Norway, Statnett SF. Since Sweden and Finland are always one area each, the system operators in these countries do not actively take part in the creation of bidding information.

The Exchange is informed of the Norwegian participants' connection points in the central grid and therefore has an overview of what areas the individual participant must place bids in.

The bidding areas are identified as *A*, *B*, *C*, etc. Sweden is always *A*, Finland is always *B*, and the different areas in Norway are *E*, *F*, etc. (Figure 3.1).

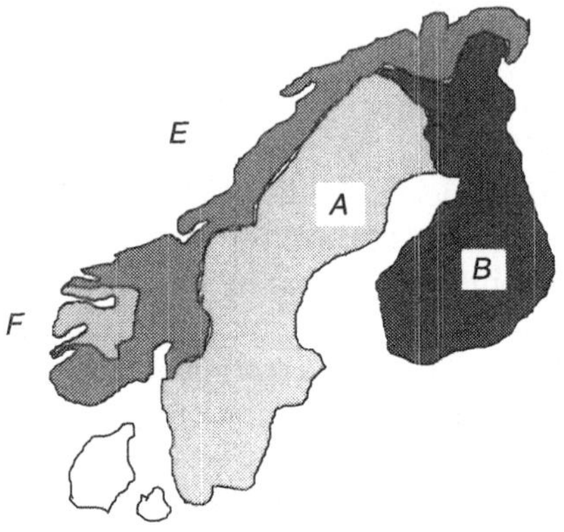

Figure 3.1 Bidding areas in Norway, Sweden and Finland, 1998

The system operator can change the area division for the current week. Participants who have already sent in bids are then automatically transferred to the new area division if it is obvious to which area the bid can be moved.

If that is not clear, the participant may have to place a new bid. Through new bidding information, the participants are informed what areas they must address their new bids and offers to.

Bid and offer form

Based on various strategies and models, the participants will set up a plan for how their own production, contractual rights and obligations in each bidding area are to be dealt with for all hours of the next day. Spot sales and purchases will form an integral part of this plan. Based on the plan, a price-differentiated bid and offer for each bidding area and each hour will be set up. The bid or offer will show purchase/sale quantities with different prices. Participants will not know the price of their own transactions before all participants have sent in their bids and the price has been calculated. Once the price has been fixed, however, each participant will receive an exchange quantity that will always correspond to that participant's price-differentiated bid or offer.

In the example presented in Figure 3.2, it is assumed that a participant has price-dependent and non-price-dependent obligations for a total of 60 MW. Of the price-dependent obligations, 20 MW has a disconnection price of 100 NOK/MWh, and 10 MW a disconnection price of 200 kr/MWh. The non-price dependant obligations are 30 MW. These

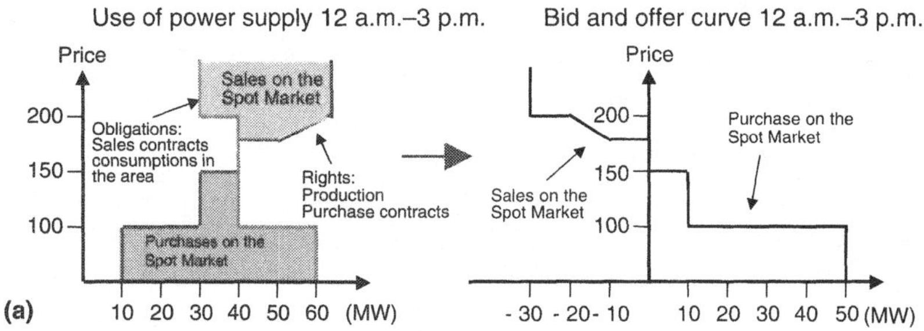

Aktør : Aker Energiverk
Week : 10/95
Area : B

Bid/offer valid for : (cross off)

Mon.	Tues.	Wed.	Thurs.	Fri.	Sat.	Sun.	Whole week
			X				

Time From - To	0	100	101	150	151	175	176	200	201	900
12-15	50	50	10	10	0	0	-10	-20	-30	-30

(b)

Figure 3.2 Bid and offer curve for a market participant, 1995: an example

obligations, which are related to sales contracts and consumption in downstream markets, form a demand curve in the left-hand diagram in Figure 3.2.

For prices below 100 NOK/MWh, the participant chooses to use 10 MW through power from bilateral contracts or its own production, and to purchase the remaining 50 MW on the spot market. At prices between 100 and 200 NOK/MWh, the participant will reduce its purchasing and use steadily more of its own production capacity and purchasing contracts. At prices above 175 NOK/MWh, the participant will sell. Sales on the spot market reach their peak at 30 MW at prices over 200 NOK/MWh.

The participant sets up a corresponding bid for all the hours he wants to report a bid. The bid, or offer, can be made valid for the entire week or for several single days. New bids or offers may be sent in daily. In our example, the participant is a seller in the spot market at prices above 175 NOK/kWh, while he is a buyer for prices below 150 NOK/kWh. The latest bid or offer received for each hour is the one used in calculating the price and exchange quantity.

The prices in the bid and offer form are treated as break-points on a continuous bid and offer curve, with linear interpolation between the points (Figure 3.2a). The bids are sent to Nord Pool in Sweden and Norway via fax or electronically in standard exchange format. An example is included in Figure 3.2b.

Price calculations on Elspot

The participants' overall bids and offers are grouped together on an offer graph (sale) and a demand graph (purchase). The price is set as the balance price at the intersection of offers and demands (the equilibrium point).

A system price (*Ps*) is calculated first, without constraints in the national grid. If the calculation shows that the power flow between two or more bidding areas exceeds the capacity limits, two or more area prices (*Po*) are calculated. The capacity fee in each price area is defined as the difference between the system price and the area price (capacity fee $= Ps - Po$).

If the price calculation shows that the capacity between the bidding areas is not exceeded, there will be only one price area, where the area price equals the system price and the capacity fee equals zero. Any additional constraint during delivery must then be handled by the *Regulating Power Market* on the Norwegian side and by the *Balance Service* on the Swedish and Finnish side. A situation without any transmission constraints is illustrated in Figure 3.3.

If the power flow between two areas exceeds capacity, the price is reduced relative to the system price in the area with a surplus (low-price area), and increased in the area with a deficit (high-price area). This stimulates higher purchases and lower sales in the area with a surplus, and higher sales and lower purchases in the area with a deficit. In this way, the price is used in the market to reduce the power flow down to capacity limits.

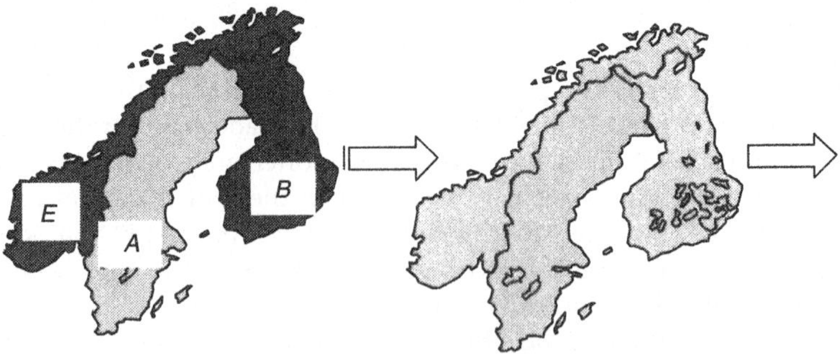

Figure 3.3 A market situation with no transmission constraints

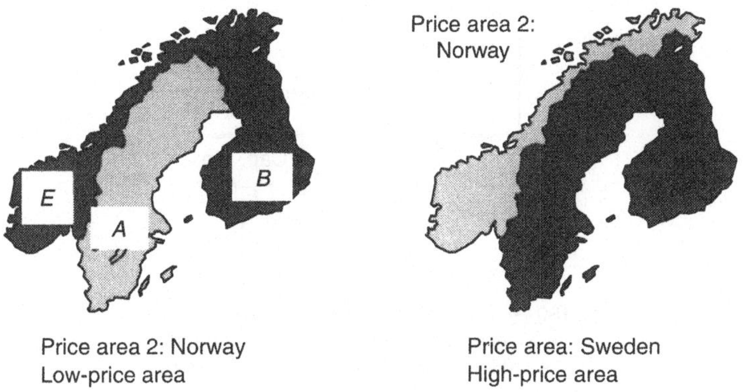

Figure 3.4 A market situation with transmission constraints

A situation with transmission constraints between Norway and Finland/Sweden is illustrated in Figure 3.4.

The mechanism for handling bottlenecks between the two price areas is illustrated in Figure 3.5. A price (*Pcap*=0) is calculated, based only on the respective areas' bids and offers. The price curve in the surplus area is then given an additional, non-price-dependent purchase that corresponds to a quantity (*Cap*) which is necessary to reach the capacity limit; and a corresponding price-dependent sale is introduced in the deficit area. This implies a parallel shift of the purchase curve in the area with a surplus and of the sales curve in the area with a shortage. This mechanism means that the entire transmission capacity can be utilised.

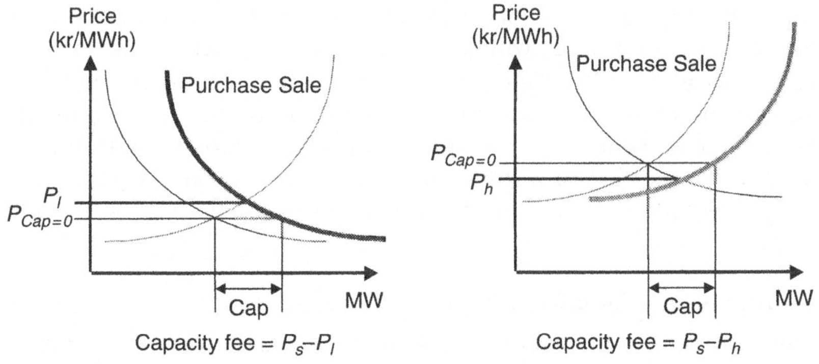

Figure 3.5 Principles for handling bottlenecks between price areas in the Nordic electricity market

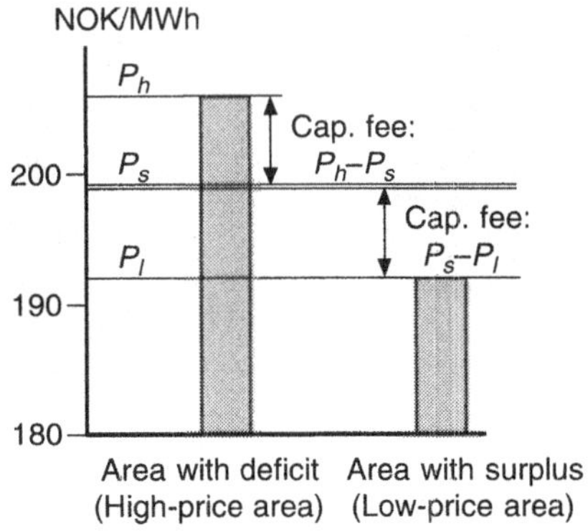

Figure 3.6 The relationship between capacity fee, system price and area prices

Capacity fee

The price signal for the participants' production planning is the area price. The area price shows the participants' total costs and income for purchases and sales of energy. The settlement for energy is based on the system price. The participants are also debited for their use of transmission capacity in the following manner: in the surplus area, the capacity fee is debited to the seller and credited to the purchaser. In the deficit area, the capacity fee is credited to the seller and debited to the purchaser. Consequently, those participants who contribute to loosening up bottlenecks will be credited the capacity fee on the national grid, and that those participants who burden the bottleneck will be debited the capacity fee.

The physical power flow will always go from the low-price area to the high-price area, hence Nord Pool purchases and sales of energy between two price areas will *always* give an *income* which corresponds to Capacity* $(P_h - P_l)$ (Figure 3.6). This income goes to the national grid. Income derived from border constraints is shared between the national grid companies on either side – i.e. Statnett and Svenska Kraftnät in the case of restrictions between Norway and Sweden, and Svenska Kraftnät and Fingrid in case of restrictions Sweden and Finland.

Treatment of bilateral contracts

The treatment of bilateral contracts depends on the national origin of the trading partners. It is therefore necessary to distinguish between internal trade and trade between parties in different countries.

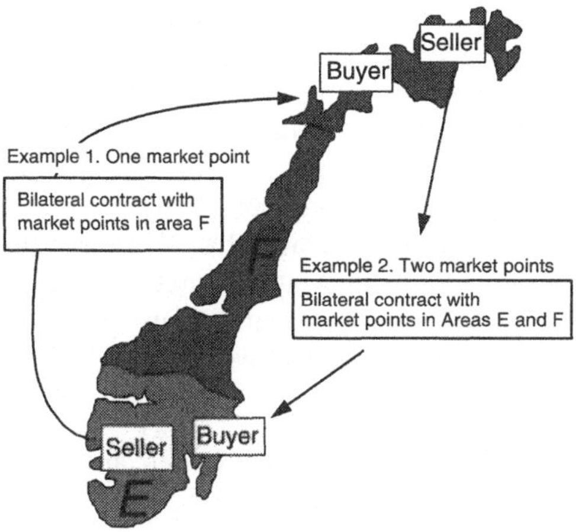

Figure 3.7 Bilateral contracts with one or two market points

Between Norwegian parties

The balance requirement means that participants must transfer exchange on bilateral contracts over the area borders as spot power (Figure 3.7). This must be taken into account when participants submit their bids.

Bilateral contracts can be handled in two different ways, depending on whether there are one or two different connection points of sale.

Example 1: One point of sale. It is presupposed that the seller has an obligation to deliver in the purchaser's area – i.e. that there is *one* point of sale for contract fulfilment. The seller is then under an obligation which must be taken into account in the bid in Area *F*. The seller must bid for the delivery as a purchase in Area *F* if he has no other way to balance the obligation.

In terms of settlement, the contractual quantity in Area *F* will be a bilateral obligation for the seller and a bilateral right for the purchaser. If the point of sale has been designated by agreement as being in the seller's area, the purchaser must offer it as a sale in Area *E* if he has no other way to balance its rights and obligations

In terms of settlement, the contractual quantity in Area *E* will be a bilateral right for the purchaser and a bilateral obligation for the seller.

Example 2: Two points of sale. It is presupposed that two points of sale have been defined, the purchaser's connection point in Area *E* and the seller's delivery point in Area *F*. In this case, both parties must take the contractual quantity into account in their bids and offers. The seller offers the agreed contractual volume as a sale in Area *F* and the purchaser bids on the same as a purchase in Area *E* if they cannot balance their obligations/rights in some other way. The contract is entered at zero in both parties' settlement.

In this way, the participants 'convert' their bilateral contract deliveries to the spot market. This means that all power flow between the bidding areas is spot power that, at all times, is included in the participants' overall bidding. Nord Pool can thus use the price mechanism in the spot market to bring the flow down to capacity limits.

Between Norway, Sweden and Finland

Bilateral contracts between Norway, Sweden and Finland have to be delivered as price hedging contracts.

A price hedging contract in its simplest form is a contract where the seller gives a price hedging against the price on the spot market. The contracts include one volume and one contractual price. If the price in the spot market exceeds the contractual price, the seller will pay the difference to the buyer – and vice versa if the spot price is lower than the agreed price.

The contracted volume may, for example, be exchanged on the spot market. This means that the volume of the contracts is transferred as spot power and both parties must follow the balance requirement as stipulated in their respective countries.

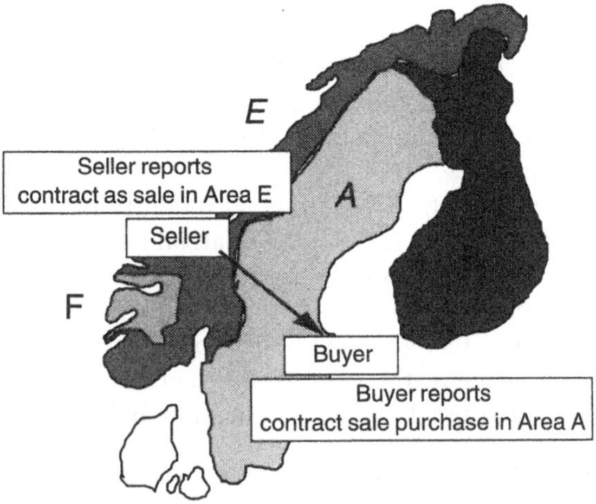

Figure 3.8 Bilateral contracts between Norway and Sweden

In the example illustrated in Figure 3.8, the seller offers the contract as a sale in Area *E* and the counterparty (i.e. the buyer) bids on the contract as a purchase in Area *A*.

Price hedging contracts ensure that energy settlement, both locally and across national borders , becomes easier for all parties involved.

The price hedging contracts utilised in the Nordic market have principally the same properties as the *Contracts of Difference* in the UK power market.

Daily routines for trading in Elspot

Each week Nord Pool distributes information about next week's trade, stating what area divisions will apply for that week's bids and offers, and in what price interval bids and offers should be reported. Once this information has been sent out, the power exchange can receive and register bids and offers for the following week. Daily trading routines are presented in Table 3.3.

Settlement routines in Elspot

The spot market has a weekly settlement. The settlement is based on the net principle – i.e. the nets of the purchase/sale, trading fees and capacity fees are settled against each other and the net amount is credited to or paid by the participant. The settlement routines are illustrated in Figure 3.9.

Table 3.3 Daily trading routines

Time	Description
–12.00	Bids for the following day are received from participants
	Bids are sent by fax or electronically in a standardised format (EDK) or via an Internet-application called *Elweb*
12.00–13.00	Price calculation is carried out immediately after all bids have been received
	Individual price reports are then sent to each participant about their trading
13.30–14.00	Deadline for complaints is half an hour
	Participants are expected to check that the results received correspond to the bid sent
	If within this time a fault is pointed out, Nord Pool will take on the participant's additional costs or, if the fault substantially affects the price, a new price will be calculated
14.00–	Distribution of general price information and other information to participants and other customers

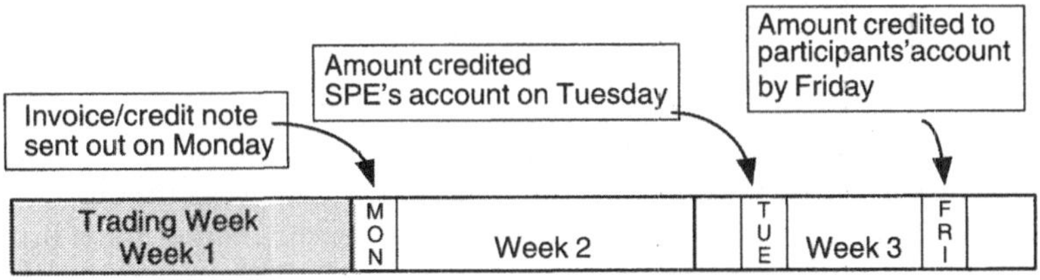

Figure 3.9 Settlement routines in the spot market

The invoice or credit note is sent to the participant every Monday or on the first working day after the weekend for all contracts that were traded the preceding week. Invoices fall due six banking days later, usually on Tuesdays, when the amount is to be at the disposal of Nord Pool in its account, with the interest-bearing date the same as the due date. Payment to net sellers is to be at their disposal three banking days later, usually on Friday.

The attachment to each invoice/credit note contains a detailed overview of the purchase and sales contracts, capacity fee, trading fees and value-added tax.

Until September 1998 Swedish and Finnish participants were required to declare their own trade according to the guidelines given by their respective Customs Authorities. The basis on which VAT has been calculated is specified in the invoice data. From October 1998, Swedish and Finnish participants are invoiced/credited for their spot trade according to Swedish and Finnish VAT respectively.

Currency exchange service

Conditions for trade in the spot market should be equal for all participants, regardless of country. The settlement routine on the spot market is relatively long, and Swedish/Finnish participants are exposed to a currency risk in the time between the day of trade and the day of settlement. Nord Pool offers a free exchange service that makes it possible for Swedish and Finnish participants to receive settlement in SEK, NOK and FIM. The exchange rates used are obtained every day from international banks immediately after the price calculation has been done.

Each settlement consists of a full week's trade and should thus be based on the same currency for each day in the one week – i.e. the currency (NOK, SEK or FIM) chosen for Monday is valid for the rest of the week.

Legal framework for the Elspot market

The legal framework for trading on the spot market specifies the mutual obligations between Nord Pool and the participant.

The legal framework distinguishes between *participants, brokers* and *clearing customers*. A *participant* is a legal person trading on his own account on the exchange. Sub-customers of a participant do not have any obligations towards the exchange. A *broker* is a legal person trading on his own account and/or on the account of clearing customers under Nord Pool's broker concept. A *clearing customer* is a legal person trading through a broker under Nord Pool's broker concept.

The broker concept

The broker processes the clearing customer's bids and is responsible for controlling that the clearing customer at all times has satisfactory security for his trading, as illustrated in Figure 3.10.

If the security posted is too low, the broker participant must post the security on behalf of the clearing customer, or reduce the customer's trading on the spot market. Settlement for trade is effected directly between Nord Pool and the clearing customer. Trading fees for the broker's clearing customers are debited to the broker. Nord Pool requires brokers to have an electronic communications link (EDK) with the power exchange.

The legal framework

The legal framework for trading in the spot market encompasses a *Participant Agreement*, a *Clearing Customer Agreement* and a *Set of Rules*.

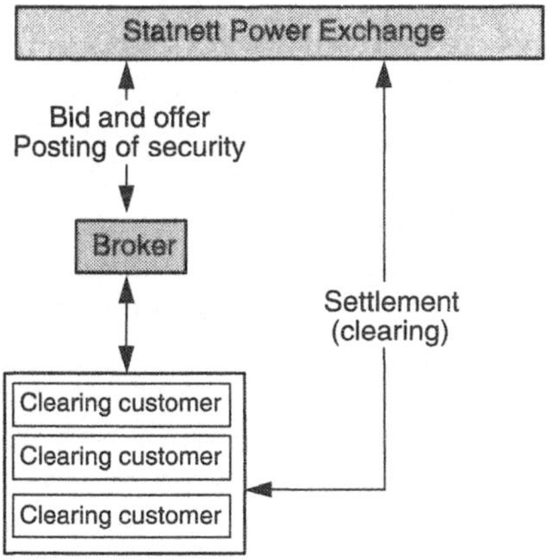

Figure 3.10 The broker participant process

This legal framework has been in place since autumn 1998. The Participant Agreement is general in its scope, the Set of Rules more specific. By signing the agreement, the signer becomes subject to the rules applicable at any given time.

The Participant Agreement sets out the procedures to be followed in the event of amendments to the rules. Signing the Participant Agreement gives the right to trade on the spot market and the Regulating Power Market. The Participant Agreement and accompanying rules regulate all matters between the participant and Nord Pool.

An approved broker participant can conduct trade on his own behalf and on behalf of his clearing customers. Broker participants must be approved by Nord Pool and must arrange for a Clearing Customer Agreement with their own clearing customers. The Clearing Customer Agreement is signed by Nord Pool and the clearing customer, with the endorsement of the broker (Figure 3.11).

Framework for trade in the Nordic exchange area

There are two types of participants trading on the Nordic power exchange: Norwegian, Swedish and Finnish participants who are registered as a company in Norway, Sweden and Finland, respectively, and broker participants who can trade on the exchange on behalf of their own clearing customers. Although they trade through the broker, such clearing customers arrange their settlements directly with Nord Pool:

- There is no border tariff between Norway and Sweden with regards to contracts on the spot market, nor between Finland and Sweden.
- The participants may only place bids in bidding areas in their home countries. It is possible to place bids in NOK, SEK and FIM, and a participant can change currency on a weekly basis, but not in the middle of a trading week.
- All participants are debited/credited the capacity fee for each given hour in the areas where they have placed bids. Norwegian, Swedish and Finnish participants trade according to the same set of rules and pay the same fees.
- In the broker participant concept, Norwegian, Swedish and Finnish broker participants can trade on behalf of a clearing customer in all three countries. Participants trading on behalf of themselves trade according to the same set of rules as broker participants. Nord Pool must approve broker participants.
- Bilateral contracts with physical delivery that have as of today been entered into by Norwegian and Swedish participants, or Swedish

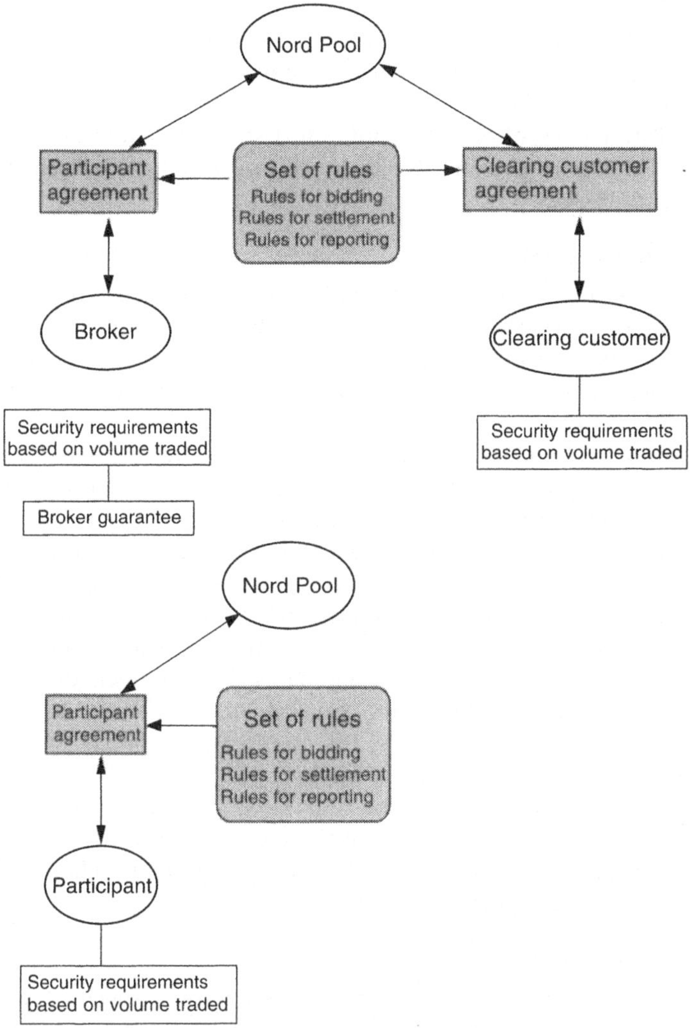

Figure 3.11 Legal framework for participants, brokers and clearing customers

and Finnish participants, may be given priority in regards to transmission. Other bilateral contracts will be treated as financial price hedging agreements.

- The security requirement is the same for Norwegian, Swedish and Finnish participants. Security may be placed by a Norwegian, Swedish or Finnish bank/finance company.

- Swedish and Finnish participants place bids to the Nord Pool office in Sweden. Nord Pool distributes a participant-specific trading confirmation to participants and a general overview to Statnett, Svenska Kraftnät and Fingrid.
- Swedish and Finnish participants must state the name of the company that is responsible for the real-time balance in Sweden and Finland, respectively.

The futures market, Eltermin

The market for financial trade with power contracts encompassed approximately 300 TWh in 1997, and of this around 15 per cent was traded on Nord Pool's Eltermin market. The rest of the transactions took place directly between buyers and sellers, with or without the support of brokers.

Eltermin is a financial market for price hedging and risk management when buying or selling electrical power. This market organises trade in standardised financial contracts – agreements between a seller and a buyer to deliver a fixed amount of power at a certain price in a specific time period. Participants can choose to price hedge purchases and sales up to three years ahead. Eltermin is an important instrument for risk management and the budgeting of future proceeds and costs in connection with power sales and purchases. The contracts do not lead to physical delivery when they become due. Financial settlement in the delivery period is done as the contracts are settled against the system price in the spot market, Elspot.

Portfolio administration for the individual participants is calculated with respect to the market value of the contracts entered into. In this way, participants are made aware of losses and profits in relation to the market value of the portfolio.

Products in Eltermin

A contract in Eltermin allows price hedging for a specified volume of power in a specific time period. A participant assuming a purchase or sale position in Eltermin is guaranteed that the transaction will be completed, at the agreed price, as a purchase or sale of a corresponding volume of power in Elspot. The contract price hedges a fixed volume of power – which remains the same for all hours in the contract – throughout the duration of the contract period, as illustrated in Figure 3.12.

Even though the actual purchase or sale of power by a participant in Elspot may vary from hour to hour throughout the contract period,

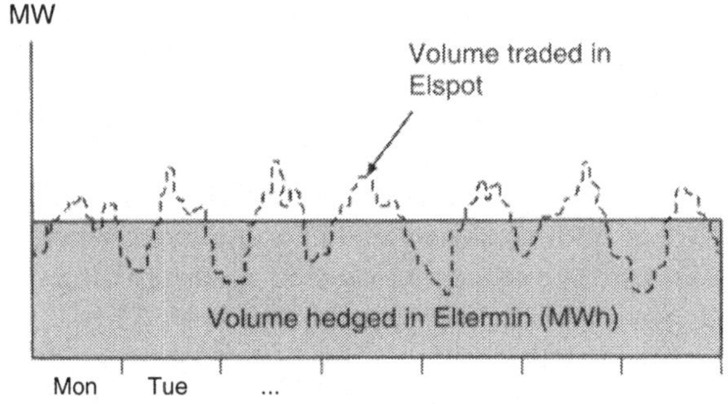

Figure 3.12 Hedging in Eltermin

the participant determines the level of purchases or sales he would like to price hedge. The greater the volume that the participant is planning to trade in Elspot without price hedging in Eltermin, the greater the participant's exposure to price fluctuations in Elspot.

Eltermin contracts can be divided into two main categories – *futures* and *forwards*. The difference between the two contract types can be found in the daily settlement of their 'trading period – i.e. up to the due day (delivery week).

For futures, the value of each of the participant's contract portfolios is calculated daily, based on changes in the market price of the contracts. The daily change in value will be financially settled between buyer and seller (market settlement). In this way, losses and profits are quickly accounted for and realised.

Forward contracts do not have cash settlement before the delivery period starts. The forward settlement will accumulate daily during the whole trading period and be realised with an equal portion every day during the delivery period. The same earnings and risks will be achieved whether trade is done in futures or forwards.

The trading horizon in the market is currently three years. Contracts may be traded for a period of up to three years ahead in time.

Futures contracts

Contracts that are due between four and seven weeks ahead in time are organised in blocks. Each block contains four weeks. When blocks fall due for delivery they are divided into weekly contracts. This facilitates a better overview of the power portfolio of participants and reduces the number of contracts to be handled each trading day. The division of blocks into weeks is performed in the following manner:

Week contracts(Uxx) The exchange splits the first block when less than four single weeks remain from the week of trading until delivery. In other words, during normal years with 52 weeks, it is possible each individual trading day to trade contracts regarding four–seven single weeks. During years containing 53 weeks, trading contracts for eight single weeks will be performed in week 45.

The delivery period is reduced by one hour when the switch is made to Daylight Saving Time, and increased by one hour when the switch is made back to Standard Time.

Forward contracts

Forward contracts can be traded either as season contracts or as year contracts in this way:

Forwards – delivery periods	
FWV1xx (Winter 1, year xx)	1 January–30 April
FWSOxx (Summer, year xx)	1 May–30 September
FWV2xx (Winter 2, year xx)	1 October–31 December
FWYRxx (Entire year xx)	1 January–31 December

The first three contracts can be traded all the way up to the start of the delivery period.

Year contracts are divided into three underlying seasons: FWV1, FWSO and FWV2. The division will be made prior to the two last trading days of the year. In other words, the trading period for year contracts is until two trading days before delivery of FWV1.

How trading in Eltermin is conducted

Eltermin contracts are traded on the Nordic Power Exchange continually between 8.00 a.m. and 3.30 p.m. every business day, Monday through Friday. During this period, participants can submit individual orders for the various products, or they can trade on orders submitted by other participants. Eltermin is computer-based; all trading is conducted via an electronic system. Participants may trade directly in the market via the electronic trading system *PowerCLICK*, or they may trade by telephone via the *help desk* at the exchange. During the trading period five–eight exchange traders work at Nord Pool's help desk, assisting participants who are trading over the phone. They also answer inquiries and assist participants who wish to make

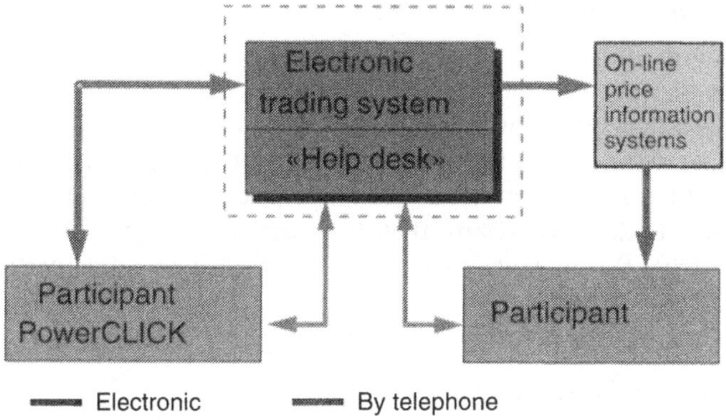

Figure 3.13 The electronic information system

a special deal. The help desk handles orders on behalf of participants by booking them into the electronic system, as illustrated in Figure 3.13.

Trading via telephone (MHS)

Participants may place sell or purchase orders by telephone to the help desk, which posts the orders on the exchange. All orders submitted by a participant are binding until the end of the trading day or until the help desk is notified of any wish to withdraw an order. Similarly, participants may also trade on orders that are already posted on the exchange and receive detailed information on prices and underlying volumes.

If trade is conducted on the orders of a participant who is not connected via EHS, Nord Pool's direct electronic trading system, the Nord Pool help desk will immediately contact the participant and confirm the trade.

Participants who trade over the telephone normally receive information about market activities via an on-line information system. These systems provide updated information on exchange prices at the current time. The on-line systems provide information about products; best purchase and sales prices in the market; last traded price; and volume of electric energy sold during a specific trading day. Some on-line services also offer historical data and analysing tools. Nord Pool's ftp-server or Web pages may provide sufficient information about activities on the exchange for participants who do not need continuously updated information.

Electronic trading (EHS)

Electronic trading using Nord Pool's EHS system was introduced in the Autumn of 1996. In order to conduct trade electronically the participants will need a PC with a PowerCLICK trading application connected to EHS via a separate line. The electronic trading system gives the participant an outline of the activity on the market – i.e. prices, volumes and turnover. Electronic trade also means that the participant can conduct trade directly with the market, giving an advantage over other participants who trade via the help desk.

The electronic system offers participants the following possibilities:

- Posting their own orders
- Trading on orders posted by other market participants
- Changing their own posted orders
- Cancelling their own posted orders.

All orders placed by participants are binding until the end of the trading day or until the participant has changed or cancelled them and received a receipt of cancellation from the exchange. There are functions enabling the participant to choose whether or not an order should remain in the market after trading has been conducted on that order.

Through the EHS electronic trading system, participants always have updated information that is accessible locally. Examples of such information include:

- The best purchase and sales prices as well as the depth of the market
- The last traded price, and highest and lowest price during the day
- The total volume underlying individual prices
- A summary of bids placed in the market by participants and a summary of trade conducted by participants during the trading day.

Participants using the EHS electronic trading system also have access to trading by telephone. Contacting the help desk at the exchange can be particularly useful when a participant wishes to place an inquiry or make a special transaction, such as a combination of contracts.

Special trading routines

After the closing of the market each day, written confirmations of transactions are dispatched by fax. Participants are given a deadline of 30 minutes to check these confirmations against their own records and notify the exchange of possible errors.

The final price for each contract is the last trade price within the purchase and sales price spread. For contracts that have not been traded, the final price is defined as the mean of the best purchase and sales prices. If this does not provide a satisfactory final price, Nord Pool may seek advice from a specially appointed final price council before setting a final price.

All telephone conversations between participants and the exchange are tape-recorded. The audio tapes may to a high degree clarify any misunderstandings that have occurred between the exchange and the participant.

Clearing and settlement routines for Eltermin

The Power Exchange has made an agreement with OM Stockholm and Norsk Oppgjørssentral ASA (NOS) to provide services in connection with the clearing and settlement of contracts traded in Eltermin. Clearing means that Nord Pool takes on the counterparty risk and guarantees payment. The clearing concept comprises a close technical integration with a number of banks, and this enables clearing and settlement to be done in a simple and efficient way.

Daily clearing routines

Every day after trade has been settled in Eltermin, all trading transactions are transferred to partners for clearing. The details in the clearing routines are summarised in Table 3.4.

Net positions in the different contract series are calculated on every individual clearing account. On the basis of the net position the security

Table 3.4 Daily clearing routines

Time	Description
08.00–15.30	The market opens at 8.00 (from 12 October 1998) and participants may trade until 15.30 hours
15.30–16.00	The market closes at 15.30 hours and final prices are determined Trading may be conducted by request to the help desk until 15.30
15.30	Written confirmations of trades are dispatched by telefax to participants.
16.00	Deadline for filing complaints is half an hour
The following trading day	
–08.30	Participants receive clearing lists for trades conducted during the previous day
–11.00	Final deadline for participants to pay security settlement amounts to deposit account or margin account

demand is calculated daily according to the security rules. Market and forward settlement is calculated against changes in the net positions (caused by purchases or sales) as well as changes in the market value of the contracts.

The depot bank sends an overview of the balance on every individual deposit account, and this is used in comparison with the daily security demand and the security placed.

On the basis of this information, clearing lists are sent to the owners of the clearing accounts via fax before 8.30 am on the first banking day after the trading day in question. Broker participants receive clearing lists for all of their clearing customers. From these clearing lists traders can deduce what instalments to make to their marginal account or deposit account.

If the daily margin call is larger than the available security, the participant is given a deadline until 11.00 a.m. on the first banking day after the trading day to arrange security. After this time Nord Pool may conduct closing trade of positions until the margin/deposit account is the same as the margin call.

Detailed description of settlement routines

Daily settlement of trade in Eltermin includes:

- *Market settlement* based on changes in the market value of participants' positions
- *Price hedging settlement* for contracts due for delivery, based on the system price in Elspot
- Calculation of a *margin requirement* equivalent to the price risks that the participant exposes the market to.

Market settlement – futures contracts

In the market settlement, the value of the net positions within each contract is adjusted according to the market value. The market value is the closing price on the last day of trading prior to the day in question. If the market price has increased since that day, participants with purchase positions will be paid an amount corresponding to the price increase multiplied by the volume. Participants with sales positions will be debited a corresponding amount.

Forward settlement – forward contracts

Forward settlement reflects the change in value from day to day of the participant's forward contracts – i.e. the difference in value on the

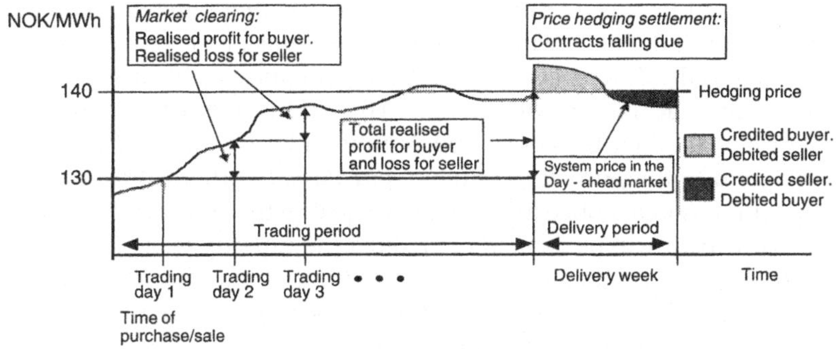

Figure 3.14 Price movements, contract U06-95

forward contracts registered on a clearing account. This variation is *not* settled daily via the deposit account, the way market settlement is done. The settlement is calculated and accumulated every day during the trade period, but only realised *after* delivery.

The example in Figure 3.14 shows the price movements for the weekly contract U06-95 each trading day from the purchase date until the due date (delivery week). Profits and losses are realised in the daily market settlement. After the last day of trading before the due date, the total profit/loss will correspond to the difference between the market price (closing price) on the last day of trading and the price at the time the transaction was carried out. In Figure 3.14, this difference is 140–130 = 10 NOK/MWh.

If the contract had been a forward contract, the loss and profit would first have been realised upon delivery. The difference is the same as for futures contracts: 10 NOK/MWh.

Price hedging settlement

Price hedging settlement is done when the product falls due to financial delivery. In the price hedging settlement the due amount is calculated daily against the difference between the system price in Elspot and the hedging price. The hedging price is a volume-weighted traded price for the last trading day of a contract due for financial delivery. If the product has not been settled during the last trading day, the hedging price will be the average of the best purchase price and sales price at closing of trade.

If the system price in Elspot is higher than the hedging price, the buyer is credited an amount equivalent to the difference multiplied by the volume. If the system price is lower than the hedging price, the buyer is debited the equivalent amount. The opposite applies to sellers.

The overall financial result for a participant letting purchase positions continue until due date will, in the above example, be a payment corresponding to the difference between the system price in the delivery week and the price at the time of purchase. This means that if the participant physically takes out the contracted volume in Elspot, his total costs will correspond to the price at the time of purchase. In other words, the participant is ensured a price for a quantity equal to the contractual volume. The participant will be debited or credited the capacity fee (explained in the description of Elspot, p. 60) at the time of the physical trade in Elspot. This will bring about an extra cost or a gain, depending on the price range in which the participant has his exchange point.

Security requirements

If a participant goes bankrupt or for some other reason defaults on his payment obligations to Nord Pool, the Exchange must enter into the participant's positions and carry out a closing transaction. This exposes Nord Pool to a risk of loss proportionate to the size of the participant's portfolio and price directions in the market. Closing purchase positions will entail a loss if the market value falls, and closing sales positions will entail a loss if the market value rises. The security requirement should cover the margin call (futures and forwards) and the accumulated losses (forwards).

The margin requirement is expressed as a percentage of the portfolio's market price. The percentage is based on an estimated price variation between two consecutive trading days and is set by Nord Pool. This percentage varies between 3 and 10 per cent , depending on the contract type. For forward contracts accumulated losses have to be covered in addition to the margin requirement. More details on this can be found in the Margin Regulations (*Sikkerhetsregler*).

The clearing list

Each day participants receive a *clearing list* specifying:

- The participant's transactions during the last day of trading
- The participant's resulting net position
- Trading prices and closing price on the last day of trading
- Changes in the contract value from the preceding day of trading
- Margin requirements
- Trading fees
- Total surplus amounts or demands for payment into margin/deposit account.

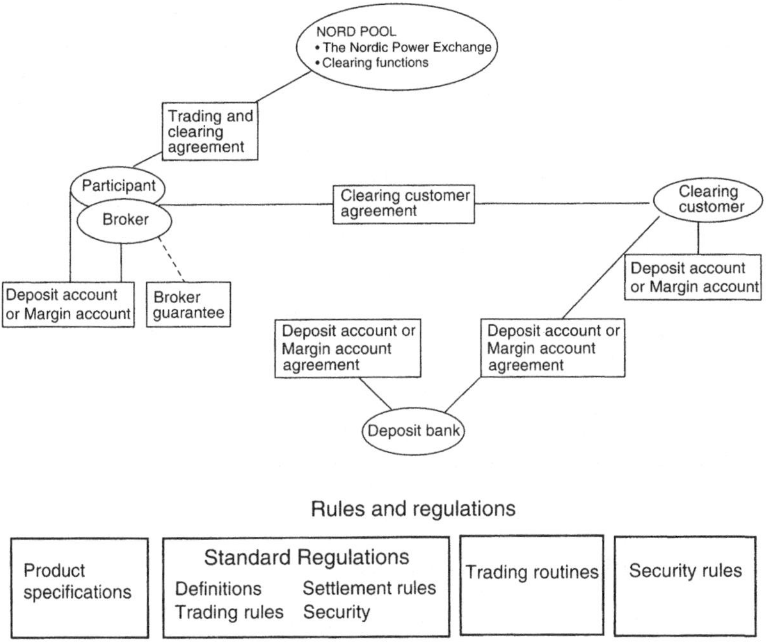

Figure 3.15 The legal framework for the Eltermin market

Legal framework for Eltermin

The various components of the contract in its entirety, including related rules, are shown in Figure 3.15.

- *The Trading and Clearing Agreement.* This is related to the Standard Regulations for trading and clearing. The Nordic Power Exchange and the participant sign the clearing agreement. The signing of the agreement incorporates the Standard Regulations, which apply at any given time.
- *The Clearing Customer Agreement.* The parties to this agreement are the broker and his customer, who is called a *clearing customer.* In this agreement the clearing customer authorises the broker to act on his behalf on the exchange, to conduct all trading, and register trading for clearing on his behalf. The agreement must be sent to the exchange for approval. The agreement furthermore confirms that the clearing customer has accepted the Standard Regulations for trading and clearing as well as the relevant supplemental agreements and additions.

- The *Deposit Account Agreement* or *Margin Account Agreement.* This is an agreement between the deposit bank for trading and clearing of financial contracts at the Nordic Power Exchange. The margin payment, which is a part of the margin requirement, is placed in the deposit account. The companies pledge this deposit account as security in favour of the Nordic Power Exchange, through the Declaration of Security. Companies with a negative security clause open a Margin Account which is not pledged, but which has underlying security in the form of a guarantee in favour of the Nordic Power Exchange.
- The *Account Access Agreement.* This gives the Nordic Power Exchange the right to debit the margin account or deposit account.
- The *Deposit Bank Agreement.* This is an agreement between the deposit banks and the Nordic Power Exchange. The agreement stipulates how daily reporting between the banks and the Nordic Power Exchange shall take place.

Alliances and future plans

In 1998 Nord Pool made an alliance with International Petroleum Exchange (IPE), which is situated in London. It is Europe's largest energy futures and options exchange, offering contracts in Brent Crude, Gas Oil and Natural Gas. A mixture of the traditional way of calling out and electronic systems are used for trading. In November 1998 the IPE announced an agreement to co-operate via electronic systems with NYMEX, the world's largest energy futures and options exchange. This uses the IPE's Energy Trading System (ETS) as a basis for the development of a new electronic trading platform.

This is an alliance between Europe's two largest energy futures, with the ultimate objective of enabling users of each market to access the contracts listed by both exchanges.

The alliance is motivated by the wish to ensure the best possible service to members and users of both exchanges. The IPE and Nord Pool believe that market participants are interested essentially in the products and contracts that are traded, rather than in the identity of the exchange that provides them. The agreement between the two exchanges is designed to ensure that companies and individuals operating within the European energy and futures industries can have the widest possible choice among exchange traded products.

In February 1999 German and Norwegian partners decided to join forces in setting up a power exchange in Leipzig. The aim of this joint venture was to contribute to the development of a liquid market for electricity contracts in Germany, based on price transparency.

Nord Pool and its German partners, Freistaat Sachsen, Land Sachsen-Anhalt, Stadt Leipzig and SACHSEN LP expected this development project to be completed by 1 August 1999.

In the letter of intent signed in February, the partners agreed to carry out a feasibility study to explore the possibility of establishing a power exchange, and to decide on the further process through to the establishment and operation of a power exchange in Leipzig. The objective is to have a fully operative exchange in the year 2000 – a power exchange offering physical contracts (short-term market contracts), forward and future contracts, and clearing. Nord Pool may in the future enter alliances with other exchanges or establish itself as a joint owner of other energy exchanges, and by the Summer of 1999 Nord Pool had established a price quotation in Western Denmark.

4
Competition and Market Power

Arve Halseth and Per Ingvar Olsen

Introduction

In this chapter, we focus on the abilities of electricity generators to exercise market power in the Norwegian and the Nordic electricity markets. The analysis is based primarily on non-co-operative cartel theory involving the use of standard game-theoretical models, with references to more complex extensions of the standard models and computerised simulations based on such models. The more complex models are needed for the discussion of the implications of stochastic variation in both demand and generating capacity in the hydropower system, whereas the simulation studies have been applied to discussions about the possibilities of exercising market power in an integrated Nordic electricity market. Basically, we assume that the ability to gain from co-ordinated behaviour on the side of the generators is dependent on a sufficient inelasticity of demand, which permits an increase of revenues through reducing the volumes supplied. The ability actually to carry out such actions successfully, however, is seen as depending largely on structural market conditions.

In the first and second sections of this chapter, we highlight the factors assumed to be important structural conditions enabling collusive behaviour in the Norwegian electricity market; these include the market structure, the ownership structure and the institutional framework in more general terms. In the third section we discuss market power in light of a more complex theoretical model applied to analyse the more specific conditions for tacit collusion in the hydropower system. In the fourth section, we discuss the outcomes of the numerical simulation model constructed to provide some quantitative measures of the impact of market co-ordination on market spot prices in the Nordic market.

This serves as a basis for discussing the potential benefits which large Nordic electricity generators may stand to gain from reducing their production output.

An essential test of the new market system has been whether it can generate real competition in both generation and supply, and resist tendencies towards the emergence of market power. Unlike the British electricity market reform, the Norwegian reform introduced competition in both generating and supply simultaneously, however with a time-lag in real terms from the introduction of the new legislation to the emergence of substantial competitive behaviour. A few follow-up regulatory interventions have also been necessary, not least in order to reduce the transaction costs to small consumers when shifting suppliers.

Norway's regulatory system is structured so as to accord greater priority to the creation of efficient competition than to the creation of efficiency in the infrastructural network distribution system. Both the new point tariff system of the network system (the 'postage stamp' system) and the obligations placed on the network owners through a system of area and high voltage line licences, place some of the important economic externalities of the competitive system in the hands of the network owners. The success of the market reform, as seen from this perspective, is partly dependent on the ability to orchestrate a market system that can operate as closely as possible to the competitive market ideal, at the expense of the collective infrastructure non-competitive system.

From nature, Norway has been gifted with substantial hydropower resources distributed throughout the country in a large number of small and medium-sized waterways – often with steep waterfalls. These geographical conditions have enabled a decentralised and site-specific development of generation and supply – frequently involving regional co-operation on larger projects, or co-operation between the state and regional/local electricity companies. Today, there are more than 2000 generating units, around 70 generating companies and more than 200 distribution companies with electricity transportation as well as supply functions. By 1990, 45 per cent of the volume supplied for general consumption was distributed through vertically integrated companies. The decentralised structure has – despite state efforts over several decades to streamline the sector – led to a vast variety of regional co-operating structures. Some regions are vertically integrated, some are semi-integrated through cross-ownership, some typically integrated through the regional political system and still others have long traditions in long-term contracting. The institutionally weakest of these structures

Table 4.1 Market shares of production, 1994

Company	Production (GWh)	Market share (%)	Accumulated (%)
Statkraft	31.432	28	28
Norsk Hydro AS	10.400	9	37
Oslo Energi	7.780	7	44
Bergenshalvøen Kom. Kraftselsk.	5.864	5	49
Lyse Kraft AS	5.291	4	54
Hafslund Ny-comed AS	2.577	2	56
Vest-Agder Energiverk	2.470	2	58
Kristiansand Energiverk	2.387	2	60
Trondheim Elektrisitetsverk	2.385	2	62
Skiensfjorden Kom. Kraftselsk.	2.253	2	64

Source: Financial reports of the largest electricity companies (1994).

have typically been challenged by the pressures from the new competitive system – especially during periods of low spot market prices, when local distribution companies have incentives to escape their ties to specific generators and buy from whoever offers a lower price.

Generating capacity involves three main elements: yearly production capacity, installed generator capacity and hydro-reservoir capacity. The distribution of national capacities of these three types varies from company to company. The ten largest generating companies in 1994 had the shares of yearly production shown in Table 4.1.

From these figures, it appears that ownership is not very concentrated – at least when judged from the figures for annual production alone. Measured by a standard concentration index like Herfindahl's index, the index is 0.1 – far lesser than the 0.18 which serves as a rule of thumb for a concentrated market. Furthermore, more than half of the production of the state owned company Statkraft is contracted long-term to energy-intensive industries on contractual terms set by the Norwegian Parliament. The second largest generator, Norsk Hydro AS, is itself a large industrial producer which uses more than it generates. The amount of electricity actually put on the market is thus even less concentrated in terms of ownership.

More important, however, is the distribution of installed generating capacity, and of reservoirs in particular. Both are to some extent owned jointly by two or more companies and, generally speaking, both generating capacity and reservoirs are more concentrated than yearly production. This implies that during dry periods several generators would be short on reservoirs and dependent on a few reservoir owners for marginal deliveries to fulfil their contracted obligations. The major reservoir owners are Statkraft SF (ca. 40 per cent), Norsk Hydro AS, Oslo Energy AS, Lyse Kraft AS and Vest-Agder Energiverk.

Electricity supply typically has retailing properties. Large consumers participate directly in the wholesale market. Some of the next-largest industrial consumers have formed co-operative companies in order to manage their common electricity trade nationally as well as internationally – a trend also observable with other large organisations like big housing co-operatives and chain stores. For small-scale business, public sector institutions and households, the electricity supply companies serve as local intermediate retailers between the wholesale markets and the consumers. Today, nearly all supply companies have a dominant position in their traditional supply area. The largest are shown in Table 4.2.

New actors have played a crucial role in the new market system. For a competitive system to work, an adequate institutional system must be established – but individual companies must also be willing to compete, to challenge their rivals in what used to be separated supply monopolies. In Norway, new, privately owned trading companies played an essential role in provoking competition among the incumbent firms. What essentially made this possible was the over-capacity of the generating system at the time of the reform, combined with a

Table 4.2 Supply shares, 1995

Company	Distribution (GWh)	Share of gen. supply (%)	Accumulated (%)
Oslo Energi	7460	10.66	10.66
Bergen Lysverker	2950	4.21	14.87
Nord-Trøndelag Energiverk	2429	3.47	18.34
Trondheim Energiverk	2332	3.33	21.67
Troms Kraftforsyning	2223	3.18	24.85
Østfold Energiverk	2072	2.96	27.81
Stavanger Energi	1831	2.62	30.43
Bærum Energi	1558	2.23	32.66
Vest-Agder Energi	1454	2.08	34.74
Skiensfj. Kom. Kraftselsk	1252	1.79	36.53

Source: *Annual Reports* for the electricity companies (1995); Statnett Årbok (1995).

row of unforeseen wet and mild years. Both elements contributed to keeping spot market prices substantially below the established contract prices between the suppliers and their customers. This enabled new actors to capture customers by bidding on short-term contracts and re-offering these with a positive margin to consumers. Publicly owned firms, seeing their consumer base shrink, responded by lowering their contract prices and by trying to recapture consumers from other suppliers – mainly in the market for large and medium sized consumers. Through this domino effect, spot market prices and contract prices had substantially converged by 1993, and trends in long-term contracting had become crucially dependent on short-term contract prices. Then, after two dry years with cold winters through 1995 and 1996, the private trading companies experienced substantial losses and later stopped trading on their own account in the highly volatile electricity market. Some merged with publicly owned electricity companies, others restricted themselves to advisory, broker and market-maker activities, and others went out of business.

The second competitive challenge to the incumbent firms has come from markets outside Norway. Regulatory conditions ensure that most trade over existing and planned cables to Sweden, Denmark and to continental Europe is organised through the open market. Foreign electricity companies – other than the now-integrated Swedish market – have to bid and ask into the pool system for trade not explicitly regulated by government-approved contracts. In this way, control by national generators of import/export relationships is substantially restricted by state control and market institutional arrangements.

The economic interest behind the integration to continental Europe is not so much that of export or import as such. From the perspective of Norway, foreign generators account for a necessary flexibility in both demand and supply to the otherwise 100 per cent hydropower system of the country; and to continental interests, the Norwegian hydropower system offers efficient short-term regulatory services to their thermal systems, at low cost. In the longer term, however, even though they are limited by the capacity of the transfer system, Norwegian pool prices should be expected to approach the marginal cost of the foreign thermal production systems, if the system works according to plan.

The potential market power problem

From time to time concern has been voiced about the possible abuse of market power on the generators' side of the market. Various elements add to this concern – for example, the well established co-operative structures from the period before the market reform, some evidence that prices might have been co-ordinated upwards during unusually wet and mild winter seasons, the limited number of sellers in the market during unusually dry periods, and some concern about apparent efforts among generators to form co-operative organisations (Sørgaard 1993). Part of this has to do with 'social coordination' at the individual level, which is explicitly excluded from the non-co-operative analytical models that we will be discussing here.

By 1994, many of the larger publicly owned regional generators had formed co-operative companies, grouping into four entities based mainly on geographical criteria. Including the largest generator Statkraft, a market structure with efficient internal co-ordination as envisaged within the four co-operative entities would have made the supply side rather concentrated. However, the Norwegian competition authorities rejected these initiatives, and only one of them (Sørkraft, in southern Norway) proved important to ongoing operations. Following the establishment of a joint Nordic market in 1996, regulatory interventions in this area have become less restrictive, as the number of generators in the joint market increased substantially, and as none of the co-operating alternatives were anywhere as large as the largest Swedish generator Vattenfall AB.

In export relationships, co-operation has been promoted. Negotiations for long-term contracting with continental electricity companies, which tend to be market monopolies in their home regions, have been organised in two Norwegian blocs – one with the eight largest publicly owned generators organised in Norsk Krafteksport AS, and the other with 25 smaller companies in Eurokraft AS. However, discipline has not always been firm, and there has been some tension between Statkraft as the most experienced actor in foreign markets and some of the next-largest companies.

A second type of concern about the competitive abilities of the system has focused on the limitations to competition in supply to small consumers. In order to promote competition, the regulator has interfered to reduce the price which each grid company can charge its customers when they shift from one supplier to another. Even though it can be argued that transaction costs owing to measurement costs, the handling of payments between an increasing number of suppliers with each network company and the risks involved for the local network company, all represent substantial costs, the regulator NVE has given top priority to supporting competition. Transaction costs to the small consumer have been reduced to almost nothing, and the question of cost recovery has been partly transferred to the general transmission tariffs. Despite this intervention, very few small consumers have actually shifted suppliers. This is probably because of the price responses of the suppliers, which have brought about a strong convergence of consumer prices. This outcome clearly indicates that the electricity market works – and, indeed, that it works quite well even at the level of potential competition.

Market power in a hydropower system

Thus, there seem to be no obvious reason to expect any substantial capability for collusive behaviour among generators, as long as we restrict ourselves to non-co-operative preconditions. We will, however, shortly present and discuss in greater detail some further problems involved in establishing collusive behaviour in a hydropower electricity market.

There have been a couple of studies of market power in the Norwegian electricity market. The theoretical approach has typically been that of economic cartel theory, with a discussion of various game-theoretic models accompanied by a discussion of empirical data (Sørgaard 1993; Olsen 1994). The game-theoretical approach presupposes that actors have specified properties like rational utility maximising behaviour, independent and complete organisational control, homogeneous products, complete information, etc. In actual markets, most of these conditions are not fulfilled; real-life market structures typically involve ambiguous and complex relationships of more or less control, conflicts of interests and influences from external economic and political regulations. Firm behaviours are typically both competitive and co-operative in multiple dimensions. The aim of simplistic modelling, however, is to concentrate on and extract what are seen as essential structures of logic in the market in question.

With the integration of the Norwegian and Swedish markets, and with the active participation of both Finland and Denmark in this market, the relevant market context to analyse is now the *Nordic* market. First, however, we should mention some of the peculiarities of a pure hydropower system like that of Norway, as concerns the conditions for collusive behaviour.

Cartel theory generally is about tacit collusion between individual utility seeking firms who know that their strategic behaviours influence the strategic behaviours of their rivals, and vice versa. That is, they are in a situation of strategic interaction on non-co-operative basis. Standard models assume that the strategic variable is either price or volume, with volume usually interpreted as either production capacity or output, where two firms play their optimal strategies in order to maximise profits. Results are then analytically compared to the efficient competitive market solution. In more complex modelling, price and volume models are integrated into multi-stage games, and the standard static models are typically modelled as repeated games representing the dynamics of the strategic interplay over time.

Non-co-operative collusion in the face of demand and capacity uncertainty

Because none of the Norwegian generators are large enough to be capable of playing any important role as a residual monopolist in the electricity market, the relevant problem to discuss seems to be a cartel situation in which several generators are capable of establishing a joint collusive regime. One model which can realistically represent some of the major problems to collusive behaviour in the hydro-electricity context has been developed by Staiger and Wolak (1992). Their aim is to portray the effects of stochastic demand in a situation with two producers and capacity constraints. This model is applicable also to a situation with stochastic capacity constraints – and that is a situation typical of the hydropower system, where production is constrained by the partly unpredictable influx of water. Accordingly, the model can be interpreted as a model for collusion under uncertain capacity utilisation rates – i.e. the relative outcome of stochastic capacity constraints and stochastic demand.

We shall not present the formal analysis here. The main results, however, are rather intuitively apparent. First, tacit collusion is easier to sustain when actual realised production capacity is unexpectedly high and/or when actual realised demand is unexpectedly low. This follows because, in such a situation, each firm is capable of presenting a credible threat to the other which prevents the other from deviating from the collusive strategy of maintaining a high price by limiting output. The content of the threat is to capture a larger market share by cutting prices (a price war) if the rival does not maintain the collusive price, and to set a competitive price in all periods thereafter. In standard cartel theory, a credible threat of such a price war will serve as a sufficient condition for sustaining the collusive outcome at any given level.

Secondly, collusion is also easier to sustain in the opposite situation, when capacity is unexpectedly low and/or demand unexpectedly high.

In this case, each firm will have a very limited capability to capture any larger market share, so that the gains from a larger volume will be more than offset by the loss from the lower price on the large volume traded. In the middle range, there is a price-war area where collusion becomes progressively more difficult to sustain as the actual realised capacity utilisation rate approaches its statistical expectation for the joint capacity utilisation rates of the two rivals. When the actual realised capacity rates increase above the expectation level, collusion becomes progressively less difficult to sustain.

Thus, according to the theory, in unexpectedly wet (large capacity) and warm (low demand) periods and in unexpectedly dry (low capacity) and cold (high demand) periods, electricity generators should find it easier to collude than in 'middle-range' periods. The event when collusion breaks down is basically determined by the relationship between the firms' expected gains from future collusive pricing – which depends on their expected ability to sustain collusion in future periods – and the one-shot benefits to be gained from deviating by delivering all one's capacity in one period before both revert to non-collusive strategies thereafter. It follows that the more firms expect collusion to be sustainable, the higher will be the expected gains from adhering to the collusive strategy and the more sustainable will be collusive behaviour.

Collusive ability

Several elements can be expected to influence beliefs about the future gains from collusive behaviour and, accordingly, the ability of an industry to sustain collusion. The distribution of ownership and capacity control rights are vital here. Collusion is more difficult to sustain when the number of generators increases. With an unlimited number of participants, the collusive outcome approaches the competitive market solution. We have seen that in Norway generating capacity is not very concentrated in terms of ownership. Some generators are themselves large industrial consumers and net buyers in the market, like Norsk Hydro AS. These can be expected to follow anti-cartel strategies in the electricity market – for example, triggering price wars when collusive behaviours are observed. For collusion to be sustainable, some sort of co-ordination other than ownership is needed, such as the proposed producer co-operatives. In the absence of joint ownership or contractual agreements on the strategic variables, however, these might have basic internal properties rather similar to that of a non-co-operative game. Each of the participating companies might choose to increase its individual market share at the expense of the co-operative by offering a slightly lower price elsewhere in the market. Thus, a loose form of co-operation might not be able to sustain the necessary internal controls.

Secondly, collusion is crucially dependent on the ability of the rivals to observe each other's pricing behaviour, to distinguish stochastic influences from strategic changes and to present credible threats of punishment in the latter case. In the hydropower system, pricing is a complex intertemporal issue based on expectations as to future influx of water, new capacities, import–export trade, cyclical variation in demand, etc. Interpreting a rival's price cut is accordingly a tricky question. There is a risk that pure stochastic influences rather than strategic price cuts will trigger price wars. In such a system, collusion is not easy to sustain.

Thirdly, positions tend to vary over time. In unexpectedly wet and mild periods various companies will be net sellers who find themselves as net buyers in dry and cold periods. Potential alliances will accordingly tend to break down as positions change. Also regional differences will change over time with changes in weather conditions. The position taken by a company will accordingly vary from year to year, even though average national reservoir levels might be unchanged. All these changes from stochastic influences make collusive strategies even more difficult to sustain.

Fourthly, price wars are very costly in the hydropower system, because the water resources used during price wars are unlikely to be bought back at a similar price in the market later on. This follows from the intertemporal price-setting of hydropower. The influx of water is free of cost, where as water to be used for electricity generation can be bought back only by paying the market price for electricity. A price war in the present period will – other things being equal – increase prices in future periods, while lowering prices in the present period, as total generating capacity is set by nature's influx of water to the system. This effect generally reduces the credibility of the collusive strategy. By contrast, the price for coal used by a thermal power plant during a price war is unlikely to influence future coal prices to any significant degree.

Strategic storage has indeed been modelled in theoretical cartel theory, for instance by Rotemberg and Saloner (1989), and their general results are at least partly applicable to the hydro-reservoir management situation. They find that strategic management of stored goods is a two-edged sword. Increased storage in order to increase the credibility of one's own collusive strategy also increases one's own incentive to leave the cartel arrangement in order to capture a larger market share. The same holds for the rival. The result adds to the logic of Staiger and Wolak's reasoning, in showing that collusion is more sustainable if the rivals have equally high or equally low storage levels. Likewise, collusion is less sustainable in the intermediate range or when producers have asymmetrical storage levels.

Fifthly, collusive pricing is illegal and politically illegitimate. The regulator, the press, consumers and politicians as well are likely to react to any evidence of collusion on the part of the generators, nor are the politically owned generating companies likely for very long to withstand strong accusations of 'anti-social behaviour.

Taken together, all these elements indicate that cartel co-ordination based on pure non-co-operative strategic behaviour seems neither easy to establish nor easy to sustain in a hydropower system. This need not mean that co-ordination cannot exist – but there will have to be important social co-operative or hierarchical elements in the market to explain the phenomenon. And, in that case, we are outside the framework of non-co-operative cartel theory.

Market power in the Nordic electricity market[1]

With the integration of the Swedish and Norwegian electricity markets from January 1996, the entry of Finland into the joint market somewhat later and the participation of Denmark and gradually Germany and the Netherlands countries, the relevant market context to analyse has, as noted, now become the *Nordic* one. Because Sweden, Finland and Denmark all have a much more concentrated electricity generating structure than does Norway, it is not obvious that expanding the market makes the execution of market power less possible than in the internal Norwegian context. In a Nordic context, the focus turns towards the analysis of the large state-owned companies: Statkraft (NOR), Vattenfall (SWE), Imatran (FIN), together with second-largest Swedish generator Sydkraft and the Danish co-operative companies Elsam and Elkraft. Together, these companies represent a large share of total Nordic generating capacity; indeed, the market share of Sweden's Vattenfall alone in the Nordic market is larger than the market share of Statkraft in the Norwegian general supply market.

Accordingly, this final section will discuss the potential for market power in the Nordic market context. We present a quantitative analysis aimed at analysing the extent to which the largest Nordic power generators stand to gain from the exercise of market power. The analysis will concentrate on how the generators might adjust the running of their existing plants – whether they consider it profitable to reduce output in order to achieve spot price increases. Thus we will not be focusing on the implications for different types of contracts, nor the longer-term perspective in which strategic interests may influence investment in new generating capacity.

Computer simulations carried out in ECON's model of the Nordic electricity market have been the operative tool for the analysis. In this model, the adaptations of strategies by the generators have been modelled on the basis of the standard non-co-operative Nash–Cournot oligopoly model. This means that the strategic variable of the game is taken to be the decision to generate some volume, and that prices are calculated as outcomes of the game. Outcomes are calculated on the basis of a Nash equilibrium in a strategic game between the generators, where the volume supplied by each individual generator is a function of his marginal production costs, his generating capacity and the price elasticity of demand. We have also modelled the extent to which the other generators strategically adjust successive volumes when observing changes in market prices (the conjectural variation or elasticity of supply). All generators are assumed to execute purely non-co-operative strategies.

Whether the individual generators will find it profitable to exercise market power depends on a great many factors. We start by considering a 'base case' where external factors such as institutional conditions, levels of consumption, production and transfer costs correspond to autumn 1995 values. Next, we consider whether the incentives to exercise market power in the model are influenced by the degree of integration between the Nordic countries, and whether this is influenced by the level of demand, here interpreted as a function of the 'underlying competitive price level' in the market.

The 'base case'

Figure 4.1 shows the positions of the largest generators under two specific conditions – first, under the assumption of perfect competition, where the price per definition equals the marginal production costs, and secondly, under the assumption of oligopolistic competition.

From Figure 4.1 we see that the largest Swedish generator *Vattenfall*, and to some extent the Finnish generator *IVO*, both have incentives to force the spot price up by reducing their market supply.

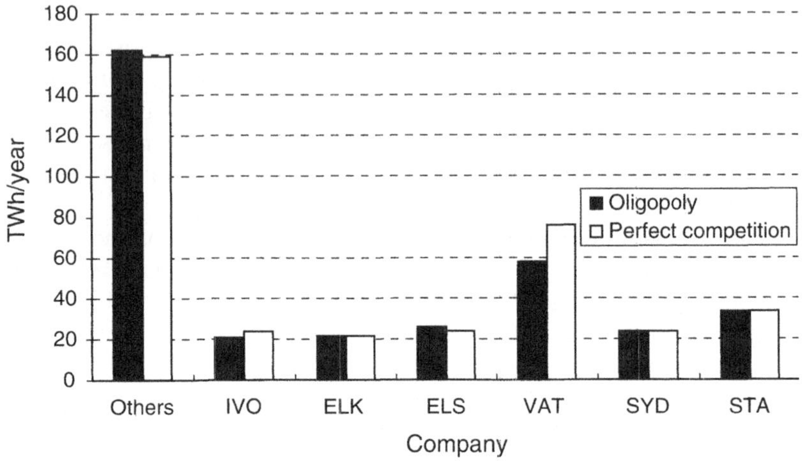

Figure 4.1 Production by company, 1995 (TWh/year)
Note: VAT: Vattenfall (SWE), SYD: Sydkraft (SWE), IVO: Imatran Voima (FIN), STA: Statkraft (NOR), ELS: Elsam (DEN), ELK: Elkraft(DEN).
Source: Halseth (1998).

Under oligopolistic conditions, the calculated price lies slightly under 2.5 ¢/kWh (cf. the Norwegian Central Grid), which is 15 per cent above the perfect competitive price equilibrium.

Vattenfall's relatively low output reflects the company's large market share, some 20 per cent of the Nordic market and around 50 per cent of total Swedish production. Whether or not it will be profitable to exercise market power depends on a two-part calculation. First, if some of the capacity is removed from the market, the economic contribution margin[2] of this production will lapse. For such a decision to be profitable, this lapse must be compensated by the increase in contribution margin for the remaining production which follows from the increased prices. The greater the market share, the greater will be the volume which achieves a larger contribution margin, making it more profitable to exercise market power to begin with.

It is interesting to note that *Statkraft* has scant incentives to reduce output, because its generating capacity is 100 per cent based on hydropower. In hydro-based plants, as noted on p. 000, the contribution margin of marginal production equals almost 100 per cent of the power price. This means that the price must increase more sharply for the company to defend a decision not to exploit all of its production capacity. The calculations thus clearly indicate that the Nordic hydropower generators – including Vattenfall, which has a nearly 50/50 hydro/nuclear capacity portfolio – will find it more profitable to utilise their hydropower-generating capacity to the full, than will generators with primarily thermal power capacities.

Figure 4.1 also shows that supply from independent non-collusive generators within the Nordic market and the Danish generators *Elsam* and *Elkraft* increased somewhat owing to the higher prices. However, the calculations also indicate that there is little capacity available at prices below 2.5 ¢/kWh among all the small generators, which otherwise would have made it unprofitable for Vattenfall and *IVO* to exercise any significant degree of market power. It is interesting that the Danish generators contribute to reducing the largest power producers' incentives to exercise market power. The home markets of these companies are (so far) sheltered and prices to end-users have remained fairly independent of prices in the overall Nordic market. This in turn means that a higher Nordic spot price will have little influence on the yield of the Danish firms, so Elsam and Elkraft may increase their yield per produced kWh through a reduction of capacity utilisation only to a limited extent.[3]

The fact that Finland's *IVO* has incentives to exercise market power reflects two interesting aspects. First, the marginal production of the company involves coal condensation. Operating costs in these plants were relatively high due to CO_2 charges (around 2.31 ¢/kWh in 1995).[4] Such taxation results in low contribution margins on the capacity being withdrawn from the market, which again increases the incentives to exercise market power. In addition, bottlenecks between Sweden and Finland create protection for IVO in the sense of limiting the extent to which the company's dominant position in the Finnish market might be substituted by import.

Bottlenecks and border tariffs[5]

In recent years, there has been a process within and between the Nordic countries for closer integration of national electricity markets. Central to the debate here has been whether such integration will influence incentives to exercise market power.

Figure 4.2 shows the effects on market prices of removing cross-border protective regulations (illustrated by border tariffs in the model) at all the Nordic interconnectors. In 1995 such tariffs were implemented on all interconnectors, except those between Denmark and Norway. In January 1996 the tariffs on the Swedish/Norwegian border were banished, and the tariffs on the Swedish/Finnish interconnectors were removed in 1998–9.

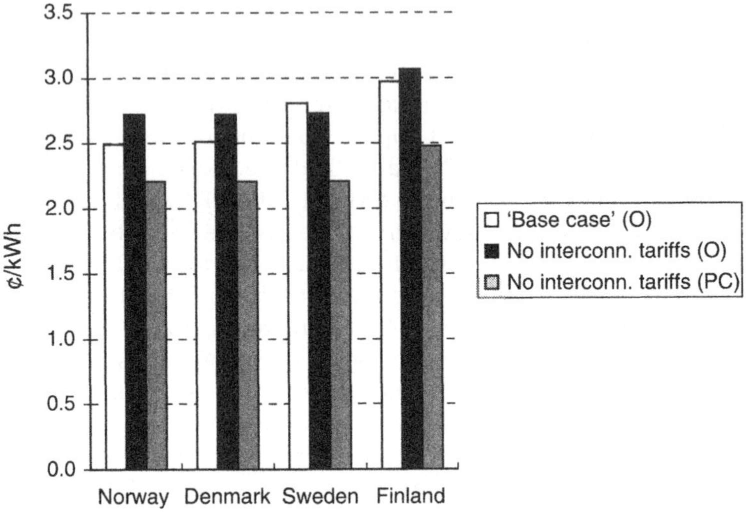

Figure 4.2 Power prices, by country 1996
Note: O: Oligoploistic competition, PC: Perfect competition. The 'price' in Denmark corresponds to the plants' marginal production costs.
Source: Halseth (1998).

The column for 'Base case (O)' shows the prices in the situation which is described under the 'Base case' – i.e. that prices in Norway and Sweden are different as a consequence of border tariffs. When these are removed ('No interconn. tariffs (O)'), prices will converge. However, we also see that a reduction in border tariffs will tend to increase Norwegian prices (and Danish production costs) more than it tends to reduce Swedish prices. The reason is that, if common Nordic prices are introduced, Vattenfall will reduce its production further, so as to keep prices up. Since there is no shelter for the Swedish market under 'Free trade' conditions, Vattenfall will be 'forced' to keep prices up in the entire Nordic market.

As for IVO, free trade paradoxically leads to even higher prices *and* increased production. This is perhaps a counter-intuitive result, since generally free trade would be expected to increase competition and reduce prices, in the Finnish market as well. However, reduced trade barriers make base-load Finnish exports to Sweden more profitable, but bottlenecks make it impossible to increase imports during peak-load periods. So Finnish net export (and production) increases, and that leads to higher overall prices and higher domestic production.

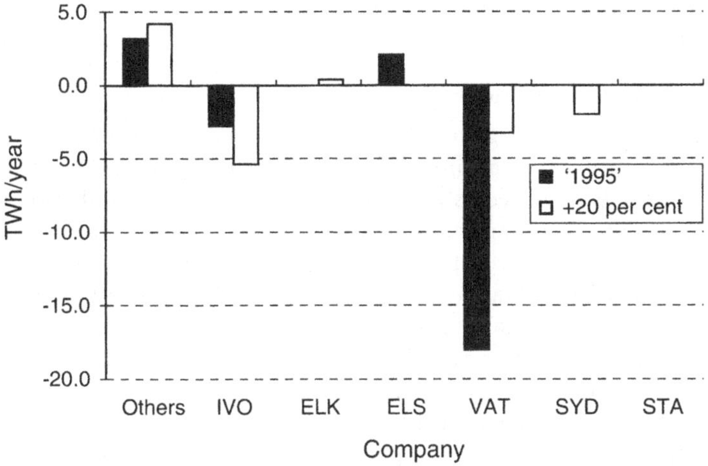

Figure 4.3 Capacity held out of the market by demand alternative, 1995
Source: Halseth (1998).

A tighter market

The basis for the analysis this far has been an underlying consumer price corresponding to the autumn 1995 level. Let us see whether the incentives to exercise market power change under the assumption of a tightening of the market with higher prices.

Figure 4.3 shows how output is distributed between companies, where '1995' equals the demand level which has been applied till now, and '+20 per cent' refers to a partial increase (20 per cent) in the underlying consumption. In the calculations, the price level increases from around 2.5 ¢/kWh to slightly less than 3.4 ¢/kWh in the Norwegian part of the market. The price under perfect competition equals 3.2 ¢/kWh.

We see that Vattenfall's incentives to exercise market power are clearly reduced. While 18 TWh/year of its generating capacity (i.e. the difference in production between oligopolistic and perfect competition) is being held out of the market with an underlying demand corresponding to that of 1995, only 3 TWh are held out under a 20 per cent increase in demand. The reason for such a large difference is that prices increase considerably in a tighter market. Increased prices mean an increased contribution margin in Vattenfall's nuclear power plants, which in turn means that the 'cost' of keeping this part of the capacity out of the market increases. The difference in production between perfect and oligopolistic competition is that the company keeps some thermal plants with marginal costs at some 3.1 ¢/kWh out of the market. Sydkraft is in the same situation.

Trade with the continent

In recent years, Norwegian power generators have seen increased trade with the continent as an interesting business opportunity. Three long-term contracts have been signed, and a corresponding number of interconnectors to Germany and the Netherlands are being planned. Swedish and Danish companies have also entered into similar agreements with continental counterparts. One element keenly debated in these agreements is the partners' exclusive right to use the cables. Some fear that the generators will execute their rights in order to increase prices by 'draining' the Nordic power market.

Calculations indicate that the new cable connections will be used for net import under perfect competition. The trade pattern reflects the system and cost differences between hydro-based systems and thermal power-based systems. Since hydro-plants are competitive for top-load production (owing to the relatively low costs related to load management and marginal generating capacity), the cables are used for export from the Nordic countries to the European continent in top-load periods. During medium- and low-load periods, capacity in the thermal power plants will normally not be exploited to the full, and production costs will reflect only fuel costs. This means it will be profitable to use the cables for import from the continent during such periods.

Calculations also indicate that the market power connected to the exclusivity of the cable connections is a limited problem. Statkraft seems to have incentives not to exploit its import possibilities to the full during medium- and low-load periods. Vattenfall, on the other hand, seems to find it profitable to export as much as possible through its connections, independent of load type. However, the fact that Statkraft has extra import possibilities contributes to limiting Vattenfall's incentives to keep nuclear capacity out of the market. This is caused partly by a reduction in Vattenfall's market share following from the net import from the continent and partly by available import capacity by Statkraft under low and medium load. Taken together, the new connections to the continent therefore reduce the problem of market power in the Nordic market.

Co-operation

The model concept may help to shed light on the question of whether the generators will profit from collaborating on keeping capacity out of the market. In the calculations, this has been illustrated by testing the degree to which varying constellations are better off by collaborating than they are when playing non-co-operative strategies represented by the Nash–Cournot equilibrium, assuming a *pro rata* reduction in supply to the market. This analysis shows that large producers will find it increasingly profitable to collaborate as more and more companies join in. This is natural because the market share increases and because competition between the generators, by definition, is reduced in terms of number of competitors and market concentration.

The next important finding is that Vattenfall participates in all profitable constellations. This reflects the fact that the costs associated with keeping volumes off the market are now distributed to some of the other generators, which gives Vattenfall a relatively larger market share at a given market price.

Finally, we find that none of the constellations where Vattenfall does *not* participate are profitable. This model result shows that if Vattenfall decides not to co-operate in keeping prices high, the company will increase its output if prices are forced up as a result of the co-operation of other generators.

Concluding remarks

In the two final sections of this chapter we have looked into the potential for execution of market power in the Norwegian and the Nordic electricity markets on the basis of two analyses: a specific analysis of the hydropower system, and a broader simulation-based analysis of the probable impact of the use of market power for short-term market strategies of large Nordic generators. The conclusions from both suggest that there exist many factors that are likely to mitigate market power.

First, there seem to be too many independent and small actors on the supply side, representing too large shares of the total generating capacity, for non-co-operative strategies to be sustainable.

Secondly, hydropower represents a large share of the system. This tends to reduce the scope for profitable strategies, except when stochastic influences cause capacity utilisation rates to be unusually high or unusually low, in which case collusive behaviours appear more likely. However, it is more costly for hydropower generators to reduce output in order to increase market prices than it is for generators with higher variable costs; furthermore, the stochastic elements on both demand and short-term capacity in the market which follow from unpredictable variations in precipitation make tacit collusion generally difficult to establish and to sustain.

Thirdly, the institutional framework and high attention from the politicians, the press and consumers will probably make generators rather cautious about maintaining the necessary levels of legitimacy.

On the other hand, the Nordic experience shows that in practice it is often difficult to understand fully or interpret price movements in the market. Market power might be exercised and sheltered within this complexity. True, when prices take unexpected turns, there will often be allegations of abuse of dominant market positions. However, such allegations have never been convincingly proved. Furthermore, the economic theory which might work in the public interest to reveal the exercise of market power is often rather inconclusive. Only minor changes in assumptions in such theoretical models could suffice to alter the conclusions substantially.

In this analysis, we have focused on the generators' short-term perspectives for given capacity investments. There exist many other dimensions of markets that are not captured by the models discussed here, and market power may obviously be exercised both in the contract markets (physical and financial) rather than in the spot market alone. In a longer-term perspective, market power might be executed in order to dominate the access of new capacity – for instance, by making it too risky for independent generators to invest in new capacity.

The concept of the non-co-operative game theory might also be too restrictive as an approach to the ways in which competitive firms and organisational actors actually relate to each other in modern market economies. Rather than being governed solely by the strict logic presented by economic theory, elements of co-ordinating behaviour might be seen as related to regulatory, normative and cognitive structures and cultures within the industry and within society in a broader sense. These structures and cultural carriers of governing and co-ordinating systems might define common frameworks – inter-industrial structures ranging from membership organisations to common historical experiences, norms and cognitive models that provide guidelines to organisational actors on how to achieve common interests without engaging in something that can be proven to be illegal collaborative behaviour. Judged in this institutional perspective, economic behaviour is perhaps better viewed as a complex activity of both rivalry and co-ordination, where the remarkable flexibility of human beings enables them to operate with a high level of complexity and despite the numerous contradictory elements involved.

Our main results from the analysis of market power – that there is limited space for collusive behaviour and a limited profitable potential for the execution of market power – are thus crucially dependent on the assumption that firms are truly and generally non-co-operative in their behaviours. And that cannot be taken entirely for granted.

Notes

1 This section of the chapter is based on Halseth (1998).
2 Contribution margin = market price *minus* variable production costs.
3 In line with the plans of opening up for competition in the Danish market, however, the Danish producers' incentives to exercise market power will be stronger.
4 The CO_2 tax was removed in 1997.
5 Tariffs charged for the use of interconnectors.

5

Risk Management in the New Electricity Trade

Per Ingvar Olsen

Introduction

The perhaps most vital test of the new market regime will be its ability to manage the excessive volatility inherent in a system with substantial capacity variations from year to year and from season to season. A related question is whether the market system will be able to deliver new investments based on individual economic rationales rather than co-ordinated political/sectoral planning. Will the competitive market system in the longer run achieve an internationally competitive price level and a level of price stability acceptable to sector actors as well as to industrial and private consumers, or will the market system be politically constrained and supplied by governance mechanisms of collective action?

In the eight years that have passed since deregulation in Norway, there have been incidents of substantial pressures on the political system to regulate prices and contracting practices in order to reduce the volatility in market prices. Following the wet and mild winter and spring of 1993, the generators nearly succeeded in a campaign to amend the Energy Act in order to set downward limits to prices. In this period, prices remained at less than 50 NOK/MWh for months on end. Instead, the generators received permission from the Ministry of Energy and Industry to export an estimated 5 TWh of surplus generating capacity on five-year fixed contracts. In the wake of the cold and dry 1996 winter and spring seasons, the converse situation emerged, with consumers and their organisations urging the government to regulate prices in order to put a ceiling on price increases. During this period, spot and futures market prices stayed above 300 NOK/MWh for a substantial period of time – up more than 50 per cent from the previous year's average. These incidents indicate that the market management of risk can become political in extreme situations where the market actors are in position to appeal to the political institutions for changes in the regulatory or institutional system. They also illustrate the excessive price variability found in a pure hydropower system.

Before the market reform, risk management as a company-relevant activity was not seen as a company-specific issue. On the contrary, risk management was regarded and treated as a joint project involving the state, the industry and the regional/local governance/ownership system. Basically, priority was given to securing stable and predictable prices to commercial, public and private consumers through absorbing the risk problem into a problem of volume management.

In order to deal with the tremendous variation in influx of water, several collective strategies were followed. First and foremost, substantial reservoir and generating capacity was constructed in order to ensure sufficient capacity to deliver at given prices also during dry and/or cold years. Second, sufficient transmission capacity was established for large-volume transmissions between regions for use in case of great stochastic variations in precipitation across regions – in particular, between the western and eastern areas of southern Norway. Third, a policy for regional security of supply was promoted in regions with less generation capacity than demand, in order to reduce the need for permanent long-distance transmission. Fourth, the grid system was linked up with the Swedish and the Danish electricity systems in order to import during dry and cold years and export surplus capacity during wet and mild years; fifth, a national market system for uncertain 'occasional' power was established as early as 1972, based on third-party access for all generators and energy-intensive industries (those having generating capacity) – a system which rested upon practices in regional systems dating back to the 1930s. In this residual market, prices were flexible and highly volatile. Consumers in general had no direct access to this market, but large and medium-sized consumers with alternative energy systems were permitted to buy indirectly at favourable tariffs, if they accepted the risk of being cut off from supply in case of shortage.

The monopoly in supply system aimed at securing each company a sufficient and predictable return. Prices in long-term contracting between regions generally followed the price leadership of the state generator, Statkraft, who completely dominated inter-regional trade and for whom prices were set yearly by the Norwegian Parliament. Regional generating costs and distribution costs had to be absorbed regionally and locally, resulting in substantially different prices across the country.

The cost of risk management in this earlier system can mainly be seen as the cost of investments in the extra capacity that was needed to keep prices stable. Despite the monopoly-based cost-plus pricing rule, the real cost of risk management can be seen as divided between consumers and the public budgets. This somewhat peculiar fact follows because public owners were generally prohibited from extracting profits from their electricity companies, and because a great number of hydropower investments received preferential loans at low interest rates from state-funded financial institutions. These elements contributed substantially to reducing the capital costs paid by consumers. This led to a rather low return on capital within the sector, however, in the absence of capital extraction by owners large enough to maintain more than sufficient solidity in most electricity companies. Also the state and consumers in regions involved in overly expensive investments in the regional generating capacity system can be seen as absorbers of the costs of this system of collective risk management.

Risk management in the hydropower electricity market system

The market reform of 1991 radically changed the mechanisms for risk management, from a collective state–sector–society project to individually-based mechanisms basically intended to be co-ordinated through competitive market transactions. With the removal of the limitations to access to the residual electricity market, price flexibility defused throughout the electricity sector over a period of two–three years, by which time prices in long-term contracting between generators and suppliers and to large and medium-sized customers became closely linked to expected future spot prices. The major exception to this radical change were Statkraft contracts to energy-intensive industries that were protected by parliament against re-negotiations.

Once the collective project of risk management had been deconstructed, and both individual firms and consumers had been exposed to substantial price risks – and with risk management turning from primarily volume to a more complex price–volume risk management challenge – a new problem emerged: the great need to develop efficient contractual markets so as to reduce the total risk experienced by all actors at a collective level through risk reallocation. Rather than trusting the capability of the market to develop a flexible contract market itself, the state took on the role as the owner and manager of the market institution (Nord Pool AS) from the collective organisation of the generators, and started working for an exchange system based on modern futures (marking to market) under the leadership of financial professionals.

However, even with an efficient market for risk, the individual price risk experienced by both electricity companies and consumers is likely to remain substantial as long as marginal prices are dependent on hydropower capacity constraints. This follows from the impact of large unpredictable changes in generating capacity over time, and has been thoroughly demonstrated in market events in Norway since deregulation. Residual risk also follows from the way electricity is sold and used. Consumers typically hold take-and-pay contracts where the actual volume extracted from the contracts varies substantially over the year and from year to year – according to, for instance, weather and general economic activity. These features of the hydropower system and the way electricity is sold to consumers mean that substantial non-hedgeable risks remain with generators, suppliers and consumers alike. Over time, this residual individual risk level is likely to be reflected in investment decisions made by the individual firms, leading to a lower level of investments than could otherwise have been achieved.

In the following, we will look at the risk challenges to the new market-based electricity trading system and discuss the capability of flexible prices and contracting to reduce risk at the collective level, before turning to the perspective of the individual firm and how it can manage its market risk at both the strategic and the tactical level of operation.

Price and volume risks

The primary source of risk in the hydropower system is the unpredictability associated with influx of water to the generating system. Contrary to fuel-based systems, the capacity of the hydropower system is constrained by energy rather than by peak load. With marginal production costs close to zero, market prices are generally to be seen as functions of the constraints on water and storage capacities. The variability of influx at a national aggregated level is illustrated in Figure 5.1 for the period 1930–90.

We can see that the generating capacity of the system changes radically with the influx of water from year to year. Some reservoirs are constructed in order to ease out generating capacity over a period of more than one year, whereas most are typically one-year reservoirs at their minimum levels each year in April–May before snow-melt in the mountains, and at their peak levels depending on demand and

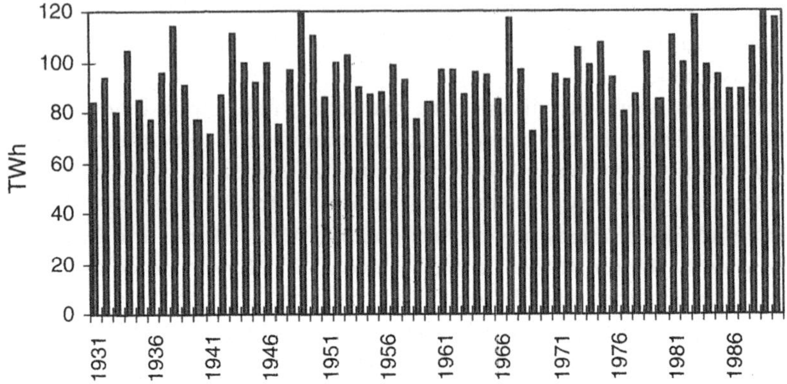

Figure 5.1 Yearly influx of water to the hydropower system, 1930–90
Source: Ministry of Energy and Industry (NOE), *Faktahefte 1996.*

precipitation sometimes in November–December. Still other reservoirs are typically restricted to short time-adjustments, for instance those constructed along major rivers. The capacity to allocate water from wet and mild to dry and cold years is accordingly limited, leaving a substantial need for demand-side flexibility to absorb the residual fluctuations in generating capacity.

Unpredictable variations in consumption are the second most important source of risk. Figure 5.2 illustrates the estimated variation in demand due to changes in temperatures in the period 1980–96.

From Figure 5.2 we see that yearly consumption differs by more than 6000 GWh between the cold years 1986 and 1988 and the mild 1991, accounting for more than 5 per cent of yearly consumption. The substantial differences are primarily caused by the large market share of electricity in the heating market.

Suppliers are generally in a position to hedge their volume risks by entering into take-and-pay-contracts with generators that transfer the volume risks directly to the generators at the cost of a risk premium. Generators, on the other hand, seem unable completely to hedge away the supply-side part of the problem. Their demand-side risk, however, could be transferred to suppliers if they entered into fixed volume contracts with the suppliers at the cost of a risk premium.

Price risk is linked with the volatility of spot market prices (Figure 5.3). These have been highly volatile ever since liberalisation in 1991. Deregulating the market resulted in a sharp price drop during 1993,

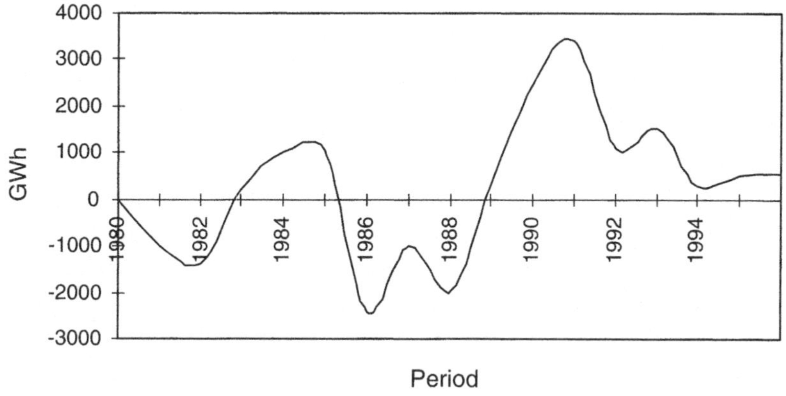

Figure 5.2 Demand variability from changes in temperatures, 1980–96
Source: Ministry of Energy and Industry (NOE), *Faktahefte 1996*.

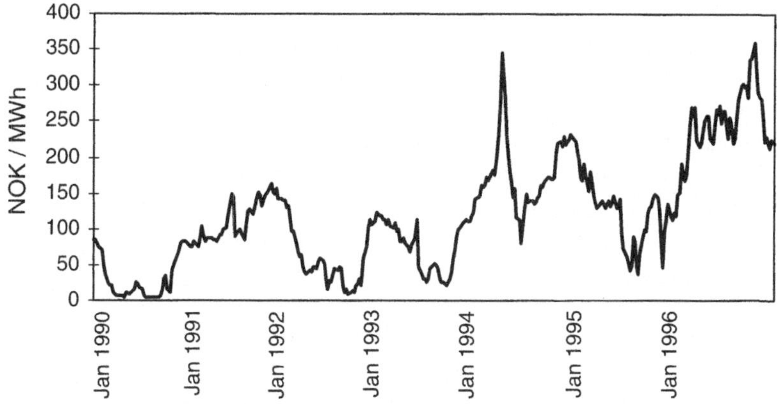

Figure 5.3 Weekly average spot market prices, 1991–6
Source: Nord Pool (1997).

when the surplus capacity of the collective-volume risk management system was put on the market; this further coincided with unusually mild and wet winters from 1990 to 1994. Year by year, however, demand has picked up with capacity, and the winters have turned colder and drier, until the very dry winter of 1996–97, leading to sharp price increases.

If prices were perfectly flexible, only generating firms among the electricity companies would have a substantial price–risk problem.

In this case, the risks would have been split between generators and consumers, whereas suppliers could have traded at a (stable) competitive margin. This implies that generators and consumers can engage in long-term fixed-price contracting in order to reduce their individual risks. This is basically the simple role of the contract markets in price risk management.

Both fixed-price contracting and the take-and-pay consumption system expose suppliers to substantial risks. As the intermediary between generators and consumers, the supplier has to cover his obligations to deliver on fixed-price contracts with purchases of contracts directly from generators or in the futures market. In order to reduce the risks involved, contracted sales should be hedged by corresponding purchasing contracts. The contracted sale, however, is uncertain and can be known only retrospectively. A cold and dry period will force the company to purchase additional volumes at high prices, while a wet and mild period will expose the supplier to attacks from rival suppliers on its consumer base, along with reducing demand in general. In this case, contracted volumes will have to be resold at low prices. In both cases, a supplier who covers his expected sales with fixed contracts will face losses.

The severity of these risk problems has been demonstrated in the Norwegian electricity market. First, during 1992 and 1993, spot market prices were low and demand sluggish due to wet and mild winters. The surplus capacity was reflected in the spot market pricing which permitted more aggressive actors to purchase spot and sell short-term contracts to large and medium-sized consumers in order to capture customers from suppliers locked in by long-term contracts at high prices. These accordingly found themselves with contracted purchases that could be returned to the spot market only with a loss. Second, during the dry winter of 1996–97, most suppliers experienced the situation that their consumers used more electricity than expected at contracted prices, and had to purchase additional contracts in order to cover their obligations at prices higher than contracted consumer prices.

To a certain extent, however, these incidents should be seen as processes of collective learning in a rather new and inexperienced market. Gradually, there will develop more advanced and skilfully constructed contracting and reservoir-management strategies more capable of managing the price and volume risks involved in the new individually allocated risk-management system. However, substantial risks at the individual level appear to remain unhedgeable at the level of the individual organisational actor.

Demand-side flexibility represents an important aspect of efficient resource allocation, as demand could potentially adjust to the uncertain variations in inflow of water to the generating system. The applied price theory of market reform presupposes that consumers respond to changing prices by adjusting their consumption or by switching between energy substitutes. Electricity consumption, however, is typically derived from capital investments in electricity-consuming equipment. For a great number of applications, no substitutes are available for electricity. In other cases, consumers are locked into electricity through investment decisions based on pricing practices before the market reform. Typically, during the 1970s and 1980s new houses were constructed with only electrical heating, whereas older houses which had been built with oil-fuelled central systems were able to change over to electrical heating at little extra cost. The converse – to build an efficient oil-based central heating system into an existing house – is clearly not as simple and inexpensive an operation.

Despite this rigidity on the consumer side, the sharp price increases of 1996–7 showed that consumer flexibility was indeed greater than could have been expected: there was a real decline in consumption of more than 7 per cent, adjusted for changes in temperatures from the previous year. Most of this was probably due to substitution from electric heating to old oil heaters and to the use of wood.

Strategic and tactical risk management

Faced with the individualised risks of the hydropower market system, organisational actors within the sector have been faced with radically new challenges. From their perspective, the state-initiated market reform has created a vacuum in terms of risk management that will have to be filled by the sectoral firms; the reform has also imposed various new regulatory constraints on how this vacuum can be filled. In particular, the new constraints are directed towards both vertical and horizontal co-ordination between organisational entities, which is quite the opposite of state policies prior to the reform. This is of course a logical governance change, given the regulator's belief in the efficiency of decentralised co-ordination in a competitive market where all actors are as autonomous as possible, in order to approach the ideal competitive market model.

One problem involved here is that the market theory itself is a reductionist one – assuming away a number of institutional factors that are in fact essential to the management of risk in market systems. Real-world risk management in market systems is likely to be a much more complex task, involving individual competition, cross-sectoral co-ordination and state–sectoral–societal co-ordination as well. At the strategic level, each individual firm might engage in all of these three levels of risk management. Firms may engage in activities aimed at influencing the institutional system and the political regulatory procedures, in networking towards other electricity companies (both tightly with specific companies or more generally within the highly organised and socialised sector), and they engage in competitive contracting and reservoir management directly aimed at managing market price and volume risks. Taken together, this complex set of risk-management strategies can be seen as the management of risk at the sectoral level.

Managing risk by the autonomous firm: contracting and reservoir management

It is usually not quite clear to the organisational actors of publicly owned electricity companies how the relevant risk ought to be defined, or for whom risk is to be managed. The standard model in finance assumes that the relevant risk is that of the well diversified equity owner. However, political owners usually have a very different attitude to risk and to managing their activities than do private equity portfolio managers. In particular, political owners tend to regard each sector independently and not as part of a public sector portfolio; they also tend to allocate resources politically both through company budgets and profits. This complexity will usually make it impossible for portfolio managers to interpret any particular risk–profit trade-off on the side of the owners. Operational risk management accordingly gets referred to some managerial level of decision-making within the company – which often might be 'arbitrarily' influenced and altered by, for instance, occasional interventions by the political owners into pricing decisions. This makes operational risk management a somewhat contradictory and often rather confusing activity.

In line with the intentions of the market reform, competitive contracting and reservoir management are the two obvious alternatives for managing price and volume risks. For those with reservoirs, reservoir management and flexible contracting are substitutes, in the sense that the individual attitude to risk can be accounted for by both. In the case of reservoir management and risk neutrality, optimal pricing is such that the marginal net present value from storing an additional unit of water, rather than producing another unit of electricity, should be equal to the market price. This pricing rule can be shown to maximise the expected return to the owner in a competitive hydropower market.

In case of non-neutral risk attitudes, the valuation of stored water should be corrected for by the owner's attitude to risk. If risk-adverse, he will prefer to store water with a marginal expected net present value lower than the market price. That difference represents his risk premium. If he is able to cover his risk completely by reservoir management in this way, contracting in competitive markets can be done in the same way as if he were risk-neutral, only directed towards maximising profits. Usually, however, generators attempt both: to hedge their risks by reservoir management and by contracting jointly. This is of course an even more complex task, as it will normally involve two different organisational departments or divisions within the firm.

Actors without reservoirs are forced to hedge their market risks by contracting. This is usually done both in the bilateral and the Nord Pool markets, each providing specific types of risk reallocations and flexibility.

Many electricity companies – in particular, the larger ones – prefer to set up a separate supply unit or to establish a subsidiary for contracting and trade in the competitive markets. This imposes a split between generating and supply within integrated companies, exposing both activities to wholesale market prices. Usually the generating division of the firm is responsible for contracting with whichever purchaser offers the best contracts, whereas the supply division is responsible for its own purchases. This organisational separation into generating and supply divisions has obvious managerial advantages, and provides an excellent opportunity to use the market for internal benchmarking. The problem, however, is on the risk-management side, because risk management by subsidiaries or even by internal divisions of the firm is likely to be inappropriate for the relevant risk management of the entire company – not to mention the diversified owners.

These markets are now generally perceived as fairly efficient in the sense that the potential for arbitrage between different types of contracts is small. This implies that actors can choose from a broad menu of contractual forms that can be used to tailor portfolios of contracts according to any particular risk exposure.

In the bilateral market, there has been a tendency towards standardisation of contract terms and restructuring into specific contractual types like base-load contracts, flexible time of use contracts, physical option contracts, etc. These are traded either directly between the contractual parties, or indirectly through a market intermediary like a broker company. Prices are sometimes linked to the spot market prices, so that there is actually a fixed-volume contract with price flexibility. Differences in prices between different types of contracts are usually caused by their implicit real-option content in terms of ability to choose when to take delivery from a given contract. In the base-load case, there is no flexibility at all, whereas in the physical-option contract, the purchaser merely holds an option to execute the contract at a given price in the future. In between these two, any type of flexibility can be designed.

The Nord Pool markets are generally divided in three: the regulatory market for contracts of differences and short-term regulatory dispatch, the physical spot market and the futures market. In a risk-management perspective, the spot and futures markets are clearly the most relevant. The spot market prices are set at 12.00 noon for the next 24-hour day starting at midnight. Prices are set on the basis of price–volume offers from both buyers and sellers for every hour. In the Swedish market, prices are set for every half hour. As soon as prices are set, bids and requests are converted into contract obligations.

The futures market is organised as a traditional market-to-market system with the pool operator Nord Pool serving as the contractual counterpart towards both sellers and buyers, and Norsk Opsjonssentral operating the clearing house. Futures are traded in weeks, blocks (four weeks) and seasons. Prices are set two years into the future. Seasons are split successively into blocks, and blocks into weeks, as delivery time approaches. Futures contracts are purely financial contracts where prices at the time of delivery are equal to spot prices. This implies that over time the futures prices of a given contract will converge towards the expected spot price at the time of delivery.

The Nord Pool market has year by year increased its relative share of market trade, and has developed its products and trade procedures into an on-line market for physical spot deliveries and for financial futures contracts (Figure 5.4).

Spot market trade typically tends to increase with the variance in inflow and temperatures. More interesting, perhaps, is the steady growth in the week market, which covers all trade in futures. Even though volumes traded are still too small to permit efficient trade of large volumes at a time, the emergence of the collective good of a highly flexible contract market is well under way, permitting companies to change their portfolio positions rapidly without significantly influencing market prices. On the other hand, large volumes are still typically traded bilaterally at prices reflecting the alternative cost in the Nord Pool markets.

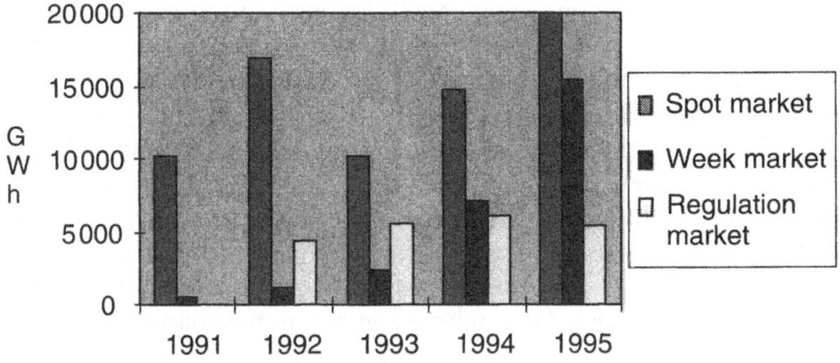

Figure 5.4 Volumes traded at the Nord Pool markets, 1991–5
Source: Nord Pool (1997).

Managing risk by extending corporate controls

The risks faced by individual electricity companies can also be approached by strategic efforts to expand managerial controls. Various options are available: one may diversify the company's assets over different technologies, over different hydrological areas, over the value chain, into other companies and into other types of economic activities. This involves strategies for mergers and acquisitions both nationally and internationally, for import–export strategic co-operation, for cross-ownership and for entering new businesses by developing existing competencies into distinct business activities, such as telecom and communications or other energy-distribution activities. Such organisational diversification strategies directly alter the need for risk management through contracting and reservoir management, as the relevant risk of each project to the company portfolio of economic activities is generally reduced.

The predominately public ownership and the restrictive concessionary laws substantially reduce flexibility in Norway's electricity sector equity market, as well as severely constraining the abilities to increase corporate controls in the manner often done in other market systems – by trading corporate stocks. Also the sectoral regulator NVE has intervened in company mergers and acquisitions, requiring corporate separation of the generation and supply business from network transportation activities as a condition for approving each particular acquisition or merger.

What has gradually developed into an important trend is the merging of electricity companies within traditionally co-operating regions, into larger regional companies. Such mergers can often be seen as demonstrating the final break-through for efforts at regional integration undertaken by both managerial elites and state officials during the previous regime. These efforts were usually obstructed by local politicians who now face the threat of being squeezed out of business by the competitive market, and who therefore seek protection by increasing corporate controls jointly with their neighbours. Ironically, the policy of the 1970s and 1980s of integrating local companies into larger regional units succeeded to a very limited extent, whereas the market system based on the need for a large number of actors has managed to break down local obstruction and create what is now seen as 'unwanted' regional integration.

In particular, Sweden's entry into a common Nordic market, bringing with it larger Swedish firms, seems to have pushed local politicians towards advocacy of regional integration as a protective strategy. The Swedish electricity system has seen a much more rapid structural change, emerging into three dominating generators – or groups of generators – with only a small tail of minor municipal independent companies. The publicly owned Norwegian companies have in general been reluctant to engage in foreign market mergers or acquisitions, being both rather small and inexperienced in that type of activity. From being a relatively slow starter, however, the state company Statkraft SF has obtained a 15 per cent share of Sweden's second-largest electricity company, Sydkraft AB.

Another strategy practised by some of the larger companies has been to form larger co-operative arrangements across broad regions of the country, like Sørkraft in Southern Norway, Nordenfjeldske Kraftselskap in Northern Norway and Østlandskraft in Eastern Norway (the latter formalised before the market reform) or between rather similar firms in different regions of the country, like the formalised OBT AS, a trading company owned jointly by the power companies of Oslo, Bergen and Trondheim. Apart from Sørkraft, which has obtained permission from the state competition authorities to form a tight co-operative structure, the others have remained rather limited approaches to real joint managerial controls – at least when judged in terms of formal structures. These larger co-operative structures emerged at the time of the very low prices during 1993, and could be seen as a joint project between generators to manage the downward price pressures in a cartel-like manner. Later increases in prices due to tighter resource constraints, however, substantially reduced the appropriateness of this strategy.

Risk management as a joint sectoral project

Despite the deliberate deconstruction of the joint state–sector–society project within the electricity sector, the electricity sector remains largely integrated and co-ordinated in several ways. Ranging from traditional regional and national co-operation, joint investment projects and industrial organisations at a high level of common sectoral identity, both organisations and individuals are linked into a variety of co-operative and network-like structures. Moreover, most top managers are graduates of the same institution, have known each other for years and regularly attend professional and sectoral meetings and seminars on matters of common interest. These sectoral 'infrastructures' serve to continue the joint project by directing common issues, facilitating the exchange of opinions and ideas and in general creating consensus on sectoral strategies.

Being engineers, many of these executives are still more concerned with the collective project of constructing an efficiently integrated technical and governance system than with increasing the competitiveness of the individual company, which is generally regarded the economists' approach. In the absence of the traditional state sector joint project of building an efficient national electricity system, many sectoral managers engage in the less ambitious project of regional integration – usually, but not always, in opposition to their political owners, who prefer to maintain a degree of direct control over budgets and pricing by holding tightly on to local property rights.

The political owners are in turn linked through the political parties and through local, regional and state political networks and institutions. In the ownership context, co-ordinated activities seem only to a limited extent to be affected by the new standards of legitimacy provided by the market reform.

The role of the state in sectoral risk management

How able electricity sector companies are to fill the risk-management vacuum entailed by the market reform will usually involve an entire range of managerial activities, from contracting and reservoir management to increasing managerial control through strategic corporate action and to participating in risk management in a joint sectoral project. Taken together, all of these constitute the risk management of the sectoral actors, which again can be seen as being both constrained by and counterplaying with the state institutions related to the electricity sector within the framework of an overall managerial risk set of activities.

As the enforcer of the competitive market reform, the Norwegian state hardly sees its role as that of the minimalist 'night watchman' state advocated by the neo-utilitarians (for instance Buchanan, Tollison and Tullock 1980) which is usually affiliated with the neo-liberal wave of market reforms of the 1980s. Rather, its role and identity as a forceful developmental state is reaffirmed by its successful market reform and by its increased sectoral controls, both in terms of ownership to essential institutions and in terms of increased regulatory authority and legitimacy supported by economic regulation and control theory. The neo-liberal reform, then, can hardly be seen as reducing the essential role of the state in the economy, but rather points at the role of the state as actively both pushing for economic efficiency, directing collective action and constraining and sanctioning local decision-making.

Accordingly, efforts to manage volatility in prices and volumes in the hydropower system can be seen as having important governmental and collective elements. First, there is the role of the state, both in increasing capacity and in improving the terms of trade with foreign electricity systems. This will to a greater extent link pricing to the more predictable thermal systems abroad and help to smooth out the variations of the hydropower system through international trade. International trade has always been predominantly governmentally regulated and co-ordinated, both towards foreign markets and internally towards the electricity industry. Indeed, the import–export regime of the new market order is perhaps best seen as a joint state–sectoral project aimed at maximising the national gains from trade, rather than as an intrinsic part of the competitive market.

Secondly, there is the regulatory system for reservoir controls. This is a centralist governance system for security of supply that places definite constraints on the individual owners' ability to manage their reservoirs.

Thirdly, the Norwegian state has a leading role in generation, transmission and market institutions through its ownership of three essential institutions: Statkraft SF, Statnett SF and Nord Pool AS (the latter jointly owned by Statnett SF and Svenska Kraftnat AB). Through these sectoral companies, the state has direct access to investment decisions in both generating and transmission as well as tight controls with the market infrastructure and links to foreign markets. Capacity investments are accordingly not dependent on decentralised decisions made by individual competing firms, but can also be undertaken directly by the state through its large sectoral companies.

Fourthly, investments are still highly regulated through the legislative concessionary system. New power plants are subjected to political decision-making processes in the government as well as the Parliament, whereas upgrading of existing plants involves only simplified procedures at the administrative level. The timing and predictability of investment decision processes are thus predominantly political.

All this points at the dominant role of the state in managing risk at the collective level, as well as explaining why sectoral actors find it attractive to construct a forceful counterplay in order to influence state activities. To legitimise such an effort, sectoral actors typically have to define their goal as that of the common social good rather than the well-being of individual firms. Hence, even though the state may have set out to deconstruct the joint state–sectoral–societal approach to managing the electricity sector and replacing it with state regulation and decentralised competition, renewed state–sectoral agendas are continuously emerging.

Incorporating the hydro-system into neighbouring thermal systems

Foreign generators have for many years provided important demand and supply flexibility to the Norwegian system. During wet and mild years, the hydropower surplus has been exported to generators in Sweden and Denmark, and in dry and cold years thermal power has been imported. The problem as seen from Norway has been that both the influx of water and the demand in Norway and Sweden tend to co-vary, owing to similarity in climate. This has meant that export prices have been very low, whereas import prices have been equally high in Norwegian foreign electricity trade.

In the wake of the market reform, several major projects and plans have been launched in order to establish electricity trade with countries like Germany, the Netherlands and the UK through cables across the North Sea. In a few years, new cables with a capacity of 1800 MW to Germany and the Netherlands will substantially increase import–export capacity. At the same time, bilateral capacities between Sweden/Denmark and Germany/Poland are also increased substantially. This new international infrastructure for electricity trade is expected to increase international trade radically and reduce price volatility in the Norwegian market, as prices will converge towards one single international price. Furthermore, the integration of a large and flexible hydropower system with large continental thermal systems will enable the Norwegian system to export short-term regulatory services at reasonable prices by exploiting technical regulatory capacity that otherwise has zero marginal value in the national market (Tables 5.1 and 5.2).

Table 5.1 Existing capacities for electricity trade to other countries (MW)

Country	Norway	Sweden	Finland	Denmark	Germany	Russia	Poland
Norway		3565	100	1040	0	50	0
Sweden	3565		1435	2680	600	0	0
Finland	100	1435		0	0	1060	0
Denmark	1040	2680	0		2000	0	0

Table 5.2 Planned capacities for electricity trade to other countries (MW)

Norway–Netherlands	600
Norway–Germany	1200
Sweden–Poland	600
Finland–Russia	450

Source: Center for Electricity Studies, BI (1997).

Additionally, initiatives are underway to reach agreement on an interconnector between Norway and the UK.

The state-owned company Statkraft SF has been the central, most experienced negotiator with continental counterparts in these arrangements, accompanied by large generators organised into two groups; Norsk Krafteksport AS and Eurokraft AS. This duopoly structure is actively supported by the Norwegian state. The new cables will be jointly owned by Statnett SF and its European counterparts. All contracts have been scrutinised by state officials, and 25-year licenses have been issued for electricity trade. Even though obtaining clear-cut control over import–export trade has become increasingly complex owing to the greater number of links and the general inclusion of Sweden into the common Nordic market, the state has a very distinctive leading edge on decentral actors in structuring the conditions for foreign trade, with dramatic consequences for the market risks of individual firms.

Regulating reservoir management

A second element of governmental risk management is the system of reservoir regulations. Reservoirs are regulated within the concessional framework, in the sense that at a given minimum level of storage, the owner cannot produce without explicit permission from the regulator, NVE. This means that the regulator's policy for security of supply might have an important influence on prices, in particular during dry and cold periods. Whether prices will increase substantially or generators will receive permission to produce at below-minimum-level storage, is basically a centralised issue which is to be decided by the regulator or by the Minister of Energy. During the period of high prices in 1996–7 with corresponding low storage levels, representatives of the power industry invited the state to increase storage capacity for security of supply by purchasing reservoir capacity. This would increase the role of centralist and collective reservoir management relative to the decentralist market-based co-ordination.

State investments and regulatory controls of decentral investments

The increased prices through 1996 led several electricity companies to produce plans for new capacity investments. A substantial number of these are projects for upgrading existing plants so as to permit increased energy production or greater generating capacity. Such investments have at least two advantages. They are subject to simplified administrative decision procedures with only limited political controversy; and each investment is relatively small and thus involves limited overall risk for the investor.

By contrast, investments in new power plants are subject to much more cumbersome procedures. Some concessions have already been granted, primarily to Statraft, to construct new power plants. From the remaining 24 TWh potential for hydropower development, around 60 per cent is owned by local and regional electricity companies, and among these are a majority of the cheapest projects. Even though some municipal and regional electricity companies have applied for concessions to construct new hydropower reservoirs and generating stations, there is a clear tendency for the joint operation of the large state-controlled energy companies Statoil AS, Norsk Hydro AS and Statkraft SF to take the lead in establishing most new generating capacity, as well as probably being in a more advantageous position to manage the political procedures related to large investment projects. In 1997 these three companies were given permission to construct two large gas-turbine power stations on the west coast of southern Norway, organised in the joint venture company Naturkraft AS.

The political treatment of concession applications has proven highly sensitive to short-term price volatility and to environmental issues. Before summer 1996, owing to the problems with the CO_2 emission policy, the application for a concession to construct gas turbines was accompanied by assurances that production would be exported to thermal power systems in other countries. Later, however, the sharp price increases due to low reservoir storage levels suddenly made it legitimate to speak of supplying domestic consumption as well.

Concluding remarks

In this chapter we have presented the issue of risk management in the electricity market as partly an activity of each individual firm, partly a sectoral and partly a state activity at the collective level of action. What is new with the Norwegian market reform in this connection is primarily the vacuum it created for risk management at the level of the individual firm, but also the reconstruction of risk management at the state–sectoral level. This change was marked both by expansion of the roles of state companies and a renewal of import–export policies. Of particular interest is the new approach to import–export permitted by the deconstruction of the large joint state–sectoral–societal project, with its implicit conflicts of power between electricity generators and energy-intensive industries that had limited international trade to short-term demand-side management. Seen in this perspective, not only did the individual electricity companies take on a new role as autonomous market actors, the state itself managed to increase its autonomy from both energy-generating and energy-consuming industries in order to more efficiently pursue strategies for national resource allocation and risk management.

Rather than being preoccupied with the simplistic interpretations of market risks typically framed within neo-classical economic theory and finance, management of risk by individual firms is seen as fundamentally imposed by and constrained by the state, as well as being embedded into a broader state–sectoral risk-managerial project in which the very same firms are participants. Indeed, precisely this complexity and multidimensionality of risk management has served to build trust: trust in the ability of Norway's new market system to manage the excessive volatility involved in the hydropower system, trust in the ability to provide adequate levels of new investments in order to maintain prices at a competitive international level, and trust in the ability to provide the long-term stability necessary to maintain general trust in the new liberalised electricity system.

Part II

Grid Management under a Competitive Regime

6
Incentives for Efficiency in Grid Operations

Eivind Magnus

Introduction[1]

In a country like Norway, grid activities from the high-voltage transmission grid down to the low-voltage distribution nets account for nearly 50 per cent of total capital investments, and represent a major share of operating costs. As these are natural monopolies, the challenge is how to avoid the abuse of monopoly power. Internationally, there are two main traditions for regulating natural monopolies such as electricity transportation. One is self-regulation based on public ownership; the other is income regulation of private companies implemented and organised by a central or regional regulator. The Norwegian model as it has been developed during the 1990s seeks to combine these two traditions – what we could term *income regulation of public companies*.

Prior to the liberalisation and restructuring of the Norwegian electricity supply industry, there was no regulator controlling net tariffs or revenue levels in electricity companies. Public ownership, it was felt, would protect consumer interests from the abuse of monopoly power. In introducing wholesale and retail competition, the Norwegian government argued that formal monopoly control of grid activities was necessary. The reform was expected to stimulate the transformation of companies from traditional infrastructure entities into commercial companies, which in turn required new regulation mechanisms for the remaining monopoly activities.

The Norwegian Water Resources and Energy Administration (NVE) was in 1991 tasked with regulating and controlling grid activities. The NVE was also set up as a licensing authority in connection with investments in large distribution plants (above 22 kV) and with granting geographical area licences. This monopoly control covers several aspects of related transportation activities. Revenue level as well as price structure and company organising are issues which have occupied the regulator ever since the market reform in 1991.

Ideally, a regulation regime should motivate firms to price their services efficiently, to ensure that product quality is satisfactory, both in the short and the long run, and to contribute to running the business in a cost-efficient way. In addition, the regime should minimise the administrative costs incurred through regulation. Experience in Norway and elsewhere has shown that these might be conflicting objectives (see ECON 1994).

In the past two decades, economic theory has focused on the constraints facing a regulator in carrying out monopoly regulation. Greatest attention has perhaps been given to the information constraint, which has at least two dimensions. First, the regulator lacks information about underlying costs (adverse selection). Secondly, the regulator is not able to observe the companies' efforts to operate efficiently (moral hazard). It is also assumed that the companies subject to regulation are better informed about the underlying costs than is the regulator, and that they know more about efficiency efforts undertaken. In practice, these information constraints prevent the regulator from implementing the preferred regulation policy. A realistic regulation policy thus becomes one that is consistent with the firms' and regulators' information structure, constraints and feasible instruments (Laffont and Tirole 1993). The asymmetry of information gives the regulated firms a strategic advantage that could be used to manipulate regulation decisions, and thereby gives rise to an information rent, which is compatible with a monopoly profit.

Regulation theory has shown that the regulator is faced with making a trade-off, between his desire to motivate cost efficiency and his wish to limit monopoly profit. Too much emphasis on reducing monopoly profit makes it difficult to stimulate cost efficiency, and vice versa. This trade-off has been addressed in the discussions between the industry, the regulator and academic institutions in the process leading to today's income-cap regulation system. In this chapter we present and discuss various mechanisms available to the regulator in general. The last part of the chapter presents and discusses the new Norwegian incentive regulation model. The focus is on how the Norwegian regulator has sought to balance the two conflicting objectives in structuring an incentive regulation scheme – between the power to motivate the utilities to operate and invest efficiently, and the ability to minimise the monopoly profit remaining in the grid companies.

In 1993, a regulation model based on rate-of-return regulation was introduced. In brief, the idea of this model was that the utilities were allowed to determine the level of income necessary in order to achieve a rate of return on grid capital one percentage point above the interest on government bonds. This model was, however, only a temporary regime. At an early stage, the regulator announced its interest in introducing an incentive-based model. In order to reduce information asymmetry, the regulator started to develop a reporting system for tariffs and accounting data, and a model for measuring efficiency differences. This work began in 1993 and was more or less finished by 1996–7. The data reporting system and the model for measuring efficiency differences enabled the regulator to establish a basis for stipulating an incentive-based regulation system which took account of individual variations in the underlying cost level and cost efficiency. This new incentive regulation model was introduced from 1 January 1997.

Regulation of income level

Introduction

The new rate-of-return regulation model for net activities introduced in 1993 meant new and radical changes for the utilities and their owners. The reform recognised the owner's right to earn interest on capital investments in grid operations. Furthermore, the income of the grid owner was now to be monitored by a central body, and not as before by the local authority. However, the new regulation model was not regarded as satisfactory, because the various companies lacked incentives for operating in a cost-efficient way. As this was a traditional cost-based regulation model, an upper limit for the company's total earnings was stipulated, based on the expenditures of the company as set out in its annual report. Operating costs and capital costs are included in this cost concept. Capital costs were determined by taking depreciation costs and adding a reasonable return on invested capital. Regulation regimes designed in this way are often termed 'rate-of-return regulation regimes'.

Lack of incentive characteristics

The incentive characteristics of the cost-based regulation models have been much discussed in the literature on regulation. In particular, three weaknesses have been pointed out. First, incentives for efficient operation will be weak if every cost reduction automatically leads to lower prices. This will be the case if prices are automatically adjusted compared to reported costs. Secondly, cost-based regulation models may influence the company's choice of input factors. Averch and Johnson (1962) have shown that rate of return regulation will change relative factor prices on capital and labour in favour of capital, as long as the allowed return on capital exceeds the capital cost of the market. Such a change in the relative prices of input factors will lead the company to choose a factor combination that is overly capital-intensive compared to what an unregulated company would choose. The third weakness concerns the possibilities for cross-subsidisation between monopoly activities and activities exposed to competition. This relates to companies with activities in several businesses, of which at least one is not regulated as a natural monopoly. In such a situation, the company will have incentives to move costs from the non-regulated to the regulated part of the enterprise.

The pure cost-based regulation model assumes that the income limit is continuously adjusted. Normally, the income limit is valid for a certain period of time. During this period, the firm may take possible gains from more efficient operation to income. Thus, there are positive incentive effects connected to this. The longer the period between the readjustments of income limit and prices, the stronger will these incentive effects be. In the Norwegian model, the regulation period was only one year, with any excess return during an accounting year paid back the year after. That was one important reason for the weak incentive properties of that model.

In some regulatory regimes, firms may not include all investments in their capital bases when their return on capital is calculated. The purpose of such a system is of course to prevent wasteful investments. The fear of not having investments acknowledged gives clear incentives. In Norway, in practice all relevant investments were included in the capital base.

Recently, there has been much discussion of whether rate-of-return regulation based on detailed control of individual actions in fact may have an effect quite the opposite of that described by Averch and Johnson. The argument is that the firms may profit by choosing a factor combination which is too little capital-intensive. Firms may limit their investments, fearing that the regulation authorities may reject the inclusion of investments as part of their capital bases, or that the capital cost is set too low.

Price-cap regulation

An alternative model to rate-of-return regulation is price-cap regulation, whereby the regulation authorities stipulate maximum prices on the monopolist's products. The company is then free to sell at prices at or below the maximum level. The company is allowed to keep any gains from cost reductions. In pure price-cap regulation regimes, maximum prices are adjusted for inflation according to a price index agreed on in advance, possibly less an exogenous factor which is supposed to reflect an expected increase in productivity in the company (this is known as the RPI-X formula in the UK). Changes in maximum prices may thus take place in two ways: either due to automatic adjustments on the basis of agreed inflation or productivity adjustments, or through a change in the actual adjustment formula.

Pure price-cap regulation will not make use of historical cost data. The reported costs of the company are thus irrelevant to its income. High costs may not be transferred to the customers through higher prices, and the company thus does not obtain any gains from cross-subsidising. The most important advantage of price-cap regulation is that there are strong incentives for increasing cost efficiency, since the company may keep parts or all of the gains connected to improvements in productivity. In practical implementations, however, the regulator must base the stipulation of caps on information from the companies, such as historical cost data.

The chief objection relates to the difficulties of stipulating relevant maximum prices and deciding on an appropriate adjustment formula. If prices are set too high, the result be similar to that of an unregulated monopoly. If they are set too low, the company may experience problems in the long run in providing adequate service to its customers.

Focal issues in connection with price-cap regulation are the time period between each evaluation of the adjustment formula, and the basis on which any such evaluations should be made. In practice, this will be a matter of choosing between the incentive effects of the regulation, and the flexibility of the system in connection with changes in basic assumptions. If the adjustment formula is changed frequently, and in a way which deprives companies of achieved efficiency gains, the incentive characteristics will deteriorate. On the other hand, an overly long period between such evaluations will make the system inflexible and incapable of responding to important changes in economic and technical framework conditions.

A practical question in connection with all price-cap regulation is how to adjust rates in line with changes in the price level for central input factors. One approach could be to use the retail or wholesale prices index. However, some regulated industries employ a combination of input factors which is not very well reflected in general indices.

For instance, capital-intensive activities will be very sensitive to the interest level. A possible solution to this problem would be to establish separate indices, based on a price composition which corresponds to the actual factor composition.

Rate-of-return regulation vs price-cap regulation

Recent economic research has shown that there need not be great differences between rate-of-return regulation and price-cap regulation as far as incentive characteristics are concerned (Laffont and Tirole 1993). Regulation models will normally not be implemented in their pure form. Under both regulatory regimes it is possible to undertake regular revision of the basis for calculating prices. In between each revision, the companies themselves will be responsible for their costs.

One difference between these models when implemented in their pure forms is the connection between previous results and the calculation of the income limit. In principle, a price-cap regulation system does not apply historical results as a basis for regulation. In practice, however, it is difficult to avoid using historical results as input when stipulating the maximum prices. Consequently, systems of maximum prices may result in punishing efficient companies through a reduction of maximum prices. Thus, a maximum price system may provide the same incentive problems concerning cost efficiency as a model based on rate-of-return regulation.

The rate-of-return regulation model followed in Norway was close to its pure version, since any deviation from the allowed rate of return was adjusted through repayment mechanisms.

Yardstick regulation

When a service such as low-voltage electricity transportation is provided by several companies, yardstick regulation could be a convenient measure for monopoly regulation.

In brief, yardstick regulation entails measuring the monopolist's costs compared to other companies delivering the same product or service in another market, letting the return of the company depend on its costs compared to the industry average. The idea is that companies which are run efficiently will be able to obtain a higher return on capital than will inefficient companies. This regulation model may be particularly relevant in power distribution, where there exist a considerable number of units between which comparisons may be made.

The literature on regulation indicates that yardstick regulation may have certain positive optimisation characteristics. For example, Shleifer

(1985) has shown that firms in an industry characterised by natural monopolies, in which firms must accept prices which depend on the cost level of firms in corresponding activities, seek to minimise costs. However, Shleifer has made some very simplified assumptions regarding the cost conditions facing different firms in different areas.

On the other hand, grid companies deliver heterogeneous products. Cost conditions vary greatly, depending on geographical and demographical factors, such as population density. This makes it very complicated to implement yardstick regulation in an appropriate way. It must be emphasised that such regulation in an industry where there are sizeable differences in underlying cost conditions may lead to unduly high profits in some firms, whereas others may experience dramatic losses (Brown 1989).

To remedy the problems of heterogeneous products, Shleifer (1985) suggests the use of statistical methods to quantify the differences in basic cost conditions. In this way, scale regulation may be applied after all. However, it has proven difficult to develop good explanatory models for cost differences in power distribution; see Iulo (1961) and Gröner (1980). The problem of heterogeneity may be reduced by grouping firms in reasonably homogeneous subsections. The challenge here is to find objective grouping criteria where coincidence does not have too great effects.

Relative changes instead of absolute costs could be used as a point of departure for comparing firms. This means that the return rate of the firms will depend on whether the development in costs is improved or impaired compared to the average for the sector. Furthermore, the statistical analysis could be concentrated around a limited number of cost components, primarily those components which are most important in terms of resource consumption in the industry in question.

Regulation under asymmetric information

The various incentive mechanisms are central in recent literature on regulation. For good overviews on this literature, see Schmalensee and Willig (1989) or Laffont and Tirole (1993). This literature builds on the theory of optimal contract agreements in so-called principal–agent relations. Here the regulator may be seen as the principal, with the regulated company being the agent.

A major issue in principal–agent theory concerns how contracts between the principal and the agent may be designed when the agent has access to better information (e.g. concerning the underlying cost conditions), or when the principal is unable to observe the efforts of the agent. When information about such issues is unevenly distributed, we have a situation of *asymmetric information*. To the regulator, the question is how the regulation mechanism should be designed when asymmetric information prevails.

The ordinary practice is to differentiate between two situations of asymmetric information: 'moral hazard', and 'adverse selection'. 'Moral hazard' refers to a situation with conditions which the firm may influence, but where these conditions are hidden from third parties, including the regulation authorities. The firm may for example choose for itself what efforts it should make in order to keep costs down to a low level. Such efforts may include increasing the staff labour intensity, improving work routines, or various aspects connected to the financial operation of the company.

A situation of 'adverse selection' refers to the underlying cost conditions relating to a company. These are conditions which the company may not influence; nevertheless, problems concerning regulation may emerge when the information relating to these conditions is unevenly distributed between the parties. The underlying cost conditions may partly be connected to *technological conditions*, although they may also refer to the company's ability to operate efficiently.

If the firm is capable of hiding or limiting the regulation authorities' insight into its abilities and efforts, the firm may, given certain assumptions, earn extra profits. These extra profits are often termed *information yield*. The issue in modern regulation literature is often how to design a regulation regime so as to ensure that as much as possible of the information yield is returned to society, at the same time as cost efficiency is taken into consideration.

The regulator's (principal's) problem is to find a regulation mechanism which, under certain restrictions, maximises the total welfare of society. The principal may not observe directly the firm's underlying cost conditions and the efforts which the management and the other employees make. However, the regulator may register the total costs of the firm, *ex post*. While the principal is expected to take common interests into consideration, the agent will pursue his own objectives. The objective function of the agent may be formulated in various ways, but it is normally dependent upon income and efforts. The agent's marginal utility of income is positive, while the marginal utility of effort is negative.

The principal is expected to have a certain amount of advance information as to the firm's underlying cost conditions beforehand. For instance, the principal can be expected to know the probability curve for certain variables connected to the firm's ability and willingness to achieve good results.

According to this theory, the requirements which must be fulfilled in order for an incentive mechanism to be optimal include the following:

- the mechanism must be incentive-compatible – i.e. giving the agent (the firm) incentives to reveal its underlying cost conditions
- all firms included in the regulation must survive in the long run.

In principle, the regulation authorities have two objectives: they will want to motivate for cost efficiency, but they will also want to limit the amount of monopoly profit left in the firms. These are conflicting objectives. If the regulation authorities desire a regime focused on incentives, they may choose price-cap regulation. However, pure price-cap regulation has poor characteristics with regard to the collection of monopoly yield, as every cost reduction will benefit the firm. The opposite is the case for cost-based regulation. Thus, the regulator will need to balance between considerations of cost efficiency and considerations of monopoly profit.

An important result stemming from this theory is that the regulator must accept that a certain monopoly profit (or information yield) is left to the firm, in order to give the firm incentives to reveal information as to its own cost conditions. The regulator needs to reward the firms that reveal their underlying cost conditions and operate efficiently. This may be achieved through implementing an incentive mechanism where the firms see that they may profit from providing correct information about their real cost conditions.

Laffont and Tirole (1993) have formulated a regulation regime which satisfies the optimisation requirements in this theory. This regime consists of a menu of different regulation contracts, from which the firms may choose their own combinations of cost sharing and reward. Contract alternatives with a low reward will generally be associated with firms that wish to absorb only a small share of future cost variations. On the other hand, contract alternatives with a high reward will be associated with firms that wish to assume greater responsibility for cost variations. The former type will be very close to a pure cost-based model, whereas the latter is close to a price-cap model.

Brown (1989) have described a regulation regime very similar to Laffont and Tirole's menu proposal. In their model, firms may commit themselves to a certain productivity improvement, and in return keep the benefits from improving productivity beyond the agreed level. If a firm commits itself to a productivity improvement of (say) 3 per cent annually, it may keep 100 per cent of the productivity improvements beyond this level. When the firms commit themselves to an improvement of 2 per cent, they may keep (e.g.) two-thirds of the improvements beyond 2 per cent, etc. Correspondingly, firms that are unwilling to commit themselves to any improvements in productivity will not be given the opportunity to enjoy any gains there may be from further improvements.

By making firms face choices of this kind, firms with great potential for improvement will want to commit themselves to a tight productivity development plan in return for the chance of a higher yield. Firms that are less certain concerning their potential for efficiency improvements will tend to choose a combination which is less ambitious regarding commitment to improving their productivity. The best firms are given incentives to operate more efficiently through tempting them with opportunities of higher yield. Firms with a smaller potential will have their costs covered, but will have to live with a lower return on capital.

Here it must be added that the incentive mechanisms prescribed by this theory have been tested in practice only to a limited extent, although recent research in this area has provided valuable new insights. Among the problems indicated by critics is the assumption that the regulator knows about cost conditions in the firms beforehand. In practice, this information may be so imprecise that it is difficult for the regulator to design a relevant menu of regulation contracts. This may be particularly difficult under complicated cost conditions, as is the case in power distribution.

The Norwegian authorities considered introducing incentive mechanisms that to a certain extent utilised the principal ideas of optimal regulation under information constraints. One possibility was to give the utilities the option of participating in incentive regulation contracts. If the option was not taken, the utility would stick to cost-based regulation, but with a relatively low rate of return. The intention behind introducing a voluntary regulation mechanism was to encourage those utilities which had potential and motivation for implementing cost-saving measures, without in general violating the ability to meet demand and quality requirements in utilities with small possibilities for cutting costs. This idea was, however, rejected by the regulator owing to the administrative burden such a incentive mechanism would impose.

The new Norwegian incentive regulation model

Income limits

As from 1 January 1997, the NVE introduced a new regulatory principle based on income caps. The main objective was to introduce stronger incentives to reduce the cost level in grid operations (NVE 1997).

The model is a kind of price-cap regulation very similar to the UK RPI-X formula. The chief difference is that an income limit is determined instead of a price cap. Through the regulation model chosen in Norway, grid operators now face fundamentally different framework conditions which will be of importance to the way in which utilities act, the value of the grid and the structure of the industry. The main features are as follows:

- Regulation periods of five years are introduced. The first period lasts from 1997 to 2001. During this period, the individual utility will have a defined annual income limit.
- The income limit is determined by the NVE on the basis of the cost level in 1994–5 and a normal rate of return on book capital as of 31 December 1995. This figure will be adjusted automatically in line with inflation.
- If the actual costs of the utility fall below the determined income, the utility may keep the gains in the form of a higher return on book capital. If costs exceed the fixed income amount, the utility will have to cover the difference itself in the form of a lower return on book capital.
- There will be requirements as to annual efficiency improvements, defined as a particular percentage of the total income amount.
- Utilities able to meet the efficiency improvement requirement will earn a rate of return equivalent to a normal rate set by the NVE. For the period 1997–2001, the NVE rate is set to 8.3 per cent; this corresponds to the risk-free rate (public bonds) plus two percentage points.
- Upper and lower limits are defined for return on capital. The limits are set at a stipulated normal rate of return ± 7 percentage points. The upper limit for 1997 equals 15.3 per cent, whereas the lower limit is set at 1.3 per cent. The normal rate of return on capital is adjusted annually in conjunction with the general level of interest.

Incentives for efficiency improvement are strengthened within the regulation period through the fact that the owner of the grid may keep

100 per cent of an efficiency gain on the margin, as long as the return on capital stays within the interval fixed by the NVE. Actual costs will not affect the determined income amount during the regulation period. The NVE has further argued that annual reductions in the determined income will be greater for utilities considered less efficient according to the NVE measurement methods for grid efficiency.

The annual adjustment of the determined maximum income is defined in one formula for determining the amount in 1997 and one formula for future adjustments. The income limit for 1997 is calculated as the sum of the following components:

- *Operating and maintenance costs*: The *average* of costs in 1994 and 1995, adjusted for the changes in the retail price index from 1994–5 to 1997.
- *Energy loss in the grid*: Average physical loss in the grid in 1994 and 1995, valued at the spot price at the relevant point of time (1997).
- *Depreciation*: The amount depreciated in 1995, adjusted for changes in the retail price index.
- *Return on capital*: Book capital as of 31 December 1995 is adjusted for the development in the retail price index (RPI). This adjusted amount is then multiplied by the NVE interest rate (8.3 per cent from 1997 to 2001). This interest rate is determined in the same way as today's return limit – i.e. as the risk-free interest rate plus a surcharge for risk.
- *Required efficiency improvements*: Finally, from the sum of the above elements, an amount based on the percentage stated in the required efficiency improvement will be subtracted. In 1997, the required rate of efficiency improvement was set at 2 per cent of the determined income amounts of all the utilities. For the period 1998–2000, individual requirements were set, on the basis of differences in measured efficiency between utilities.

In the first year of the regulation regime, the following formula (somewhat simplified) defines the initial income:[2]

$$IT_{e97} = [(DV_H + AVS_H + BFK_H * r) * I_{97} + NT_H * P_{97}] * (1 - EFK_{97})$$

By the end of the year, the determined income amount will be adjusted by using the actual spot price instead of the estimated price used in advance to fix the income amount. All elements marked with an *H* have been determined according to the base period 1994–5. *r*, *I*, and *P* are factors which should adjust for changes in variables over which neither the plant nor the NVE has any control. The last element reflects the NVE requirements for efficiency improvements in the first year.

Adjustment of the determined income for 1998 and later years is given by the following formula:

$$Income_{n+1} = [Income_n * (RPI_{n+1}/RPI_n)] * (1 - EFK) * (1 + G_{n+1}/2)$$

where G is the annual growth in the transportation volume.

This means that the income amount for 1998–2001 will equal the income amount for 1997 adjusted for changes in the RPI, and further requirements of efficiency improvements for 1998–2001 and 50 per cent of anticipated growth in the volume transported.

In special cases, particularly in the case of a readjustment towards a considerably higher degree of capitalisation, the upper limit may be of importance. In general, however, the upper and lower limits are likely to be of little importance, particularly during the first years.

The pressure for efficiency improvements

For 1997, the required efficiency improvement was stipulated at 2 per cent of total fixed income. For the regulation period 1998–2002 the required efficiency improvements were based on NVE's measurements of the utilities' individual cost efficiency, giving a range between 1.5 and 4.5 per cent. Utilities with a high score were placed at the lower end of the interval, while utilities assessed to be least cost-efficient got requirements at the upper end. In addition to this explicit requirement, the current regime includes one element which will contribute to increasing the total pressure for efficiency improvement:

- If inflation remains low, the total amount for capital costs will increase less than what a normal renewal of the grid should indicate. High inflation may produce the opposite effect.

It is possible that many utilities have over-invested and renewed their installations too early. In that case, there is a considerable potential for reducing capital costs by postponing grid renewal for a few years.

The effects of the required efficiency improvements may prove to differ considerably from one electricity utility to another, depending on the size of 1994–5 costs and where they are in relation to the renewal cycle of the grid. Utilities that have renewed important parts of their grid before the end of 1995 will face a more favourable income amount and may probably be better able to reduce their capital costs in the years to come. Utilities that either had high *real* costs in 1994–5 or small capitalised amounts and thus high *accounting* costs, will also face a more favourable initial income amount. To the extent that reported costs for 1994–5 include various non-capitalised investments, the cost basis for the income amount may be too high. Companies in which not all real investments have been capitalised may achieve considerable 'efficiency improvements' simply by altering their accounting practices.

With their new model, the NVE has shown a will to push through cost reductions. The NVE's success as a regulator will probably be evaluated in relation to its results in this area.

Grid value

The value of the grids is influenced by the utilities' ability to carry out efficiency improvement measures relative to the income amounts determined by the NVE. The value is influenced by the rate of return to be set for investments in the grid, taking into the risk connected to this type of activity. Increased risk in many respects contributes to increasing the owners' required rate of return from grid activities. Simply put, this means that grid operators must either increase their earnings in order to maintain levels at today's level, or that the value is reduced if earnings cannot be increased sufficiently. Only in exceptional cases will the value of the grid equal its book value. The sum of efficiency potential, tax liabilities and increased risk may result in both higher and lower grid values.

To increase grid-value beyond today's booked capital value of the grid, the utility will need to cut costs considerably. A utility's controllable costs are largely connected to salaries, and many of today's owners will find it difficult to make cuts in staff. Possibilities of cost reductions of this type will thus vary greatly. Also highly relevant here will be the point of departure (1994 cost levels) and the extent to which the utility has already carried out efficiency improvements.

Regulatory risk

The regulation regime which was in force up to 31 December 1996 gave grid companies full certainty as to obtaining a reasonable return on capital. High costs could usually be transferred to the customers through increased distribution tariffs within the maximum return as determined by the NVE. If the company's return was equal to the maximum return, then the value of the grid was by definition equal to its book value, as long as the cost of capital equalled the NVE rate.

The introduction of the new regulation regime, combined with a general liability to tax, has changed the situation for grid activities in Norway. They are now more *exposed to risk*.

The most important aspects of uncertainty are:

- Annual productivity requirements. How and to what extent will they be adjusted during the regulation period?
- Development of the capital base. How will the limit for capital costs and the capital base develop in the long run?
- How will efficiency improvements in one period affect the income limit to be set for the period?

Cost developments and the ability to exploit possibilities for efficiency increases will influence the value of the grid directly. As for value, it may produce effects in both directions, since owners may keep the gain if they make improvements beyond the authorities' requirement, but will also have to endure the loss if they fail to meet the requirement. Furthermore, the regulation regime represents an uncertainty in itself, in that adjustments of the income amount, any extraordinary changes during the five-year period, etc. will increase the risk as seen from the owner's point of view.

Regulatory risk is a factor connected to changes in the possibilities of return, which may come about as a result of unexpected changes in design and practice of the regulation regime. The uncertainty connected to the actual design of the system is now reduced, since the NVE has chosen a model. On the other hand, this is also a system which may influence the utilities' profitability possibilities to a much greater extent than earlier. Total regulatory risk is thus affected by two factors, working in opposite directions. Whether the regulation risk has increased or decreased is thus an empirical question.

Regulation model and structural changes

The new regulation model has the following effects on the economic situation for grid activities:

- Through the required efficiency improvement, utilities will be forced to implement considerable efficiency measures in order to obtain a normal return on capital.
- On the margin, the economic incentives for improving cost efficiency have been considerably strengthened.
- The return on capital in grid activities has become uncertain. It depends on NVE decisions, the plant's ability to implement cost-reducing measures and general factors such as inflation.

- The regulation model will have different effects for different units. Utilities with a certain degree of inefficiency have initially received high income amounts and have therefore been able to realise a higher return on capital than plants which already have implemented efficiency measures.
- When electricity utilities merge, the new utility will have an income amount which equals the sum of the previously separate utilities. This means that realisation of economies of scale will result in a higher return on capital for the merged utility.

The model thus prepares for leaving to the grid owners any realisable economies of scale, through the establishment of greater organisational units inside the distribution activities, as long as the return remains within the permitted interval for the rate of return. Preferably, such mergers should be made between neighbouring utilities, in order to obtain natural planning units. The question is how the new regulation model will affect the markets players' interest in participating in mergers which are profitable in a socio-economic perspective.

We have pointed out that the model provides possibilities for increased return on capital, but also that the uncertainty has increased due to increased regulatory risk. Combined with tight requirements of increased productivity, the question is whether this may put the grid values under pressure. However, a fall in grid values, if any, is not equivalent to saying that mergers have become uninteresting from a commercial point of view. The decisive factor is whether the owners may increase the value of the capital which is laid down in the grids, through participating in future mergers. Transaction prices recently paid for grid operations in Norway indicate increasing grid values.

An important question is whether the potential for increased return on capital in distribution activities will be regarded as sufficient, in view of the increased regulatory risk. This uncertainty will remain particularly great until experience has been accumulated as to how the regulation model is practised. As utilities gradually gain such experience, their interest in mergers may be strengthened through a reduction in regulatory risk. Another question is whether interest in merging neighbouring utilities has been strengthened through the alteration we now have seen. Various aspects here may work in opposite directions. To the extent that synergy effects are strongest between neighbouring utilities, the model will, *ceteris paribus,* make merger between neighbouring utilities most interesting. On the other hand, as we have noted, the model may have different effects for different utilities. There is thus still the danger that 'unfortunate utilities' may become unattractive partners for neighbouring utilities. That means we cannot rule out the possibility that the new regulation model can create difficulties in building up natural planning units in particular regions.

Conclusion

The Norwegian regulation authorities (NVE) have chosen to base the regulation of grid activities in Norwegian electricity utilities on income limits. These limits are determined on the basis of historical accounting items, and set requirements as to productivity improvements. The NVE has also published results based on efficiency measurements and signalled that future productivity requirements will depend on the utilities' results regarding these measurements. The model that has been adopted provides the utilities with very strong incentives to increase the efficiency of their operations. Norwegian electricity utilities must be prepared to undertake considerable changes and rearrangements to satisfy the productivity requirements which the NVE has signalled for the period 1998 to 2001.

One controversial item in the NVE's regulation system is the relatively tight requirements regarding efficiency improvements. These are determined individually and are based on the efficiency measurements. In view of the limitations of any such method, there is a certain risk that the individual utility may experience problems in covering the necessary transfer costs, as productivity requirements may be too demanding.

A more flexible model would introduce greater freedom of choice regarding required efficiency improvements. The possibilities for return on capital would then be graded according to the level of efficiency improvement to which the plant had committed itself. Consideration was given to implementing such a model, but this was rejected for administrative reasons.

Notes

1 This article is based on Magnus (1994), Magnus and Bråten (1996a) and Magnus and Bråten (1996b), EFFEN Marked.

2 The following notations have been used:

DV_H = historical operation and maintenance costs = $(DV_{94}+DV_{95})/2$ – i.e. the average of costs in 1994 and 1995

NT_H = historical physical energy losses in the grid = $(NT_{94}+NT_{95})/2$; this corresponds to the average net loss, as measured in kWh in 1994 and 1995

BFK_H = book capital as at 31 December 1995
AVS_H = depreciation in 1995
$I_t = RPI_t/RPI_{95}$ – i.e. the RPI for the relevant year, divided by the RPI for 1995
r is the NVE interest rate which is stipulated for each regulation period
P_t is the spot price in year t
EFK_t is the percentage requirement of efficiency improvement in year t.

7
Efficiency and Cost in Distribution Companies[1]

Jan Bråten and Eivind Magnus

Introduction

In the eight-year period following the 1991 regulatory reform, increased attention has been given to cost levels in transmission networks owned and operated by Norwegian utilities. As a consequence of the new regulatory principles, utilities must now make a clear administrative and operative distinction between network activities and those activities which are exposed to competition, by keeping separate accounts for their various activities. Utilities must also specify transportation costs when billing their customers. This means that information about the cost level in the networks is today available to the public.

This greater focus on cost efficiency in the transmission network-is also due to the new incentive regulation regime for net tariffs introduced by the monopoly supervisor, the NVE (Norwegian Water Resources and Energy Administration). The new regulatory regime, which is based on individual income caps, makes possible a higher rate of return in utilities which are able to reduce short- and long-term slack.

The increased attention to internal cost efficiency in network operations has also initiated research into the development of methods for calculating transmission network efficiency in utilities. Improved methods for measuring cost efficiency have various applications, with the choice of methodology depending on the user's need. The regulator may utilise the measurements so as to learn more about the cost function of transmission activities and thereby reduce the information problem in carrying out tariff regulation. The regulator also publishes indicators of cost efficiency in individual utilities to establish public pressure to get inefficient units to cut their costs.

Information on the potential for efficiency improvement could be used by utility management to initiate and support cost-reduction measures. While the regulator primarily needs indicators for overall efficiency, management in the utilities will be more interested in pinpointing any slack in the various subactivities.

The cost of distribution per kWh varies considerably among regional grids and among the nearly 200 local distribution companies. Costs in NOK per MWh for 69 representative distribution companies are shown in Figure 7.1. The 69 companies are the participants in the 1996 benchmarking with the value-chain model; they represent approximately 65 per cent of the market.

Figure 7.1 shows significant differences in costs per unit of energy. The major part of these differences is explained by differing population densities in the areas covered by various companies, (as reflected, for example, in the length of transportation to each customer), and by variations in natural conditions. The rest can be explained as differences in efficiency.

Electricity is frequently used for domestic heating in Norway. This accounts in part for the very high consumption, on average around 20 000 kWh per household per year. Because electricity is used for heating, the distribution system has been constructed with the ability to carry high loads.

This chapter is divided in two sections. The first discusses the role of efficiency measurements to reduce information rent in carrying out monopoly regulation. The second discusses and compares two

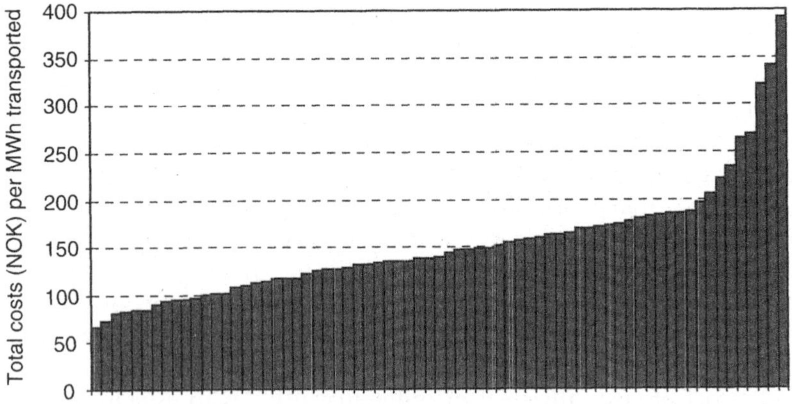

Figure 7.1 Total costs per MWh in 69 Norwegian distribution companies, 1996

different models currently used in the Norwegian Electricity supply industry.

Incentive effects of efficiency measurements

Introduction

An important activity for the NVE has been to develop methodologies for cost comparisons and efficiency measurements. In this section we investigate possible incentive effects of this activity, and discuss how methods for measuring cost differences could be used to reduce the information constraint in implementing incentive-based regulation.

In principle, cost comparisons and efficiency measurements may play a role in relation to efficiency improvements in the grid in two ways. They may be applied by the electricity companies as a measure for achieving greater efficiency, or they may be applied by the regulation authorities in their work with regulation or control of the electricity utilities' costs and revenues. In both cases, efficiency measurements will contribute positively to promoting efficiency. Efficiency measurements may bring about a more conscious attitude among owners and managers concerning the potential for efficiency gains, and may serve the owners as a management tool. This means that efficiency measurements may play an important role independent of how the regulation principles are actually designed in practice.

Efficiency measurements as a regulation mechanism

Reduction of information yield

As noted already, a main problem in designing the control of monopolies is that the authorities lack complete information on the necessary costs related to efficient operation; moreover, that information is unevenly distributed between the regulator and the firms (asymmetric information). A major concern in regulation theory has been to show what consequences imperfect information may have for the principles of an optimal regulation regime. Asymmetric information means that the regulator must balance the collection of the monopoly profit and the incentive characteristics of the regulation system. In other words, the monopoly control must allow some of the monopoly profit to remain in the firms in order to motivate them to increase their efficiency.

The regulation authorities' information problem may be lessened if the regulation applies to several companies producing corresponding services under identical technological conditions. By making comparisons of costs and analysing cost differences, the regulation authorities may gain information which then may be used to design a regulation system more in line with the overall objectives.

The purpose of this section is to discuss how cost comparisons and efficiency measurements may be exploited in connection with monopoly control, and the assumptions which must be satisfied in order for the measurement methods to improve the characteristics of the monopoly control. To this end, we will take a closer look at the importance of uncertain rewards.

Efficiency measurements as a formal part of income regulation

In a pure *rate-of-return regulation system* (see Chapter 6), companies are certain to cover their costs in the long run, in addition to receiving a return on invested capital which corresponds to the level stipulated by the authorities at any given time. It has been thoroughly documented, both in theory and practice, that rate-of-return regulation has weak incentive characteristics. However, cost comparisons may be used to grade the return. Electricity utilities which are efficiently run, indicated by the measuring system employed, may receive a higher return on capital than less efficient units. In this way, efficiency measuring have directly financial consequences for the electricity utilities.

Similarly, the results from efficiency measurements may play a role in *price-cap regulation systems*. Here, the regulation authorities face the problem of fixing the correct price cap. If the cap is set too high, too much monopoly profit will remain in the companies. If it is set too low, companies may suffer long-range problems in maintaining a satisfactory quality level. Through cost analyses and efficiency measurements, the regulation authorities may obtain access to information which can help them set more correct price caps.

Cost comparisons and asymmetric information

To the extent that cost comparisons can influence the revenue of the electricity utilities, asymmetric information between utilities and the regulator may affect the reporting which the utilities must undertake in order to provide data for cost comparisons. If the electricity utilities enjoy a great information advantage, the usefulness of such comparisons may be limited.

The methods developed for cost comparisons in electricity distribution in Norway require data on the conditions under which the electricity utilities must operate, as well as on the costs connected to grid activities. In both respects, the authorities are dependent on data from the utilities. Asymmetric information may become a particularly great problem if the regulation authorities cannot easily control or verify the data. As for data on costs, the utilities may have economic incentives to report costs lower than those forming the basis for the point tariffs. To avoid this problem, the authorities must be able to make consistency tests of the data reported to the regulation authorities and the data which form the basis for the point tariffs.

The control of data reported in connection with cost comparisons means extra costs for the regulator. To keep these costs from becoming too high, the number of controls must be limited; moreover, control routines should be structured to give the electricity utilities incentives for reporting as accurately as possible. The latter may possibly also be achieved through making it clear in advance that utilities reporting good results will be controlled in any case.

Uncertain rewards

Introduction

In the following, we will consider the complications that may arise if the regulator fails to register the cost-reducing efforts made by the utilities – in other words, if the reward from increased efforts becomes uncertain. To what extent does uncertainty in connection with rewards influence the strength of the incentives in the different regulation models? And to what extent do measurement methods affect this uncertainty?

Imperfect correlation and attitude towards risk

The economic literature has shown that uncertain rewards do not constitute a problem as long as the market players are risk-neutral (Sandmo and Hagen 1992). In this particular situation, risk-neutrality entails that the players act on the basis of their expected reward. For players of this type, it is sufficient to know that there is a positive correlation between effort and reward. If we assume that the players are risk-neutral, the required characteristics of the measurement methods become relatively modest. It is sufficient that the comparisons made contribute to a positive expectation among the players that increased efforts do pay off. Under such circumstances, it will also be possible to establish a measurement regime with yardstick regulation which meets the regulator's objectives – to motivate the firms to choose an optimal level of effort without demanding monopoly profit in return.

The assumption of risk-neutral players may, however, be unrealistic. An interesting question is what implications risk-aversion will have for the design of the monopoly control system, given that the connection between effort and reward is uncertain. From traditional risk theory we know that risk-averse players demand compensation for accepting higher risk. In a situation of regulation, this may mean that the regulation authorities must increase the reward in order to motivate the plants to greater efficiency. With both an imperfect connection between effort and reward, and risk-averse players, it will no longer be possible to motivate companies to step up their efforts without ceding some monopoly profit, even under yardstick regulation.

Uncertain rewards and regulatory risk

The general conclusion from economic theory is that risk-averse players require financial compensation in order to accept increased risk. If the incentive mechanism of the regulation system is based on financial rewards, uncertainty as to the size of the reward will mean that the utilities, *ceteris paribus*, will demand a higher reward in order for the mechanism to yield the desired incentive effects. The greater the uncertainty, the greater will be the required reward.

This result may be generalised as regards uncertainty concerning future framework conditions as well, often spoken of as *regulatory risk*. When risk-averse utilities experience regulatory risk, it becomes more uncertain whether increased effort today will be rewarded tomorrow. The greater the regulatory risk, the greater reward the utility will expect to receive under a future regulation regime in order to undertake the burden of implementing cost-reducing measures.

Publication of efficiency differences

The authorities could chose to limit their involvement to collection, analysis and publication of cost data, in order to give the general public access to information concerning which plants are run efficiently and which are not. In this situation, the results will have no direct consequences for the utility's income. The idea is that publishing this type of information will serve to motivate the individual plant, at the same time as the customers' and owners' basis for making inefficient plants increase their efficiency is improved. Such a mechanism is often termed *pillory competition*. Cost comparisons and efficiency measurements used in this way may also help to improve the complaints arrangement, since it will be easier to determine whether the utility is in fact efficiently operated.

Voluntary efficiency measurements

In Norway, the utilities themselves carry out efficiency comparisons on a voluntary basis. Such efficiency comparisons put efficiency on the agenda and give the board of directors, politicians, important customers and the general public a basis for scrutinising the efficiency of the local electricity utility. This in turn means that new players are introduced on the scene, and that may create political pressure in favour of increased efficiency. While measurements may motivate change, they may also provide a tool for controlling the implementation of an efficiency improvement process, as they may help the owners identify appropriate operational efficiency objectives.

In addition to information on efficiency comparisons, public attention towards other utilities' implementation or planning of considerable cost reductions may reduce political barriers against efficiency improvements. The very existence of pioneers in efficiency improvement may contribute to increasing the pressure for enhanced efficiency, or possibly reduce the political cost of efficiency improvement for the others. For one thing, efficiency improvements will be put on the public agenda and viewed as a normal process which others may benefit from copying. Secondly, those who increase their efficiency will demonstrate what other utilities may achieve; finally, others may benefit from the lessons learnt by the pioneers.

Summary

Cost comparisons and efficiency measurements may contribute to reducing the regulator's information problem under regulation of natural monopolies. They may also be used in the utilities' internal work with efficiency improvements. If the measurement methods employed had provided the regulator with perfect information about the underlying cost conditions, they would simultaneously have solved the central problems of regulation. The results yielded by the measurement methods could then have been used as input to determine the correct income limits, so as to cover the electricity utilities' costs accurately. In practice, however, measurements are imperfect. The methods at hand and the available data can at best provide a reasonably correct picture of cost developments.

If the results of the measuring affect the electricity plants' revenues directly, any information advantage the plants may have could be used to influence the reporting on which the measuring depends. It is thus important that the data should be verifiable and that necessary control routines can be carried out.

The role to be played by cost comparisons and efficiency measurements is partly dependent on whether the methods can capture real efficiency improvements, and how robust they are in relation to the utilities' possibilities of affecting the measurement result. If there is too much 'noise' in the measurements, the reward connected to the result of the cost comparisons will be influenced by random factors. In that case, the utilities' risk-aversion will have to be taken into consideration in the practical design of the regulation system. Since risk-aversion may be the most realistic assumption, the ability of the measurement method to reflect real efficiency improvements may have consequences for how the regulation authorities design the reward mechanisms.

Two models for efficiency measurements in Norwegian grid operations

With more than 200 utilities active in grid operations, efficiency measurements have been seen as a useful tool for the Norwegian regulator to improve the basis for income regulation. The challenge has been to develop a methodology capable of distinguishing between differences in underlying cost conditions and differences in cost-efficiency, given the heterogeneity of the individual concession areas.

In this section we first present a benchmarking technique[2] tailor-made for transmission network activities. In recent years this technique has been adopted by Norwegian utilities representing more than 60 per cent of the distribution market. Their goal is to locate slack and to provide motivation for cost-reducing activities. Secondly, we discuss the overall potential for reduced cost in the short and long term, based on the benchmarking technique presented, using data from 1994–6. Thirdly we compare the basic principles and empirical results with the Data Envelopment Analysis Method (DEA) used by the NVE for regulating purposes.

The Value Chain Model

This methodology was introduced by a Norwegian company, Energidata, in 1994 and was then adapted for use by a group of regional grid companies. In co-operation between ECON and Energidata, the method was modified in 1994–5 for application among local distribution companies. In the following, we will focus on the use of the method for local distribution companies.

The Value Chain Model (VCM) views the distribution of electricity as a transportation activity – the transportation of effect to end-users from nodes connecting the distribution system to the generation and transmission systems. This transportation activity involves capital investments in transformers, lines, etc., physical energy losses, maintenance and administrative services.

The electric utility operates in a specific area. The level and composition of its transportation activity – the product of the distribution services which it supplies – will be influenced by the specific conditions of the geographical area served – the level and composition of electricity demand, population density, topography, etc. Since these conditions vary significantly from utility to utility, cost comparisons based on total cost figures have little relevance when we want to evaluate the efficiency. The VCM splits the distribution network into subactivities, allocates total reported operating cost among the subactivities, and then compares cost efficiency between subactivities in different utilities by using the 'best-practice' method. The method has been implemented both between regional nets and between local distribution companies in Norway. The presentation here will focus on how it has been implemented between distribution companies.

The model distinguishes between main activities and secondary activities, where the main activities comprise a high-tension network, distribution transformers (typically transformation from 22 kV to 230 V), low-tension network and customer services, as illustrated in Figure 7.2. The division of activities is based on standard distribution of costs as reported by Norwegian local grid companies, and reported costs is employed as a measure of the resources used in each activity.

Owing to differing local conditions, the necessary costs in each subactivity will vary among utilities. In order to take account of these

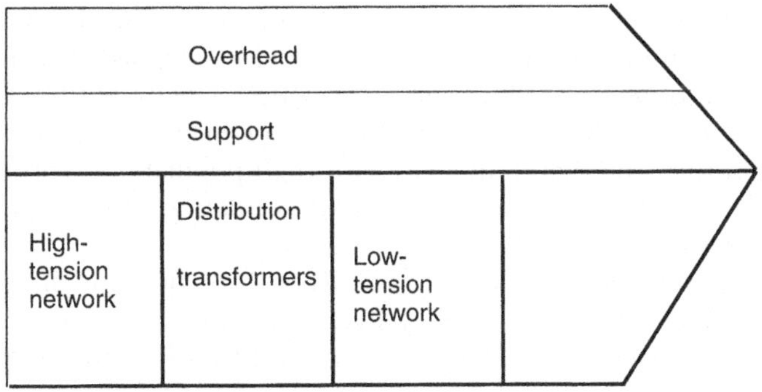

Figure 7.2 Electricity distribution divided into subactivities

differences, every subactivity receives a work-load factor, which is used to define the efficient cost for each subactivity. Conceptually, these factors should reflect the underlying work load associated with each subactivity. The work-load factor for the high-voltage network sub-activity is, for instance, related to the total length of that part of the network. The cost-efficiency factor is, by definition, the ratio between the operating cost and the work-load factor: in the model efficiency is computed as if there are constant returns to scale. Thus, a suboptimal scale will result in a lower score on computed efficiency.

The formulation of work-load factors for the individual subactivity is the crucial element of the method. Factors are formulated to reflect differences in the concession areas related to the structure of consumer demand, population density, etc. which are seen as important cost-drivers. When these factors are correctly specified, we can make comparisons reflecting differences in cost efficiency. The goal has been to relate the cost-drivers to parameters outside the control of the individual utility. In practice, however, it has been difficult to find theoretically well founded parameters for the load factors that will at the same time not be influenced by the utility. In the present use of the model, parameter have been accepted that may, in the long run, be influenced by the policy of the utility.

For the high-voltage network subactivity, the work-load factor is defined as the length of the network, multiplied by the average maximum load in the same net to the power of 0.4. This is to reflect the fact that necessary total costs are assumed to be proportional to the length of transportation for a given capacity, but increase only by 0.4 with the capacity of the net. Hence, the work-load factor reflects the transportation volume provided by this activity.

For distribution transformers, the work-load factor has been defined as the maximum load in the network. It could be argued that the total transformation costs are lower in areas with concentrated transformation, yielding an overly low work-load factor in utilities serving rural areas. On the other hand, in areas with high population density, utilities are often forced by environmental regulations to choose more expensive solutions.

For the low-voltage network, the work-load factor is simply the length of that network. The work-load factor for customer services is the number of customers served by the utility, while the number of employees serves the work-load factor for general overhead activities. For supportive activities, the work-load factor is the total estimated building costs for the net, used as an indicator of the size of the net. Consideration has been given to adjusting the net parameters for varying geographic and climatic conditions. This has not been done in the present model.

The potential for cost reductions in a subactivity is defined as the difference between the cost-efficiency factor and a normative-efficiency factor, here based on the 'best-practice' method. When the method was developed, the idea was to set the normative-efficiency factor as the lowest observed efficiency factor in the sample for each particular subactivity. However, owing to inaccurate data, this method will tend to over-estimate the potential for increased efficiency. The demarcation line between the different subactivities is not perfect and although there is a common standard for the allocation of costs between subactivities, there are significant variations in the way different utilities report costs. Thus, the reported total costs are more accurate than the reported costs in each subactivity. Very low costs relative to the load factor in a specific subactivity can be a result of either data noise (e.g. the utility reporting 'too low costs' in the subactivity) or good performance in the subactivity. If a utility is reporting too low costs in one activity, it is likely to report too high costs in others.

To avoid under-estimation of the necessary costs in each subactivity, an alternative method is used. First the average ratio between costs and load factors for each subactivity is determined for the whole sample. The ratios form a vector, A. The ratios can be interpreted as expressions of average efficiency. A utility's actual costs (C_{ui}) can then be compared with the costs it would have, if it had the average rate of efficiency in each subactivity (C_{Ai}). The utility with best total performance is defined as the utility with the lowest value of the expression $e_i = (C_{ui} - C_{Ai})/C_{ui}$. For the best utility, e will be a negative figure. The next step is to determine the normative-efficiency factors for each subactivity. This is done by defining a new vector $N = s * A$. The variable s is a scalar and is given by the equation $s = C_b/C_{Ab}$, where C_b is the actual costs in the utility with best total performance and C_{Ab} is the costs this utility would have, if it had the average rate of efficiency in all activities. We can then replace the average ratio vector, A, with the new normative vector, N, and for every company we can compute the normative total costs, C_N, as the vector product of N and the load factors. For the utility with best total performance, we will then have $C_{ui} = C_b = C_N$. For all the other observations we will have $C_{ui} > C_N$. Finally, we can define the total potential for cost reductions in a utility as $C_{ui} - C_N$; the relative potential is given by $E = (C_{ui} - C_N)/ C_{ui}$.

As a result of the method applied, one utility will be defined as efficient (e.g. with no potential to cut costs) whereas the remaining utilities will have their efficiency defined relative to the performance of the best observation.

Potential for cost reduction according to the VCM

The methodology has been tested on data from 1994, 1995 and 1996. Analyses have been done both with a limited concept of costs (e.g. the operating costs) and with total costs. The latter has included also a standard estimated profit of 7 per cent of the capital.

Figure 7.3 illustrates the relationship between reported total costs in individual utilities and the potential for cost reduction for 69 utilities in 1995. The minimum cost is calculated on the basis of the cost level in the utility with lowest observed cost, after work-load factors have been taken into consideration. The difference between reported cost and the minimum cost is defined as the potential for cost reduction. Note that, in this case, utility number one has no potential for cost reductions relative to the others, as it is the most efficient unit of the sample.

The most efficient company in this study is Stavanger Energi. This distribution company has approximately 50 000 customers, clearly a large enterprise by Norwegian standards. In general there is no significant correlation between the computed total efficiency and the size of the utility. Assuming that there are increasing returns to scale in electricity

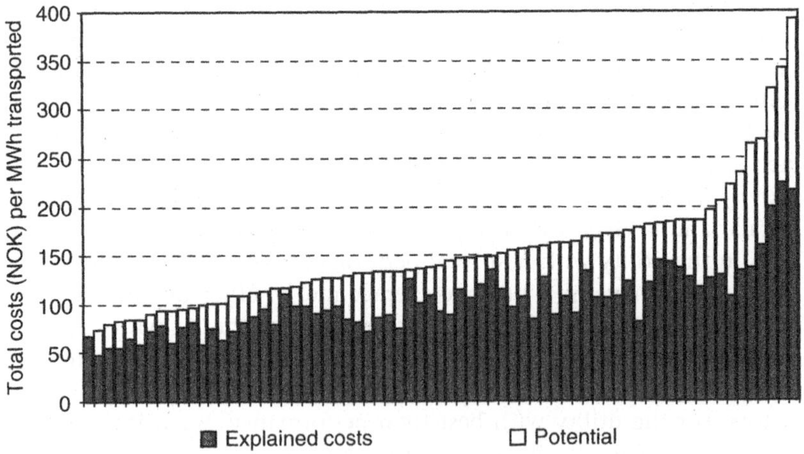

Figure 7.3 Potential for efficiency gains in 69 Norwegian utilities with grid operation, 1995

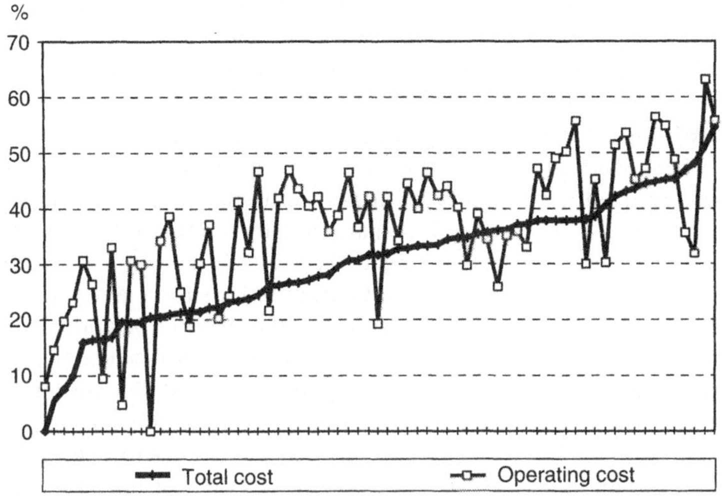

Figure 7.4 Estimated potential for cutting costs in 69 Norwegian distribution companies, per cent, 1995

distribution, this indicates that the larger companies have not in general exploited their greater opportunities to cut costs.

The average potential for reduction in total costs is estimated at 30 per cent. If we restrict the analysis to operating costs, which is in general about 50 per cent of the total costs in the local distribution companies, the average potential for reductions is estimated to be approximately 36 per cent of operating costs. The distribution of the potentials for cutting costs is shown in Figure 7.4, where utilities are grouped according to their estimated total potential.

The correlation between the two measures of efficiency is 0.7. Efficiency in relation to operating costs may be interpreted as a short-term efficiency, whereas efficiency in relation to total costs also involves long-term efficiency. The overall impression from the application of the VCM is that local distribution companies in Norway have a significant potential to increase their efficiency. The application of the method on regional grids indicates that these companies have an even higher cost-cutting potential than do the local distribution companies.

The DEA method

The Data Envelopment Method (DEA method) goes back to Farrell (1957) and has been used in several industries both in the private and public sectors.[3] The method seeks to reveal technical inefficiency. The computation is based on a set of input factors in the production process and product aspects (or products) specified in technical terms. Figure 7.5 shows the basic principles of the method in simplified form, with two input factors and one product (or product aspect).

The DEA method assumes that if a given quantity of a product can be produced with two different input combinations, then the same quantity can also be produced with any linear combination of the same two input combinations. Turning to Figure 7.5, if *A* and *B* represent two companies with observed input combinations for a given quantity of production, any point on the straight line between *A* and *B* is also supposed to be possible input combinations that can produce the same amount. Based on this assumption it is possible to define an efficient front, illustrated in Figure 7.5 as the broken line passing through *A*, *B*, *C* and *E*. Any point on the front is considered to represent a technically efficient combination. Hence a utility using *D* is not efficient, but it should be able to move down to the straight line *BC* at *D'*. The line from *D* to *D'* defines the potential for cost reduction, given a proportional reduction in all input factors. The technical efficiency of *D* is defined by the fraction *D'O*/*DO*, which is a number lower than 1. Thus, the companies who are on the efficient front get an efficiency indicator of 1, whereas the others are accorded lower values. The DEA method could be specified either with an assumption of constant returns to scale or with variable returns to scale.

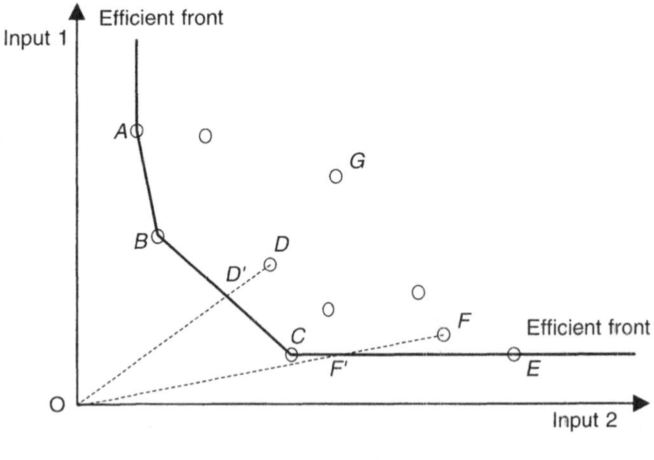

Figure 7.5 The DEA method with one product and two inputs

The regulator, the Norwegian Water Resources and Energy Administration (NVE), has applied the DEA method to the approximately 200 local distribution companies in Norway. An analysis based on data from 1994 was published in early 1996. Practical implementation was done by using four input parameters and three product aspects. The input parameters used were man-years, purchases of services and commodities, energy losses and capital, where 'capital' was defined as the book value of the company's assets. The three product aspects were the length of the high-voltage grid, the number of customers and total energy delivered over the year.

Technical efficiency according to NVE's DEA model

The regulator, NVE, published data about the technical efficiency of 195 distribution companies in the spring 1996. With reference to uncertainty concerning the quality of input data, NVE did not publish the exact indicator of technical efficiency for each company. Instead, the companies were put in groups covering different ranges of efficiency. The result is shown in Figure 7.6.

Several of the big companies belong to the efficient front group with no *revealed* technical inefficiency. One problem with the DEA method is that many observations are required to define the efficient front. Nevertheless, also the DEA method indicates that, for the majority of companies, efficiency is still relatively low.

Comparison of results

Bråten (1996) has compared the results yielded by the two methods for 48 companies that have been examined by both methods, using data

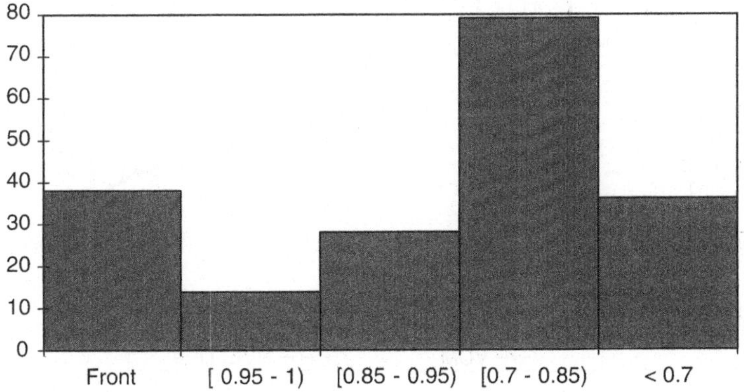

Figure 7.6 Number of companies belonging to different efficiency groups

from 1994. For this comparison, the computed relative potential for cost reductions for each company in the VCM was transformed to a cost-efficiency indicator, E', given by

$$E' = 1 - E$$

where E is the relative potential for cutting costs. The indicator, E', then takes the value 1 for the most efficient observation (where E is zero) and values lower than 1 for all others. Thus, E' takes the same form as the indicator of technical efficiency computed by the DEA method. Since NVE has not published the exact values of the technical efficiency indicators, we have assigned the mean value of each group interval to all the members of each group: thus, all the members in the group with technical efficiency in the range 0.85–0.95 have been given the value 0.90. Members of the group with indicator values lower than 0.7 have been given the value 0.65. The results of this comparison are illustrated in Figure 7.7.

As Figure 7.7 shows, the correlation is not very strong for the two methods. The correlation coefficient is only 0.54.

With four exceptions, the values of the DEA indicator are higher than the values of the VCM indicator. To a large extent this can be explained by differences in the efficiency concepts of the two methods: The VCM studies cost efficiency, whereas the DEA studies technical efficiency – and a company can be technically efficient without being

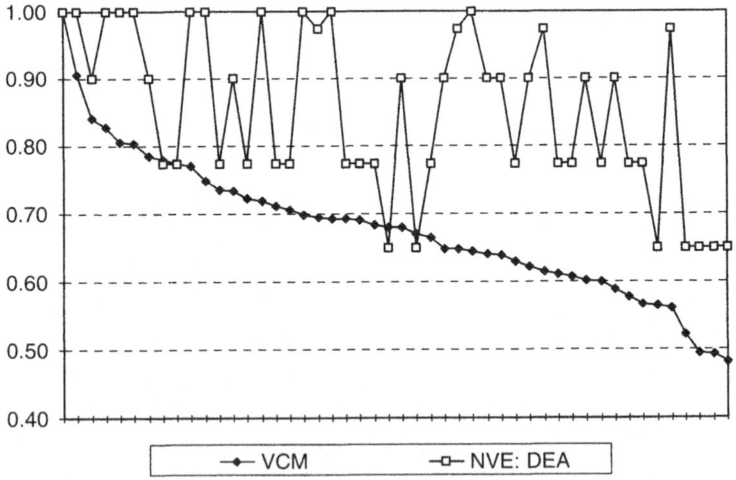

Figure 7.7 Comparing the results for the DEA and VCM indicators

cost-efficient. Moreover, the DEA method requires several observations to establish the efficient front. There will be a tendency for companies that are different in some sense – for example, in having an unusual composition of product aspects or of inputs – will be found efficient by the DEA method. Company *A*, in Figure 7.5 is an example of this. A company like this may not be very cost-efficient, but the DEA method is not able to reveal that *A* is technically inefficient. This may explain why some of the companies that are performing poorly in the VCM are classified as technically efficient by the DEA.

Differences in the basic methodology are not the only reason for the low correlation. A closer study Bråten (1996) reveals that there are several probable reasons for the low correlation in the results of the two methods. These reasons are partly related to differences in the *definitions* of input variables in the two methods and partly to errors in reported data. An example of the first is that in the DEA only the length of the high-voltage grid is taken into account, while the VCM also counts the length of the low-tension net. Thus, the DEA favours grids where the high-voltage net is long relative to the low-voltage net. This may be of some importance since the ratio low-voltage/high-voltage varies from 1/1 up to 5/1. These differences may in part be explained by the different topography and patterns of housing in various parts of the country. According to the NVE, there is also some doubt concerning the quality of the data on the length of the low-tension net.

General problems in measuring efficiency in distribution

A high correlation between the results of the two methods would have increased the credibility of both. On the other hand, the revealed weak correlation does not provide us with a conclusive argument as to which of the two methods more correctly depicts the true efficiency of the various companies. This will remain a theoretical debate, a debate that may influence how the two methods are actually implemented in the years to come. For both methods, the greatest challenge is how to handle a problem which they clearly have in common. This problem is connected to the fact that in an industry like electricity transmission, a great part of the costs will be related to the construction and maintenance of the grid. With a life-cycle of 40 years or more, this means that the reported costs in a specific year may not reflect very accurately the long-run average costs of a grid.

In the utilities, the book value of assets is based on linear depreciation, typically 30 years. Average age varies significantly, which means that there are also great differences in the size of book values relative to the size of the grids. Furthermore, there are also variations in book values because the book values historically has been set in different ways. These differences in book values and grid age represent a problem for the two described methods of measuring utility efficiency, since they both use book value as an input to describe the capital costs. Hence, companies with very low book values tend to emerge as the typical winners in both methods.

The problem of allocating costs over the years also appears in a similar context: the demarcation line between maintenance costs and investments is not sharp, and different companies use different criteria. Maintenance costs may also vary with the age of the grid, and investments typically vary between periods. Both methods try to exclude the investments from the descriptions of input to production, but they both rely on the way each company distinguishes between investments and maintenance – and there is clear evidence that this varies greatly from company to company, and also that it has undergone considerable change recently. Previously a large part of investments were reported as maintenance costs, whereas now there is a tendency to report a greater share as investments. The difference between the two alternatives is obvious: reporting the expenses as investments will spread the costs over a long period, while reporting them as maintenance will increase reported costs in the relevant year with the full sum of the expense. These differences in the placing of the demarcation between investment and maintenance introduce serious noise into the data of both methods. The VCM uses costs where investments are excluded; in the DEA, the input factors of man-year and purchases are both adjusted for the rate of reported investments.

Concluding remarks

In Norway's new regulatory regime, operating from 1997, the intention is to provide grid companies with stronger incentives to increase efficiency. For each company, a maximum income figure is stipulated, based on its reported costs in 1994–5 and adjusted for inflation and a specified demanded increase in efficiency. In 1997 all companies had to cut total costs by 2 per cent compared to the 1994–5 level to achieve normal profits. From 1998 the regulator, the NVE, differentiated the cuts in maximum income according to the company's efficiency according to the DEA method. These individual cuts ranged from 1.5 per cent for the most efficient companies to 4.5 per cent for those with a sizeable potential for cost reductions. The aim is that in the long run, the incentives are to benefit a high *level* of efficiency and not just *relative improvements* in efficiency. To achieve this, the regulator needs a good method for measuring efficiency. The regulator also intends to publish the results from the DEA and from other measures of efficiency, so as to enforce the pressure from the municipal owners and from the customers for greater efficiency. The higher the credibility of the methods, the more pressure will be generated by making the results public.

The VCM is used by most of the larger companies. It is used to motivate cost-cutting strategies, and some companies have started to use the results as a platform for further benchmarking. There is a clear need for improved means of measuring efficiency – for the regulator, and for the management and owners of the grids. We have shown how two methods, the VCM and the DEA, as implemented today, have definite weaknesses. This indicates there are good reasons for continuing research to improve these methods and the way in which they are implemented.

Notes

1 This chapter is based on Bråten (1996) and Magnus and Bråten (1996). *To metoder for effektivitetsmåling i distribusjon,* commissioned by the Research Council of Norway and the Norwegian Electricity Federation.
2 The basic principles were developed by Energidata AS in close co-operation with some utilities, and refined through a series of R&D projects commissioned by EnFO.
3 See also Charnes and Cooper (1985).

8
Owner Attitudes and Public-company Behaviour in a Restructured Electricity Sector[1]

Eivind Magnus

Introduction

A large majority of the Norwegian electricity companies engaged in grid, production and supply activities are public enterprises owned by local municipalities or county authorities. Before the market reform, these companies regarded themselves as public service entities responsible for providing the communities with long-term stable electricity supplies. Normally, they were organised as an integrated part of the local administration. The economic objective was to cover cost, and they operated subject to the expectation that any economic surplus from their activities would be transferred to their consumers in the form of low electricity prices.

After the electricity reform, the Norwegian government motivated local authorities to develop commercial entities through corporatisation of the local utilities, even though their main activity was electricity distribution and as such they were considered as natural monopolies. Faced with new challenges in a market-based power sector, many municipalities were reorganised as limited companies, still owned by the same authority. Normally their objective was restated: it was now profit maximisation. According to the government, the reorientation and corporatisation of former municipalities necessitated the development of monopoly regulation similar to the case of those private monopolies in the USA and UK. The new policy was also a consequence of poor performance among utilities, especially within grid operations. Lack of economic incentives had resulted in high operating costs and over-capacity; see Andersen and Høisveen (1995).

A question often raised in this context is whether the market reform, despite the reorganisation to limited companies, has altered the economic objectives of owners and top management. Has the market reform changed company priorities, or are they still influenced by traditional public service expectations? To what extent are the public owners motivated to promote higher productivity by the prospect of achieving higher profitability? What influence have the public owners on the internal decision-making process in the utilities? To what extent are owners willing or able to transfer any economic rewards to the decision-makers within the utilities?

To shed light on these questions, ECON undertook a research project in 1996 aimed at mapping the objectives and role in the decision process of individuals representing the owners of Norwegian electricity utilities with distribution operations. This project was commissioned by the NVE. The survey involved a combination of in-depth interviews and an extensive questionnaire. In the pilot-study phase, in-depth interviews were undertaken with the chief executive officer (CEO), the head of grid operations (HoD) and the chairman of the board (CoB) of six utilities. On this basis a questionnaire with 44 separate questions was developed and sent to a total of 40 utilities. Of these, 37 answered, representing 92.5 per cent of the sample and 57.2 per cent of the Norwegian market in terms of number of customers. The results from the questionnaire were analysed and related to utility size, concession area and price policy.

This study is the first empirical work carried out in Norway to investigate how the economic reform has influenced attitudes among public owners and top management. It should be seen as a contribution to public-choice theories and their focus on the cost minimisation incentives to politicians and administrators charged with running a public enterprise. Central to this theory is the question of how well the political process represents the taxpayers' interest. Public companies are not run by taxpayers, but by civil service administrators and politicians. These individuals have their own objective functions which, by means of the political process, are accountable to voter preferences. Civil service administrators maximise utility functions which include the size of their discretionary budgets as arguments, while politicians are assumed to engage in vote maximising strategies. Thus these individuals take decisions based on the weak influence of voter preferences for cost efficiency (Pollitt 1995).

The study was undertaken in 1996 – in other words, five years after the electricity reform was implemented, but before the incentive regulation model had been introduced. At this point, the NVE had announced that a new regulation model was in the pipeline, so we can assume that utilities expected pressures for higher efficiency to be forthcoming.

Dividend policy as an indicator for owner goals

The key question in this study was to what extent the electricity reform had altered preferences among individuals charged with running the utilities. An important element was therefore to develop indicators for changing preferences. One such indicator was dividend policy, which has changed radically after the reform. It was registered that more utilities paid dividends to the owner, and that dividend payments were increasing. An important question was therefore to what extent changes in dividend policies indicated changes in the goals of the owners.

Electricity supply is characterised by high investment costs and long length of service of the facilities involved. There is considerable flexibility in the timing of investments. Many companies also have large financial reserves. This means that in the short run they can increase dividends without increasing prices, either by consuming financial reserves or by postponing investments.

Low dividend payments could be motivated by the need to finance investments or to firm up the company's financial position, and are not as such an indication that the owners want to keep tariffs low. On the other hand, a policy aimed at high or increasing dividends is in conflict with low prices. A utility owner with a sound financial position could increase dividends without raising prices. Such a choice would indicate, however, that dividends are seen as more important than reducing prices.

The Norwegian utilities' grid management systems were all subject to a rate-of-return regulation in the period under study (see Chapter 6). As long as the cap on the rate of return was not violated, the owner was free to stipulate the tariff level. An interesting question to investigate was the relationship between dividend policy and tariff policy, since in the long run there is a trade-off between high dividend and low tariffs to the customers.

Efficiency improvements make it possible to lower tariffs while also increasing dividends. Still any reduction in prices will, *ceteris paribus*, be at the expense of the rate of return on capital, and therefore in the long run will lead to lower dividends. Correspondingly, as any dividend payment could have been used to reduce prices, dividends are a sure proof that the owners do not exclusively prefer lower prices.

Table 8.1 Distribution of a given increase in the company' surplus, average

Alternative	CEO (%)	HoD (%)	CoB (%)
Lower prices	43	42	34
Increased investments	12	7	13
Increased equity	27	36	31
Increased dividends	18	16	22

Respondents were asked how they would distribute a given increase in the surplus after natural replacement and renewal of the network have been taken into consideration (Table 8.1).

All groups gave highest priority to lower prices. CEOs and HoDs stressed lower prices more than twice as much as increased dividends. Board chairmen, representing the owners, put more emphasis on dividends over lower prices than did the executives, but the differences were quite small. On an unweighted basis the chairmen too leant towards price reductions rather than towards increased dividends, but when the figures were weighted for utility size, the priority was more or less even (28 per cent vs 30 per cent). This meant that in the bigger companies, chairman tended to give greater priority to higher dividends rather than to lower prices. To a lesser degree this was also the case for CEOs, but not for HoDs.

It is interesting to note that even five years after the reform was implemented, lower prices remained the most preferred objective. This indicates that the transition to more commercial focus was only in the beginning phase.

In order to map the dynamics in dividend policy as an indicator for changing priorities, the utilities were asked both how attitudes towards dividends had changed over the last four years and how these attitudes were expected to change over the coming four years.

Respondents clearly indicated that, after deregulation in 1991, the owners had started emphasising higher dividends and increased efficiency, whereas their emphasis on low prices remained unaltered. There were no significant differences between the three groups. However, no significant negative correlation could be established between a higher emphasis on increased and a lower or stable emphasis on low prices. This suggests that it had not been obvious to the respondents that there was a choice between the two, and that many opted to have their cake and eat it too.

The study confirms that there were expectations that the pressure for higher dividends would increase in the future. A full 84 per cent of the utilities expected their owners to demand higher dividends in the four years to come. Emphasis on increased dividends was greater in the larger companies.

So far the research indicated that in 1996 – five years after the Energy Act was implemented – cost minimisation was the commanding objective, but that a large majority expected more focus on dividend payments in the future. However, since there were significant variations between individuals, we wanted to see whether there were specific characteristics among the utilities that emphasised high dividends.

What characterises utilities emphasising high dividends?

Utilities were grouped according to the tendency to emphasise high dividend payments (Table 8.2). The purpose was to analyse the correlation in terms of key variables such as utility size, cost level and rate of return.

The concession areas served by the individual utilities vary according to population density and topographical and climatic variables. Utilities serving rural concession areas with low population density

Table 8.2 Average values of key indicators, 1993–6

Average values	Highest emphasis on dividend	Average emphasis on dividend	Lowest emphasis on dividend
Number of customers	65 613	18 794	32 914
Energy sales per customer (kWH)	28 668	25 806	25 604
Meter network per customer (metres)	104	140	131
Price level (øre/kWh)	17	17	18
Operating cost per customer (deviation from average) (%)	4	−6	−3
Operating cost per meter network (deviation from average) (%)	27	−15	−6
Rate of return (1993) (%)	10.2	7.7	10.0
Rate of return (1994) (%)	6.8	6.5	6.5
Rate of return (1995) (%)	7.1	7.1	6.7
Rate of return (1996) (%)	6.1	6.7	6.7
Preferred rate of return (1996) without any rate cap (%)	6.9	7.5	8

and unfavourable topography have high underlying distribution costs relative to utilities serving typically urban areas. As a proxy variable for the degree of favourable conditions within concession areas, the length of the network per customer was chosen.

We found that high emphasis on dividend was more frequent among the largest utilities, who also tended to serve concession areas with a greater population density. Perhaps surprisingly, we found no correlation between a strong emphasis on dividends and the achieved and desired rate of return. When respondents were asked what rate of return they would set for 1996 if not hindered by the cap set by the NVE, the result showed a negative correlation. Utilities with the strongest emphasis on dividends would set a rate of return of 6.9 per cent on average, whereas those with the weakest emphasis would choose a rate of 8 per cent. This result is clearly counter-intuitive; on the other hand, in view of the small sample, the discretion involved in answering a hypothetical question of this sort and the small margins, no firm conclusions should be drawn here.

Respondents were also asked how a windfall profit would be allocated between different purposes (Table 8.3). In the group with lowest emphasis on dividend, 40 per cent would be allocated to the customers through tariff reductions, whereas in the group with highest emphasis on dividend, only 34 per cent would be allocated to customers. As indicated, we found a clear inverse relationship between the tendency to prefer dividends and to reduce tariffs.

The survey also showed that the most dividend-oriented companies could be assumed to be somewhat less efficient than the average, which meant they had the greatest potential for efficiency improvements. They were thus in a position to finance an increase in dividends through cost-cutting. Moreover, these companies were the ones that expected a stronger pressure for efficiency improvement than the average, and they needed to have more firm and binding efficiency

Table 8.3 How would a windfall profit be allocated between different purposes (%)? Utilities grouped according to the tendency to emphasise dividend

Allocation	Highest emphasis on dividend	Average emphasis on dividend	Lowest emphasis on dividend
Reduced tariffs	34	42	40
Accelerate investments	9	4	15
Increase financial solidity	30	29	33
Increase dividend	27	24	12

Table 8.4 Assumed potential for cost cuts relative to tariffs

Potential cost cuts	Highest emphasis on dividend (%)	Average emphasis on dividend (%)	Lowest emphasis on dividend (%)
Within four years	13.7	12.2	9.1
In the long term	23.2	21.5	17.2

Table 8.5 Bonus wages: attitudes among Chairmen of the Board

Attitude	Positive	Reluctant	Negative	No answer
Highest emphasis on dividend	4	3	1	1
Average emphasis on dividend	3	3	2	1
Lowest emphasis on dividend	1	9	7	1

improvements plans. The nine most dividend-oriented companies estimated their potential for efficiency gains to be 13.7 per cent over the next four years, and in the long run 23.2 per cent. By contrast, the 18 least dividend-oriented companies estimated their potential efficiency gain to be much less, 9.1 per cent and 17.2 per cent respectively (Table 8.4).

As we see from Table 8.5, the Chairmen of the Board (CoB) in the dividend-oriented utilities were in general more positive to the idea of introducing incentive wage systems than the others. However, no significant differences were found between the groups as to what extent incentive wage systems actually had been introduced. Furthermore, disagreement between different parties within the political ownership tended to be less in the group with lowest emphasis on dividends. That indicates that changes in dividend policy were a controversial issue.

What keeps prices down?

Utilities are free to set their distributions tariffs, as long as the cap on the rate of return is not breached. A precondition was that the utility was efficiently run, but in practice tariffs were very seldom reduced by the regulator for this reason under the post-reform regime (1991–7). If the utilities were profit maximising entities, they could be expected consistently to choose the highest allowable rate of return. This was not the case, as shown in Table 8.6.

Part of the rise of the proportion taking the highest allowed rate from 1993 to 1994 can be attributed to the sharp fall in the allowed

Table 8.6 Maximum and actual rate of return, electricity distribution, 1993–5

	1993 (%)	1994 (%)	1995 (%)
Maximum allowed rate of return	11	7	7.5
Utilities employing maximum rate (of total no. utilities)	24.2	50.2	36.6
– weighted for company size	29.8	71.4	57.6
Average rate of return	7.6	5.6	5.6
– weighted for company size	9.5	6.4	6.6

Source: NVE (1997).

rate. Many companies preferred to even out tariffs and rates of return from one year to another, so they adjusted their rate of return less than the changes in the ceiling. This was also the case from 1994 to 1995, when the top rate again rose slightly. Adjusting for company size, we found that a significantly higher percentage employed the highest allowed rate, indicating that the bigger companies were more likely to use the maximum rate.

Two-thirds of the CoBs in the utilities with low population density took the tariffs of adjacent utilities into consideration when setting their own. This suggests that utilities serving high-cost areas felt uncomfortable if they should compare unfavourably with their neighbours. For utilities serving low-cost areas that can more easily compare themselves favourably with adjacent utilities, the proportion was 44 per cent. For joint stock companies the figure was 67 per cent vs 44 per cent for other companies. This may indicate that joint stock companies had gone further in their restructuring and adaptation to a deregulated market, and therefore were more aware that one criterion for success was how they compared with other companies. It might also be that a more critical eye was put upon the more independent joint stock companies.

Cost comparison between utilities through benchmarking techniques can also influence pricing. A full 59 per cent of the CEOs thought that the owners could be influenced to lower the utility's rate of return and thereby its tariffs if it were shown to be inefficient. This view was shared by 39 per cent of the chairmen. Again joint stock companies seemed more strongly influenced by comparison with others; moreover, the difference between CEOs and CoBs is less for these companies.

These results indicate that price policy was influenced by a complex set of factors, the most important one perhaps being cost comparisons with neighbouring utilities. That no correlation was found between emphasis on dividend and observed rate of return could be explained by the utilities that emphasised dividends being in a better financial position to increase dividends without raising tariffs. That in turn could support a theory that pricing policy was subject to satisfying rather than profit maximising.

Potential for efficiency gains and barriers to efficiency improvements

An important motive for the reform in the Norwegian Electricity sector was the lack of pressure for cost efficiency both in production and grid activities. Thus, the ECON survey sought to register awareness of the potential for efficiency gains, and to what extent the management felt a pressure to implement cost-reducing measures.

Among CoBs, 63 per cent expected the owners to put greater emphasis on efficiency improvements in the coming four years; 26 per cent expected some strengthening of this objective; and only 11 per cent expected no change at all. The figures for CEOs and HoDs were similar, and there was little variation across different forms of company organisation and framework conditions. Some 75 per cent of the utilities took part in the benchmarking exercise 'Norwegian grid operator championship'; a similar proportion had used comparative data provided by the NVE and other methods to map out their own efficiency. Perhaps somewhat surprisingly, the initiative to take part in this 'championship' came exclusively from the administration of the company, not from the board or the owners. One-quarter of the participants had not even presented the results to their board.

All but one of the 96 respondents agreed that the deregulation after 1991 had led to greater pressure for efficiency improvements and a more distinct customer orientation. Even so, 37.5 per cent felt that without stronger external pressures, no real improvement in efficiency would occur, whereas 46 per cent disagreed. HoDs were more likely to disagree with this statement. When respondents were asked to choose between reasons for expecting stronger pressure in the future, no clear pattern emerged. Changes in the regulatory regime, increased public awareness of efficiency in general and electricity supply in particular, and more active and goal-oriented owners each scored around 25 per cent. (We should here remember that this study was underaken before the new income-gap regulation system had been implemented.)

The utilities' own estimates of the potential for efficiency improvements were more or less in line with the benchmarking studies reported in the previous chapter. Estimates are given in Table 8.7.

Table 8.7 Estimated efficiency potential in own utility

Period	CEO (%)	HoD (%)	CoB (%)
Over next four years	11.0	9.2	12.6
Long-term	20.5	16.9	22.1

Table 8.8 Ranking of alternatives when 20% of staff is superfluous

Alternative	CEOs (%)	HoDs (%)	CoBs (%)
Push investments forward	18	9	12
Dismiss superfluous labour	8	10	11
Soft downsizing	45	51	48
Seek new business opportunities	30	30	21

HoDs had more conservative estimates than the other two groups; they were also less likely to see a need for stronger external pressure to bring about increased efficiency. CoBs of larger utilities estimated the efficiency potential to be somewhat higher than the average chairman. Estimates were much higher in utilities with favourable topographical and other area-specific conditions. This was consistent with the hypothesis that utilities with unfavourable area-specific conditions would be more efficient than the others, possibly because they would have been more acutely aware of their own cost disadvantage.

Half of the companies had firm and binding efficiency improvement plans. In general, the larger companies had come furthest in this respect. The half with the best framework conditions, also believed to have the best prospects for efficiency gains, were found to have a significantly higher proportion of binding plans.

More than one-quarter of the utilities had an agreement with employees or owners which restricted its ability to improve efficiency, whether by restricting staff downsizing or the closure of local branch offices. Only 53 per cent of CEOs and 33 per cent of CoBs confirmed that measures had been taken to reduce over-staffing. This is low, considering that 76 per cent of CEOs and 68 per cent of HoDs would prefer to alter the composition of their staff to reflect current needs, which would indicate that some groups of workers should be slimmed down.

In a hypothetical situation where 20 per cent of the staff were in fact superfluous, respondents were asked to rank four responses by allocating 100 points between them. Priorities are presented in Table 8.8, and show that so-called 'soft downsizing' – voluntary agreements and

Table 8.9 Possibility of dismissing superfluous labour, CEOs

Possibility	Joint stock companies (%)	Others (%)
Generally possible	8	6
Under special circumstances	33	11
Possible, but controversial	58	69
Impossible	0	11

natural attrition – scored five times higher than outright dismissal of the superfluous staff. This implies that the overstaffing could last for a long time and be only gradually reduced.

CEOs were more reliant on pushing forward investments in replacement and renewal of the network than were HoDs and CoBs, whereas all groups were keen on finding new business opportunities – going into new geographical areas and/or offering new services in the home area. The CEOs were also asked to describe the possibility of dismissing labour from a political point of view. The result is given in Table 8.9, where we note a significant difference between joint stock companies and others.

Of the CEOs, 23 per cent responded that dismissal had become easier, 74 per cent reported no change and only one of the CEOs felt it had become more difficult.

One-quarter of the companies had profit-sharing agreements, probably mostly at the higher management level. The CEOs and chairmen were asked about their opinion of the owner's attitude towards profit-sharing agreements. All in all, the positives and the negatives were in balance, but the CoBs had a more negative impression than the CEOs, and joint stock companies and companies with the best framework conditions were more positive. On average, respondents felt that between 16 per cent and 23 per cent of the results of efficiency gains should benefit the employees through bonuses or salary increases. CoBs represented the lower of these estimates.

By and large these results indicate that the representatives of owners and top management were aware of the potential for increased cost efficiency, but the commitment to implement radical cost-saving measures was generally weak. Barriers to efficiency improvement were still present, but reduced compared to the pre-reform situation.

Investment decisions

It is generally expected that investment planning and optimal investment decisions would play a major role in the long-term efficiency of the companies. The ECON survey indicates that the utilities, while aware of this, also used investment for other purposes than long-term efficiency and profitability.

On the one hand, both CEOs and HoDs ranked improvement in investment planning as the most important factor to improve overall efficiency (CoBs also placed this high on their list). Nearly two-thirds of the companies were found to have developed long-term investment budgeting, and 82 per cent of CEOs responded that the company after 1993 had implemented measures to improve the investment strategy. Still, one-third of CEOs agreed that over-investment still took place in their company.

As shown above in Table 8.1 (p. 161), more than 10 per cent of extra funds available would be allocated to extra investment in the grid, over and above what was needed according to the natural rate of replacement and repair. A full 60 per cent of CoBs and 44 per cent of CEOs would spend some of the available funds for such investment. In a separate question, respondents were asked to make priorities between seven different measures if company revenues should drop by 20 per cent. Even though the understanding was that this drop would be permanent, a cut in investment was the most frequent response.

As shown in Table 8.8 (p. 168), CEOs would rather respond by pushing forward investment in response to over-staffing than by dismissing someone, and the HoDs and CoBs put more or less the same weight on the two options. A small majority of both CEOs and chairman would use increased investment as a means of keeping superfluous labour in their jobs.

These responses strongly suggest that the timing and level of investment was only partly set with long-term efficiency in mind, and that the investment was a cushion against unforeseen or distressing developments. Except for the greater emphasis on investment as a means of absorbing superfluous labour, there are no significant differences between the CEOs and chairmen in this respect.

Perceptions of ownership roles

In this survey, the CoB was taken to represent the owner's point of view. The board is appointed by the local governments that own the utility. Board membership is to reflect the strength of the various political parties in the municipal or county assembly, but increasingly personal competence has come to play a more central role in the selection process. Chairmen were asked to describe their perception of the board's relationship to the owners; and the answers are given in Table 8.10.

Table 8.10 Chairmen's perception of board, affirmative answers

Assertion	Affirmative (%)
One or more of the board members holds key political position in the municipality that owns the utility	72
The board has received instructions from the owners with respect to financial management (rate of return, pricing)	31
The board has a high degree of independence from the owners	58
The board is formally independent, but is composed with a view to the interests and wishes of the owners	78
The board identifies more strongly with the needs of the company than with those of the owners	64

These responses suggest that after the political authorities have appointed members to the board, the board enjoys a high level of independence. It is interesting to note that a clear majority of the CoBs feel that the board identifies more strongly with the company than with the owner. This might help explain why for the most part there were only relatively minor differences in the attitudes expressed by the CEO and the CoB in questions where the owner would be likely to have interests different from those of the administration and staff, such as dividends, manning and profit-sharing.

The administration of the company and the CoB differed considerably when asked to evaluate their respective influence. When it came to ranking the influence in investment decisions by allocating 100 points, there was a tendency to consider oneself as more important than others perceived (Table 8.11).

The CoBs thought the board had as much influence as the CEO and the HoD, whereas the CEOs and HoDs obviously thought that the board's influence was quite low. Similarly, 91 per cent of CEOs confirmed that the essentials of overall investments plans were based on proposals from the administration, with only small alterations made by the board. Among the CoBs, 69 per cent agreed, whereas the others chose alternatives where the board had more influence.

Perceptions of the board's competence and motivation also differ considerably. CEOs and HoDs expressed a greater felt need to strengthen the qualifications of the board, especially in financial and

Table 8.11 Estimation of level of influence on concrete investment decisions

Influence	CEO	HoD	CoB
The board	13	9	32
CEO	35	24	36
HoD/technical officer	51	64	32
Total	99	97	100

general management issues, than the CoBs did. The need to strengthen financial competence was perceived to be especially acute in joint stock companies – most likely owing to the heavier legal responsibilities placed on the board in such companies.

CoBs considered their board to be highly motivated, scoring them an average of 1.64 on a scale of zero to two. CEOs had a different opinion, scoring motivation at 1.26 on average. In joint stock companies, the scores were 1.58 and 0.80, respectively. This must be taken as a sign that the CEOs are not overly pleased with their boards in joint stock companies, where a board member carries more responsibility. It might be that in turning the utility into a joint stock company the administration had expected the political authorities to appoint a board that was more skilled and motivated than was actually the case.

Conclusions

The survey reported here has documented that radical changes have taken place as regards the fundamental priorities of the public owners of Norwegian utilities after the reform was implemented in 1991. The market reform and the prospect for incentive regulation of transportation tariffs were the main driving force for this new orientation.

To what extent does this study support the idea using incentive regulation to control net tariffs in public firms? Price-cap regulation, which was implemented in transmission and distribution from 1 January 1997, assumed that public owners with a potential to achieve higher rates of return would be motivated to demand cost-reducing measures within the utilities. An important precondition was that the utilities were profit-oriented. If not, the traditional incentive regulation system would not be effective.

The results presented in this study show considerable variation from company to company. The traditional view that the local electricity company is primarily a public entity for providing low-priced electricity to local consumers was in 1996 still dominant in the remote areas and among the smaller companies. It was mainly among the larger entities in urban areas that we found a tendency to put more emphasis on dividend and profit. Owners were in general more in favour of dividends compared to the representatives of the management. Among the largest utilities, the representatives of the owners gave higher priority to dividends than to low tariffs. Large utilities serving urban areas, often organised as limited companies with several owners, were clearly more profit-oriented than were the traditional small utilities serving rural areas.

Low tariffs remained the most preferred objective of owners and management alike. However, there was a significant change in attitude since implementation of the reform, a process which was expected to continue in the foreseeable future. The study indicates that owners have been reluctant to increase dividends if such a policy would lead to *increasing* tariffs. The observed tendency to put greater emphasis on dividend payments could therefore be related to the fact that a majority of the utilities were in a favourable financial situation and therefore able to increase dividends without being forced to raise tariffs. The reform has revealed a sizeable potential for cost reductions in monopoly activities. Representatives of the management as well as the owners agreed that there was a massive potential here.

The study indicated that commitments to implement radical efficiency programmes were weak, supporting the view that incentive regulation was necessary to initiate radical measures for increased cost efficiency. Nearly half the respondents considered stronger incentives necessary as a supporting mechanism for introducing binding cost-saving programmes. However, many respondents held that the net regulation regime was not the only factor of importance. Public attention to distribution cost levels in general was regarded as equally important here. This means that adequate methods need to be developed for cost comparisons where differences in the underlying cost conditions are adjusted for; further, that tariff information should be gathered, analysed and distributed to the public.

If economic incentives are to be used to achieve higher productivity, the rewards will have to be allocated to all parties involved, including the staff and management. In this connection, the reluctance to implement incentive wages could be an important obstacle.

The general question raised in this study was how the Norwegian market reform has changed attitudes among the public owners and top management. There is no doubt that important changes had taken place, and that public ownership was not an invincible obstacle for implementing new goals in the utilities. On the other hand, we found a considerable amount of variation, and the underlying commitment to introduce radical measures for more cost efficiency was relatively weak in many utilities.

The premise that market reform would promote market-oriented managers and owners was only partially documented in this survey. Traditional attitudes as to fundamental priorities remained an important factor in the Norwegian electricity industry. Public owners still regarded utilities as a vehicle to provide the public with electricity supply at low cost, and would not in general adopt profit maximising as their main objective.

Note

1 This chapter is based on ECON (1986).

Part III

The Norwegian Model in a Nordic and a European Context

9
Trade and Competition in the Nordic Context

Arve Halseth and Jan Arild Snoen

Introduction

Trade in electricity has always been important for understanding the short-term balance in the Norwegian electricity market. Since 1996, with the integration between the Norwegian and Swedish markets, competition among producers has increased significantly, and trade possibilities exert a direct influence on the market price in both countries.

Why is trade between the Nordic countries profitable? One reason is the variation in precipitation and inflow in the hydropower system, which represents 99 per cent of the Norwegian generation capacity and 50 per cent of the capacity in Sweden. Trade contributes to stabilising the market: it is possible to 'export' to the conventional thermal-based system, mainly in Denmark and Finland, during periods with high precipitation and 'import' in periods of drought. Secondly, the costs related to up-start and shut-down of generation are low in hydropower plants, compared to traditional coal- and gas-fired plants and to nuclear plants. This gives an economic rationale for peak-load deliveries from hydro-systems to thermal-based systems, and the other way around in base-load periods. Lastly, there are considerable differences in excess capacity between the Nordic countries.

The different characteristics between hydro- and thermal-based systems make it potentially profitable to build new interconnectors between Norway and Germany/the Netherlands. The basic idea is to exchange electric power on the basis of differences in marginal costs in the thermal systems and the Norwegian pool price. Such agreements secure the Norwegian participants a relatively high price for peak-load export. This export can most likely be aborted in case of drought in the hydro-system, at which point base-load import to Norway becomes most profitable for both parts. It is expected that, over time, the interconnectors will provide net import to the Norwegian market, and therefore contribute to a lower price level than would have been the case with no trade between Norway and the Continent.

In Norway, there are powerful political interests related to how the trade is organised. Owing to relatively low electricity prices over the past 20 years, the manufacturing industry has enjoyed an important competitive advantage internationally. In addition, it was traditionally the electricity generators that had exclusive control of all foreign trade in electricity. When discussions around market reforms started in Sweden and Finland, the question of whether Norway should continue to regulate foreign trade was hotly debated. In December 1995 the discussion resulted in a government White Paper proposing free trade between the Norwegian and Swedish markets. This was a controversial decision.

Economic analysis indicates that free trade in the Nordic region serves to increase Norwegian welfare. Restricting foreign trade will let the producers exploit their market power to increase export revenues or lower the costs of import. Prices will therefore tend to increase on average, and most participants in the market will be worse off. Calculations on a numeric model for the Nordic electricity markets confirms this. Results from this model also show that even though regulations may mean reduced import costs in Norway, domestic prices rise, and the loss in consumer surplus, is higher than the increase in producer surplus.

Trade restrictions will also mean greater instability in market prices owing to natural variations in precipitation. It can also be argued that all of the Nordic countries will benefit from free trade in a short- and medium-term perspective. This indicates that the various countries have mutual interests in utilising the common electricity system.

In this chapter we will discuss the rationale for trade from an economic point of view. We wish to show estimates of the benefit related to foreign trade in electricity under differing assumptions about how this trade is regulated. It must, however, be stressed that economic aspects are not the sole factor that will need to be taken into account. The process towards a fully integrated Nordic electricity market will also involve other difficult questions: among these are when it is profitable to increase interconnector capacity and who shall cover the costs, as well as how to deal with environmental issues in an international context. We will also look into these aspects in this chapter.

Production and trade in the Nordic countries

Trade in the Norwegian electricity market is dominated by bilateral contracts between producers, distributors, brokers, traders and end-users. Organised market places, such as the Norwegian–Swedish power bourse Nord Pool and a few independent bourses, are involved in a smaller, but growing share of the total trade volume.

Norway

Norwegian power production is almost 100 per cent hydro-based. Median production capacity is approximately 112.5 TWh/year. Compared to most other countries, Norway has a high number of independent producers. The largest producer is Statkraft, with a market share of 30 per cent, of which half is sold to the energy-intensive industries on advantageous long-term contracts, on conditions set by the Norwegian Parliament (the Storting). There is, however, a tendency for producers to establish alliances, although the competition authorities (*Konkurransetilsynet*) so far have sharply restricted the scope of such alliances. The OBT group (consisting of Oslo Energi, Bergenshalvøens Kommunale Kraftselskap and Trondheim Energiverk) has a 13 per cent market share, whereas Interkraft (Skiensfjordens Kommunale Kraftselskap, Vest-Agder Energiverk, Aust-Agder Kraftverk and Kristiansand Energiverk) controls 8.2 per cent of production.

Norwegian consumption is divided nearly equally among households, power-intensive industry (where prices and terms are decided by the Storting) and other trade and industry, including services and the public sector.

Trends in Norwegian electricity consumption are shown in Figure 9.1. Excluding the power-intensive industry, the underlying growth rate from 1984 to 1994 was 2.5 per cent p.a., but the overall consumption growth was held down by the shrinkage of the power-intensive industry. Owing to a slow-down in their markets, nationally and internationally, power consumption in this sector decreased by 1.5 per cent p.a. in the same period. Figure 9.1 also indicates how temperature fluctuations affect consumption. Such temperature fluctuations represent a constant source of imbalances in the Nordic electricity market.

Sweden

Production capacity in Sweden is dominated by hydro- and nuclear power, supplemented by coal-fired combined heat and power plants (CHP). In addition several oil-fired plants are available; owing to the

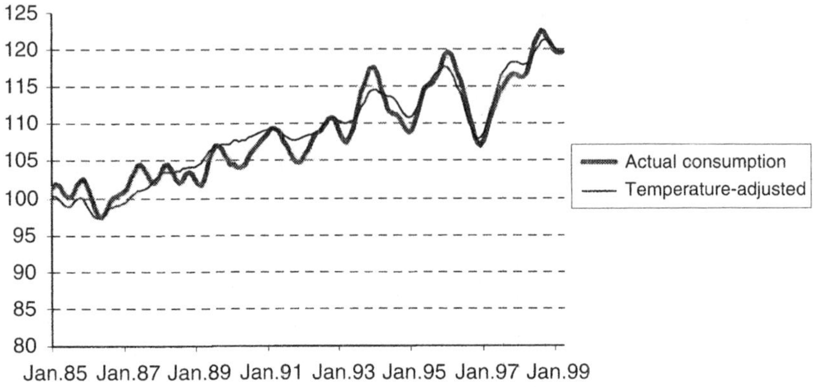

Figure 9.1 Trends in actual and temperature-adjusted electricity consumption, Norway, TWh, 1984–95
Source: ECON, NVE.

high operating costs, these are used only when markets are unusually tight, as was the case in the autumn of 1996. Median hydro-capacity is 64 TWh and nuclear capacity is 70 TWh, based on a 80 per cent regularity. Fossil fuel production varies considerably, and was less than 9 TWh in 1997.

The Swedish market is highly concentrated. State-owned Vattenfall controls more than 50 per cent of production capacity, Sydkraft 25 per cent and most of the rest is controlled by four other producers. In recent years the market has become even more concentrated through mergers and cross-ownership. Electricity consumption in Sweden is shown in Figure 9.2. After 1988 no clear trend can be discerned, neither for industry nor households.

Finland

Median hydropower production capacity in Finland is 12 TWh/year. CHP is 16 TWh/year and nuclear up to 18 TWh/year, based on the unusual high regular level of approximately 90 per cent in the four Finnish nuclear power plants. Other fossil fuel capacity is 9 TWh/year. The state-owned producer IVO/Fortum[1] controls one-third of production, and Pohjolan Voima (PVO), owned by a few power-intensive companies (mainly pulp and paper), controls somewhat less. Half of consumption takes place in industry, whereas households have a 30 per cent share and the service sector 20 per cent. Consumption has grown steadily by

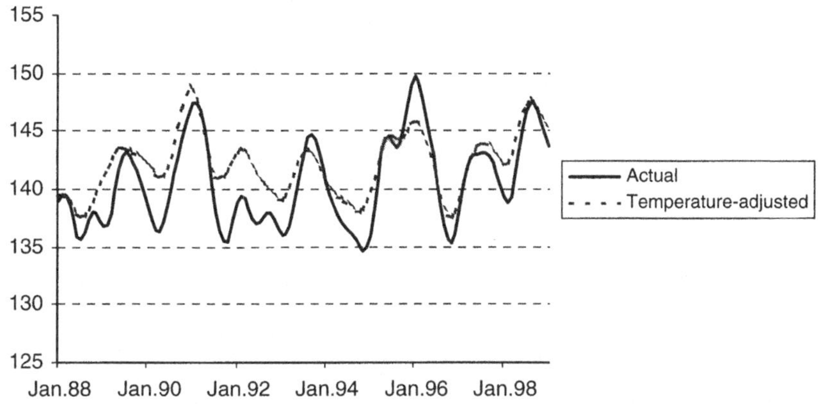

Figure 9.2 Trends in actual and temperature adjusted electricity consumption, Sweden, TWh, 1985–94
Source: Statistiska Centralbyrån; ECON.

approximately 2 per cent p.a. over the last 10 years. In this period, all sectors have experienced a growth in consumption.

Denmark

Coal-based CHP and conventional thermal plants dominate Danish production, with a small (7 per cent) share for oil-fuelled plants. In recent years, smaller independent decentralised power plants, often owned by industry, have become increasingly important, as the government has created strong economic incentives to expand this capacity. The market share of decentralised plants is already above 10 per cent and increasing. Fossil fuels dominate also in decentralised plants, but biofuels are playing an increasingly important role.

The other production companies are formally owned by the distributors. In Jutland and Fyn (Funen), the main producer is ELSAM, which also owns the transmission grid and has co-ordinating responsibility. In Zealand, Sjællandske Kraftværker is the dominant producer and has the co-ordinating responsibility, whereas ELKRAFT runs the transmission grid. Jutland/Fyn and Zealand are not connected, but there are plans for a sea cable to link the two areas. High costs and, for the time being, negligible transmission need between the two areas have led to the postponement of this project. Denmark is the only Nordic country that has not liberalised its electricity market, which is still run as

Table 9.1 Electricity production in the Nordic countries, 1998, TWh

Source	Norway	Sweden	Finland	Denmark
Hydro	116.3	73.7	14.6	–
Wind	–	0.3	–	2.7
Nuclear	–	70.5	21.0	–
Other thermal	0.7	9.8	31.6	36.4
Total	116.9	154.3	67.2	39.0

Note: – = not available.
Source: Nordel (1996).

co-operative regional monopolies. Liberalisation is now under way, and the market will be completely open by the end of 2002.

Electricity consumption is increasing steadily, but growth rates are falling. Consumption is much more stable from year to year in Denmark than elsewhere in the Nordic countries (Table 9.1). This is mainly because yearly climate changes do not play such a large role, and because Denmark has very little of the heavy industry that is so dependant on international business cycles. Consumption is more or less equally divided among households, industry and the service sectors.

Incentives for inter-Nordic trade

There are powerful economic incentives for trade between a thermal-based system and a hydro-based one. A thermal-based system is dimensioned according to peak-load demand. During base-load periods over the course of the day, there will be spare production capacity, as long as fuel is available. During peak load, the marginal costs are therefore the full cost of building a peak-load plant and variable base-load operating costs (mainly fuels). The costs of peak-load plants can be as high as 50–60 øre/kWh, owing to the short operating period, which leads to high *cost of capital* per kWh. The costs of starting-up and closing-down plants also contribute to the cost differentials between peak- and base-load production.

In a hydro-based system, total production capacity is determined by total water flows. New capacity can be acquired only through developing additional hydro-projects. This way the costs of expanding base-load capacity will be higher than in a thermal-based system, given that the least costly hydro-projects have already been developed, and that the costs of developing new (and, by definition, marginal) hydro-projects are higher than the operating costs of thermal power plants.

A hydro-based system must have enough installed capacity to cover peak-load demand, but the cost of increasing installed capacity is lower for hydro-plants than for thermal power plants. As long as there is enough water storage capacity to switch production between base-load and peak-load periods, the cost of increasing peak load production capacity is no more than the cost of an extra turbine and generator. The costs of starting up and closing down plants are also lower in hydro-plants than in thermal power plants.

The cost structure of hydro-and thermal based electricity systems is illustrated in Figure 9.3.

Based on the differences in production capacity described above, short-term power exchange would be advantageous to all Nordic countries. However, national interests are not always compatible.

- Norway would profit from comprehensive integration with the neighbouring countries owing to its near-total dependence on hydropower. It is important for Norwegian companies to reach agreements based on peak-load exports and base-load imports. Such agreements also must cover security of supply during drought, so that export commitments can be aborted under these circumstances.
- Denmark, and to a lesser extent Finland, would want to import from Norway during peak load. Power exchange between Sweden and Norway is less advantageous, as Sweden also is heavily hydro-based.
- Sweden, Finland and Denmark will probably have to base expansion of their production capacity on coal or gas-fired plants. This means

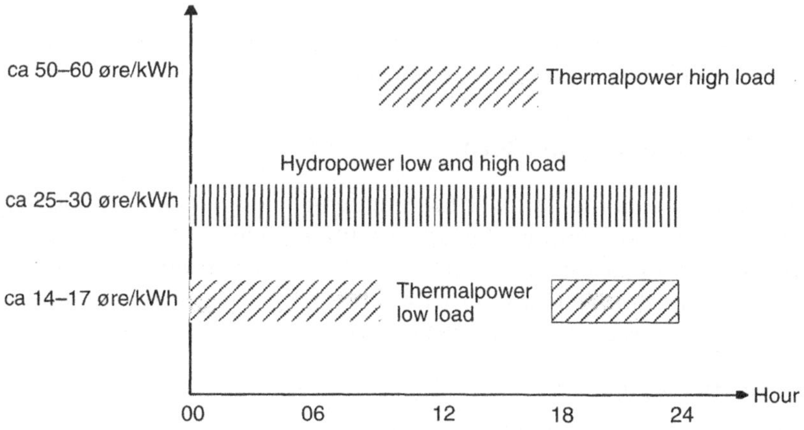

Figure 9.3 Cost structure in hydro- and thermal based electricity systems

weak long-term incentives for large-scale trade between these countries, unless they pursue very different policies in terms of restrictions on new construction for environmental reasons.

These differences in national interests explain the Norwegian desire to keep foreign operators out of the Norwegian market and to base trade on long-term power exchange agreements.

In recent years, Norway has to a larger extent based its international electricity trade on long-term bilateral power exchange contracts with the thermal-based systems of neighbouring countries. Statkraft has renegotiated its contract with ELSAM in Jutland along such lines. In 1993 Statkraft and Germany's PreussenElektra entered into an agreement due to become operational by 2003 (Viking Cable). A second agreement, between the Norwegian consortium Norsk Krafteksport and the Dutch company SEP (Nor-Ned Cable), was meant to be running from 2001, but was delayed. The last one – Euro Cable – involves the consortium Eurokraft and the German consortium EuroStrom, and will according to plans be running from 2003. All three contracts have now been approved by the Norwegian authorities, and are based on Norwegian exports during peak-load periods, with an option to import thermal-based electricity during base load. The cable projects were postponed during 1999 owing to contractual disagreements between the parties and uncertainty as to the effects of deregulation on continental electricity prices.

In Sweden and Finland deregulation of the national markets is unlikely to be very effective because of the high level of concentration and consequent market power. In these countries, competition and efficiency will probably be enhanced by letting foreign companies into the market, both as providers and buyers.

Trade in the medium term

Above the economic rational for long-term trade has been discussed, but trade is also a means of evening out temporary imbalances in the systems. Many factors may create significant fluctuations in the long-term trends. It is therefore important to highlight both the long-term and short-terms aspects of electricity trade.

Capacity imbalances

At any time there will be several factors that explain why production capacity not necessarily is optimised on the demand side. Electricity generation is characterised by long lead-times, long life expectancy of plants and high capital intensity. Government intervention and regulations, and a change of emphasis over time mean that the investors will have to take into account political risk. Moreover, market developments are difficult to predict. Periods of excess capacity or under-capacity are therefore to be expected. As this imbalance in production capacity will at any given time be unequally distributed among countries, so a strong basis for trade will exist.

In normal years, the Nordic market is characterised by significant spare capacity. This is reflected in the fact that spot prices on the Norwegian (and later Norwegian–Swedish) bourse normally have been significantly lower than the full costs of new production capacity. Most of the excess capacity is found in Denmark and Finland. Since 1988, production capacity in Denmark has increased considerably more than consumption, owing largely to the expansion of decentralised industry-owned CHP plants. In Finland spare capacity has been reduced in recent years. If the potential for integrating the hydro-and thermal-based systems is realised, spare capacity in the Nordic system is enough to cover consumption growth for many years to come. Denmark and Finland would then no longer be net importers from Norway and Sweden, but would become net exporters of base load by utilising more of their excess capacity.

Variations in water inflow

In Norway and Sweden water inflow varies significantly, depending on to precipitation – by as much as ±25–30 TWh/year. To a large extent, these variations will be absorbed by the storage capacity in the dams. Short-term trade between the Nordic countries also contributes to balance inflow variations.

Exogenous shocks

The level of demand for electricity is highly dependent on business cycles and changes in the overall economy, especially in the power-intensive industries, such as pulp/paper and metal production, that play an important role in the economies of Norway, Finland and Sweden. A slump or an increase in world market demand for the products from these industries can have a significant impact on overall national electricity demand. If these impacts are not symmetric in all countries – which they seldom will be – trade can serve to even out the resulting national power imbalances.

Changes in fuel costs, whether brought about by changes in international energy markets or by changes in taxation, will alter the terms of trade between hydro- and nuclear-based systems on the one hand and thermal-based systems on the other. Such changes can also influence the total demand for electricity, as many consumers in Norway, Sweden and Finland have the option to choose between oil and electricity for heating purposes.

Market power

Production capacity in the Nordic countries is highly concentrated, with the six largest producers controlling more than 60 per cent of production.

An extensive literature on market power explains how high market shares can, under certain circumstances, give such companies an incentive to reduce their capacity utilisation in order to drive up prices. Incentives for using market power increase when price elasticities are low, market share is high and if the competitors are unlikely to increase their output significantly if prices rise. If concentration on the supply side is higher in some countries, this will create incentives for trade. For example, if Swedish Vattenfall uses its market power to reduce its production, Danish producers could increase their export into the Swedish market, owing to the higher prices that Vattenfall's actions will produce. Such questions of market power are discussed in depth in Chapter 4.

The effect of Nordic electricity trade

In the following, ECON's numerical electricity market model will be used to estimate the effect of trade in a short-term perspective. These simulations are based on the existing market balance – i.e. production and transmission capacity and underlying consumption as of early 1995. In this model the producers employ their market power to maximise profits according to the Nash–Cournot oligopoly model.

Reference scenario

Figure 9.4 shows how prices in the national markets would be if no cross-border trade took place. These prices are an average of wet, dry and normal years. The differences between the countries are caused partly by technical and economic characteristics of the power systems, to the balance between production capacity and consumption, and by the level of concentration on the supply side. To illustrate the importance of market power, prices have also been calculated on the assumption that market power is not used.

In the absence of trade, Norwegian prices would be about 18 øre/kWh, with no difference between base load and peak load. Although consumption is somewhat less than median production, prices are quite high compared to Denmark and Finland. This is owing to very high prices during drought, which pushes up the average. In Denmark and Finland, price differences between base and peak load are due to costs associated with starting-up and closing-down thermal power plants.

In the Nash–Cournot model, Swedish producers would profit from pushing prices up to near the cost of new capacity from independent producers. This level is thought to be approx. 30 øre/kWh (the 'upper limit' in Figure 9.4). To achieve this price level, production in nuclear power plants would have to be reduced to 70 per cent–75 per cent of normal capacity utilisation. If the model is based on free competition (i.e. no market power), the price would be approximately 18 øre/kWh. Deregulation of the Swedish market would thus lead to higher prices, given the existing market structure, if no external trade were possible. Below we have presupposed that Swedish producers are not able (for political or other reasons) to exploit their market power fully, but can only reduce nuclear production by 10 per cent, resulting in a price of approximately 20 øre/kWh.

In Finland we estimate that IVO/Fortum will find it profitable to push prices 2 øre/kWh higher than under free competition.

In Norway, producers can exercise market power by letting water run unused past the turbines. According to the estimates, such 'dumping'

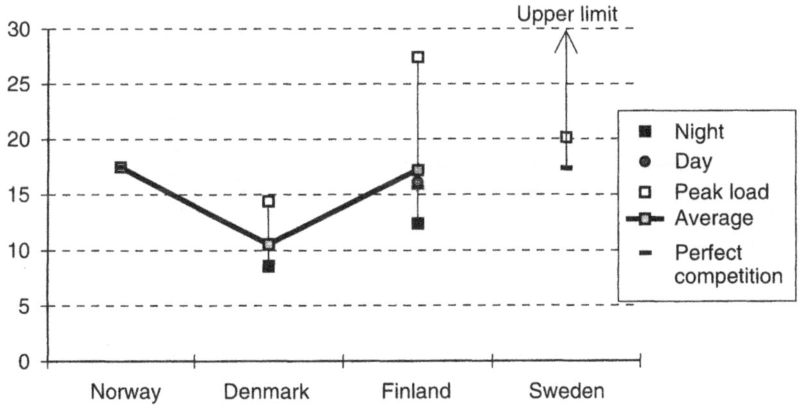

Figure 9.4 Electricity prices in the Nordic countries, no external trade, øre/kWh, 1995

of water seems to be unprofitable. Not reflected in the estimates and figure is the possibility of exercising market power by reallocating production over the course of the year.

In Denmark, where the electricity sector is organised as statutory monopolies, end-user prices reflect total production costs. In a discussion of Nordic trade, marginal production costs will determine the producers' adaptation, and these prices are reflected in Figure 9.4.

Open trade

In an open trade regime between the Nordic countries, the model estimates prices as shown in Figure 9.5. 'Open trade' means that a common *'postage stamp system'* is established and that the cost of cross-border transmission is set so as to cover only transmission losses, if bottlenecks are not taken into account. Under the existing regime, import and export taxes are considerable. In addition, there are high taxes on Finnish coal-fired plants, which creates distortions not reflected in our estimates.

Open trade will equalise prices between countries and load levels, but this equalisation is limited by transmission capacity and transmission costs. In Finland the differential between base load and peak load still remains, owing to a bottleneck in transmission capacity with Sweden. The equalisation of prices reflects a reduction in the costs of

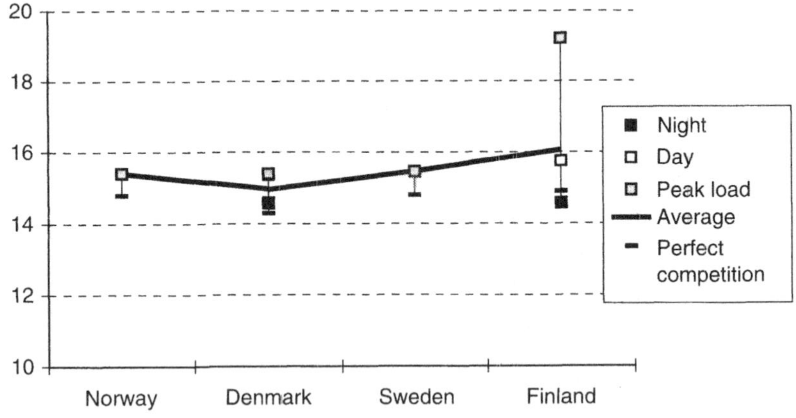

Figure 9.5 Electricity prices in the Nordic countries, free external trade, øre/kWh, 1995

starting-up and closing-down plants during peak load in the thermal-based systems, owing to imports of hydropower from Norway and Sweden.

Average prices in Norway are reduced through access to cheaper base-load imports from thermal systems during drought periods. The risk of extreme price volatility in Norway owing to low inflows is also dramatically reduced in an open trade system. In a closed system, low inflow will result in prices near 50øre/kWh, and strong inflow will push prices nearly towards zero (as happened in the summer of 1995). Under an open trade regime, prices will be 12–22øre/kWh for 90 per cent of the time.

Trade patterns

Trade patterns between the Nordic countries in a normal year are shown in Figure 9.6. Denmark exports to Sweden and Norway during base load but, more surprisingly, does not import during peak load. Denmark's plants are operated to cover internal consumption also during peak load; running them also during base load saves the costs of starting-up and closing-down, and excess production is exported. Finland exports to Sweden during the night time, and this is reversed during peak load. Sweden exports to Germany during peak load.

This pattern illustrates the interaction between a hydro-based and a thermal-based electricity system. Hydropower enjoys a comparative advantage during peak load, and any excess capacity in the thermal

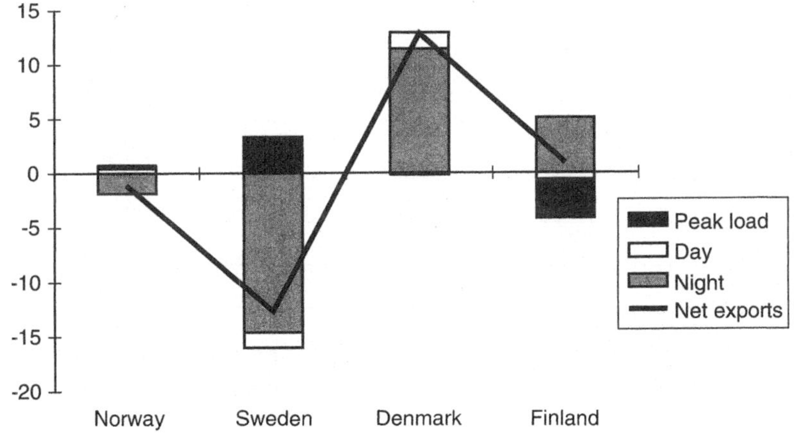

Figure 9.6 Intra-Nordic trade, TWh, 1995

systems is utilised during base load to deliver relatively cheap energy to the hydro-systems. The model has also been used to calculate how trade patterns vary with precipitation. Predictably, low inflows lead to higher exports from Finland and Denmark to Norway and Sweden. During wet years, both coal and nuclear production is reduced. The latter indicates that Swedish producers have incentives for limiting price reductions owing to higher water inflow by closing down nuclear production.

Welfare gains from trade

Figure 9.7 shows the total welfare gains (producer surplus and consumer surplus) of trade between the Nordic countries. These results reflect how the lower prices brought about by open trade lead to a larger increase in consumer surplus than the reduction in producer surplus and the import costs combined. The welfare gain in Norway is caused mainly by a reduction in the price spread based on differences in precipitation. In a normal year, access to relatively inexpensive imports eases the pressure on the national market balance. In Sweden prices are reduced owing to increased competition. Although average prices (on a hourly basis) in Finland are not significantly affected, consumer surplus increases owing to the smaller price differentials between peak load and base load (average prices decrease on a volume-weighted basis). This advantage is larger than the fall in producer surplus, yielding a net gain. In Denmark open trade opens up markets for the large excess capacity. As long as the Nordic market price is higher

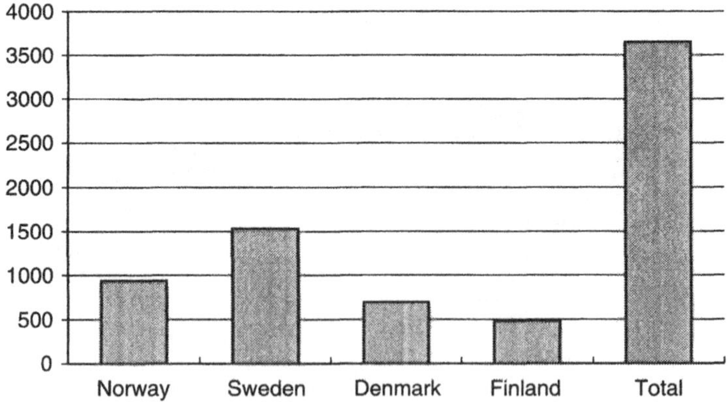

Figure 9.7 Welfare gains due to open trade, million NOK, 1995

than marginal operating costs in Denmark, export will act to increase producer surplus.

Long-term power exchange agreements with the continent

The economic basis for electricity trade between Norway and the continent rests on the economic and technical characteristics of a hydro-based electricity system on the one hand and a thermal-based one on the other, as described above. Below we will examine the effect of long-term power-exchange agreements (PEAs) on trade patterns and Norwegian electricity prices in the years 1998, 2005 and 2010. Other trade arrangements will not be examined here. Long-term power-exchange agreements include commitments for Norwegian producers to export during peak load. During base and medium load the flow is determined by differences between market prices in Norway and the marginal operating costs on the continent.

These estimates were made in 1994 with the help of ECON's electricity market model (ECON 1994).[2] All estimates are based on a normal year. The reference scenario has been developed for comparison purposes only, and cannot be treated as a prognosis for future developments. In this reference scenario, the most important developments are as follows:

- The Norwegian, Swedish and Finnish market is integrated and a common 'postage stamp system' established in 1998. Danish producers have access to the Nordic market on non-discriminatory terms.
- Transmission capacity between the Nordic countries is expanded by a 600 MW cable between Jutland and Zealand in Denmark by 1997 between Finland and Sweden by 2010 (600 MW) and upgrading of transmission capacity between Norway and Sweden by 700 MW in 2005.
- Consumption in all Nordic countries increases by 1.5 per cent p.a., except in Finland, where the increase is 2 per cent p.a., and in the Norwegian power-intensive industry, where consumption remains stable. This growth is mainly covered by using excess capacity in Finland and Denmark up to 2005, and thereafter through new gas-fired plants in Norway.
- Prices increase from 15.7 øre/kWh in 1995 to 25.7 øre/kWh by 2010. In the beginning of the period prices are kept high through Vattenfall's and IVO/Fortum's exercise of market power. At the end

of the period, the reduction of excess capacity and need to build new production capacity result in a significant price increase.

- Norway acts as an important transit country for electricity from Jutland to Sweden. Sweden becomes a major importer.

Three new cables are constructed in connection with the three long-term power-exchange agreements described above, each with a capacity of 600 MW. In our estimates, the third contract is operational from 2010 and not 2003, as has since been negotiated.

In addition, the existing contract between Statkraft and ELSAM has been renegotiated as a long-term power-exchange agreement, effective from 1996. Peak load capacity is 600 MW. In addition, deliveries to PreussenElektra through the Danish grid started in 1998, with a peak-load capacity of 400 MW.

Our estimates are based on a marginal operating cost during base load on the continent of 13.75 øre/kWh, and a transmission cost of 1.25 øre/kWh. When market prices in Norway fall below 12.5 øre/kWh, this triggers export; import is triggered by a market price above 15 øre/kWh. If a wedge between Norwegian prices and marginal costs on the continent appears, owing to the cables running full, the profit is shared equally between the two parties.

Figure 9.8 shows the result of the model on Norwegian electricity trade balance in the reference scenario and with the long-term power-exchange agreements.

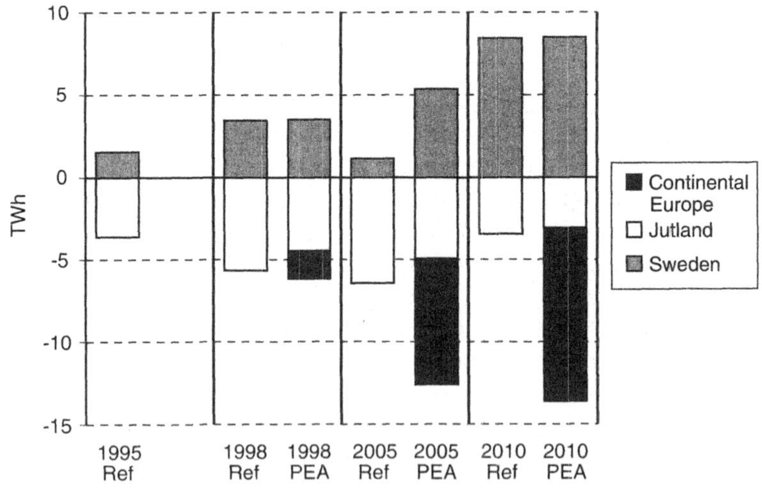

Figure 9.8 Norwegian balance of electricity trade, TWh, 1995–2010

The most important changes are the following:

- Net exports from Norway is reduced marginally in 2005, but significantly (10 TWh/year) by 2010.
- Norway's role as a transit country for Sweden is strengthened. More than 60 per cent of the imports from the continent are re-exported to Sweden.
- In the medium term, some of the imports from Denmark are replaced by imports from Germany and the Netherlands. By 2010, imports from Denmark are almost the same as in the reference scenario.
- Import capacity during base load is fully utilised both in 2005 and in 2010.

The basic effects of exchange agreements on wholesale electricity prices are shown in Figure 9.9. Our intention is not to model actual prices in 2005 and 2010, but to illustrate the impact of such agreements. Actual prices are therefore not shown, as other factors have influenced the price levels since the model was run, and because such figures very easily become outdated.

In the short run the renegotiated ELSAM agreement and transit to Germany lead to marginally lower prices. The reason is that net import increases owing to lower marginal operating costs in Germany than in

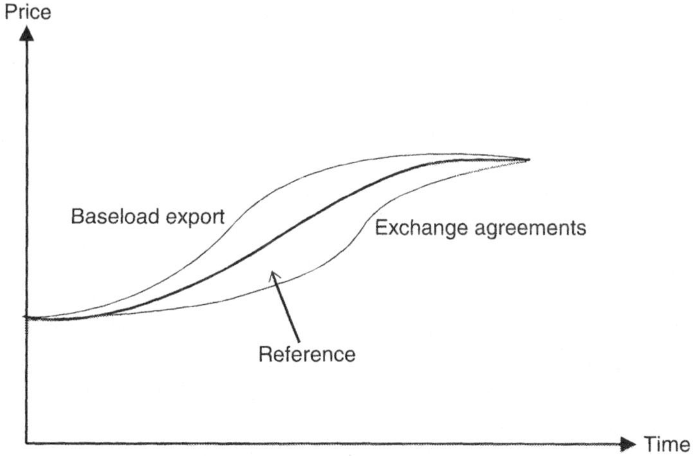

Figure 9.9 Impact of power exchange agreements on Norwegian electricity prices

Denmark. The larger price differential in the medium term is caused by the fact that the new cables ease the pressure in the Nordic market. In the long term, the differential fades away, because capacity in the cables is fully utilised and new production capacity has to be constructed in the Nordic countries. In such a situation, prices in the Nordic market will be determined by the cost of investment in production capacity, not the price levels in the surrounding countries.

In the long term, the price differential between base load and peak load increases. The price differential between winter and summer is also higher than in the reference scenario. The price differential increases because the new cables give rise to a significant energy surplus during base load, so that peak-load prices must be relatively high to make it profitable to invest in new production capacity to cover additional demand.

Producers manage their storage magazines to optimise production during peak-load periods. Even though peak-load prices in the winter are higher, the model indicates that the price differential is not great enough to make it profitable to invest in new effect capacity.

Exclusive access to cables

The Norwegian contract partners in the long-term power-exchange agreement have been granted exclusive access to the existing cable to Denmark and to the three new cables to the continent. The underlying economic rationale here is to put the Norwegian exporters in a stronger position to secure a greater share of the profits from the agreements, by pushing prices nearer the marginal production costs of the buyer. If there were free access to the cables, foreign companies could buy peak-load deliveries in the market at prices far below the costs of production on the continent. Foreign companies could also reap all the gain from exploiting excess base-load capacity. German and Dutch companies are therefore prohibited from trading directly in the Norwegian/Swedish spot market.

This exclusiveness creates another problem, as the Norwegian contracting parties can use the cables to 'dump' electricity abroad, in order to increase prices in the Nordic market. 'Dumping' in this context means that the producers sell electricity abroad, even though Norwegian spot prices are higher than the marginal cost in the continent, or that high spot prices do not trigger imports. The Norwegian authorities have sought to discourage dumping though the licensing conditions, but asymmetric information makes this task difficult.

The importance of exclusiveness is tested in the model, presupposing that Statkraft and the producers on the continent act so as to maximise their combined income. This results in only marginally higher wholesale prices, compared to a situation where the intent of the licensing conditions is fulfilled. The main reason for this result is that as early as 1998 the profit of importing at 15 øre/kWh and reselling at 17.5 øre/kWh is enough to ensure that the whole import capacity during base load is utilised over the year. Because Statkraft has only a 5 per cent share of the Nordic market (when the long-term contracts with power-intensive industry are excluded), the cost of pushing up prices by withholding supply would be higher than the gains to be made from higher prices.

Notes

1 IVO enter merged with the petroleum company Neste to form Fortum (see as pp. 208, 210, 221–3).

2 A few recent developments have altered the basis for the estimates somewhat. The third interconnector to the continent will come into operation in 2003, instead of 2010, and the cable connecting Jutland and Fyn will be postponed. These changes do not alter the general conclusions here.

10
Structure and Strategy in the Nordic Power Market

Atle Midttun

Emergence of the Nordic internal market

Finland (in spring 1995) and Sweden (in January 1996) implemented electricity market reforms very much inspired by the Norwegian initiative, but also modelled on the UK and the liberal EU initiatives. With the recent liberalisation of Sweden and Finland, in addition to the early market reform in Norway, the Nordic countries (with Denmark gradually attached in a semi-liberal position) now constitute an internal free trade market. The three Nordic countries are thereby putting into practice a more far-reaching liberal market system which eclipses even the EU Commission's most ambitious plans for an internal European Market.

A characteristic feature of the Nordic reforms is their neutrality to ownership. As opposed to the UK reform, they did not include privatisation, but largely left public ownership intact. We are in other words dealing with a system dominated by competitive public capitalism, but which also features considerable input of private capitalism, particularly in the Swedish and Finnish cases. The peculiar mixture of public ownership and competitive exposure reflects a Nordic tradition of pragmatic social democracy. Characteristically, the Nordic reforms were introduced and implemented by both Conservative and Social Democratic governments, and except for some lagging by the conservative Bildt Government in Sweden, the reforms raised little political controversy. Even in the Swedish case, the reform was implemented by the Social Democratic Carlsson Government in the final round.

The existence of three neighbouring liberalised systems with extensive interconnections, inherited from the old NORDEL co-operation, has created the preconditions for an integrated Nordic electricity market. Since the advent of the Nordic market reforms, this opportunity has been actively exploited by the build-up of Nordic trade institutions and a flourishing inter-Nordic trade. In the first round, the Norwegian and Swedish markets were merged through a common bourse arrangement, owned and jointly administered by the two national grid companies Statnett and Svenska Kraftnät. The Finnish system has also integrated with the Swedish–Norwegian system.

The extensive freedom of trade between the three countries creates structural and strategic challenges to the Nordic electricity industry. In terms of size, ownership, structure, industrial configuration and restrictions on ownership transfer, the three countries differ significantly. Finnish, Norwegian and Swedish industry therefore participate in inter-Nordic competition on somewhat different terms despite extensive cultural, social, political and institutional similarities.

Owing to the late deregulation of Danish electricity industry, we have omitted it from this discussion, which focusses on actual Nordic deregulation experiences in the mid-1990s. The Icelandic system is completely independent of the mainland Nordicone, and has therefore not been included in this discussion.

Structural traditions

Historical roots

According to the historian Thue (1995) differences in the character and the localisation of the natural resources are crucial factors influencing the organisational pattern of the Nordic electricity supply industry. At an early stage hydropower constituted the major resource foundation in all the three countries. However, compared to Sweden and Finland, the Norwegian resources have had a more advantageous geographical spread compared to consumption centres, they have been more varied with respect to size, and they have been more favourable to utilise. This is why the Norwegian electricity industry has found it far easier than its counterparts in Sweden and Finland to develop local small-scale projects, and a strong tradition of municipal regulation and control of electricity production and distribution. In Sweden and Finland, the less easily available hydro-resources have favoured organisations and institutions with considerable capital, resources and competence. This tendency was strengthened by the need for longer transmission cables between hydro-facilities and consumers in Sweden and Finland.

Thus, the accessibility of resources for both small-scale and large-scale utilisation provided the foundation for a divided development in Norway, comprising small, local, and large industrial and central facilities. In Sweden and Finland, with resource bases less open to small-scale utilisation, small-scale solutions were less prominent.

In addition, the Norwegian decentralised municipal model has been strengthened by a long-standing restrictive regulatory regime. Fear of comprehensive foreign investments in Norwegian natural resources led to the passing of the so-called 'concession laws' at the beginning of this century. These laws basically reserved hydropower construction for public actors. For this reason the Norwegian power-intensive industry (electrochemicals, electrometals and paper and pulp) has not been able to play the same central role in electricity production as in Swedish and Finnish industry.

More recently, the development of nuclear power has also contributed to the establishment of organisational differences in the Nordic electricity industry. The build-up of a nuclear industry in Sweden and Finland has involved larger needs for capital and competence, as well as entailing a need for co-ordination on a regional, national and Nordic level. The Norwegian power industry has remained non-nuclear, and thus has not faced the same pressure for co-ordination. Instead, it has been able to continue its hydropower strategy with a mixture of small-scale and large-scale projects. In line with Norway's municipalistic tradition, co-ordination to meet advantages of scale in large hydropower projects has been achieved through municipal and regional collaboration, often in conjunction with active engagement from the State Power Works (Statkraft).

Nordic structural configurations

Nordic electricity production was by the mid-1990s predominantly organised as a publicly owned economy with a sizeable share of the production facilities in municipal and state hands (Table 10.1). Public ownership predominates among the big Norwegian companies: 81 per cent, followed by Sweden 72 per cent and with Finland in a slightly more balanced position at 59 per cent. In Finland, extensive industrial ownership has modified direct public ownership in power supply. However, many of the big Finnish industrial companies are state-owned, and indirect state ownership therefore plays an important role in Finland.

The extensive public ownership in the Nordic electricity industry, inherited from the pre-reform period, means that capital gains in the

Table 10.1 Ownership structure for Nordic generators, 1994

	Institutional owners (%)	Governmental owners (%)	Municipal/ regional owners (%)	Electricity industry owners (%)	Industrial owners (%)	Unknown (%)
Norway	7	41	40	7	5	0
Sweden	13	55	17	6	6	0
Finland	2	44	15	10	27	0

Source: Midttun and Handelande (1999) and *Annual Reports* for the 20 biggest producers in Finland, Norway and Sweden (1994).

companies to be made under the new market competition will be for the benefit of local and central public budgets. It also implies that political decision-makers will hold strategic positions in guiding the industry in its reformation to commercial practice. These close links between commerce and politics at the company level also translate into ties between company decision-making and decision-making at the energy policy level. The political ties may work two ways: on the one hand, they may allow society to hold Nordic electricity industry socially responsible; on the other, public ownership may also pave way for a pragmatic regulation sympathetic to industrial needs.

Within the context of 'socialised capitalism', however, the Swedish and Norwegian models imply rather different predispositions. The dominance of state capitalistic ownership in Sweden leads to a more centralised model than the dominant municipal ownership in Norway, which favours decentralised small entities. Even though the municipal supply system operates side by side with large-scale industrial production in power-intensive companies and considerable state production, a main part of the Norwegian system has remained deeply rooted in local policy, and is currently redirecting itself away from a locally oriented business-strategic perspective.

The strong state engagement gives Swedish electricity industry greater flexibility to re-configure and set a firmer focus on a national and international field of operation. The volume of the state-owned company Vattenfall is sufficient to give the company substantial scale and strategic advantages compared to the smaller municipal companies. The Swedish state company also has the advantage of a well established political tradition for differentiating between political and commercial activity.

In addition to the differences in scale there is a difference in models of operation. State-run corporations tend to be more functionally differentiated and professional than smaller municipal enterprises. In the latter, corporate management is usually more directly confronted with political preferences and commitments.

Ownership by heavy industry stands out as a Finnish speciality in the electricity field. The linkage between heavy industry and electricity production has until recently been manifested through the existence of a separate industrial electricity grid. The recent establishment of Fingrid has now integrated the public and industrial grid into one company. However there remains an integrated system of load-sharing organised by an industry-owned power company, which operates relatively autonomously in the Nordic power market. Thus, the Finnish heavy industry electricity cluster is largely in a position to operate an industrial self-supply system for electricity within the new Nordic electricity market.

Institutional ownership, which is most widespread in Sweden, also represents a certain modification of the 'socialised capitalist' model and constitutes a basis within the electricity industry that, under a commercial regime, may facilitate commercially-based industrial restructuring. In Norway, these ownership forms are more weakly represented.

The 'socialised capitalism' model is even stronger on the distribution than on the production side (Table 10.2). Again, however, there are sizeable differences among the Nordic countries. Municipal ownership has played a dominant role in Norway and Finland, and the state-owned companies have traditionally been kept totally out of supply. By contrast, Sweden has traditionally provided the state company with a significant role also on the supply side.

Table 10.2 Ownership structure in Nordic supply companies, 1994

	Institutional owners (%)	**Governmental owners** (%)	**Municipal/ regional owners** (%)	**Electricity industry owners** (%)	**Industrial owners** (%)	**Unknown** (%)
Norway	0	0	100	0	0	0
Sweden	16	24	45	18	2	4
Finland	2	0	81	12	6	1

Source: Midttun and Handelande (1999) and *Annual Reports* for the 20 biggest distributors in Finland, Norway and Sweden (1994).

Size

Dissimilarities in institutional traditions and resource bases have also contributed to differences in size between the Nordic companies. These differences have traditionally been most dramatic on the generation side, illustrated by the fact that, at the beginning of the 1990s, Swedish Vattenfall controlled two and a half times and three times the capacity of Norwegian Statkraft and Finnish IVO, respectively. Although the proportions have moderated, this pattern – with the Swedish companies outsizing the Norwegian companies, which in turn outsize the Finnish companies – also applies when we compare the 20 biggest generators in the three countries (Table 10.3).

The same pattern is also found on the supply side, although the difference between the Swedish and Norwegian companies is reduced. Also worth noting is the fact that the supply companies have generally been far less centralised than the generation companies, which generally have been three times bigger.

Focusing on the individual companies, we note that the picture of the largest Nordic generators is characterised by the exceptional position of Vattenfall, with generation of more than 75 TWh. It is followed by Statkraft, IVO and Sydkraft, generating between 30 and 35 TWh. Then follow Teollisuuden Voima and Norsk Hydro, with generation of more than 10 TWh. The next group is made up of primarily Swedish companies, but also Norwegian ones, generating between 10 and 5 TWh. This group is led by Stockholm and Oslo Energi. The last group consists of smaller companies generating between 5 and 2.5 TWh, and is dominated by Norwegian companies like Trondheim Energiverk, Vest-Agder Energiverk and Nord-Trøndelag Elektrisitetsverk. Also in this

Table 10.3 Company size: Norway and Finland compared with Sweden, 1994

	Av. size of 20 largest generators (%) (TWh)	**Size of largest generator (%) (TWh)**	**Av. size of 20 largest suppliers (%) (TWh)**	**Size of largest supplier (%) (TWh)**
Sweden	100 (8.2)	100 (75.3)	100 (2.7)	100 (12.2)
Norway[a]	57 (4.7)	43 (32.4)	60 (1.6)	65 (7.9)
Finland[a]	33 (2.7)	29 (22.2)	44 (1.2)	42 (5.1)

Note: [a]Percentage figures for Norwegian and Finnish companies have been calculated using Swedish companies as basis.
Source: Midttun and Handelande (1999) and *Annual Reports* from the 20 biggest producers in Norway, Finland and Sweden (1994).

group are the Finnish companies Kemijoki OY and Helsingfors Elektrisitetsverk, as well as the Swedish companies Scandinavian Elverk and Graningeverken AB (see Figure 10.1).

Focusing on the supply side means reducing the scale considerably, but does not change the ranking among the Nordic companies. The Swedish companies are dominant among the largest Nordic suppliers. Vattenfall again stand out compared to the other large Swedish companies including Sydkraft, Stockholm Energi, Uddeholm, and Gøteborg Energi (Figure 10.2). The only two Norwegian companies that can be compared to this group are Oslo Energi and Bergen Lysverker, ranked as second and last, respectively. In Finland, there is only one company within this size range, Helsingfors Energi.

Norwegian companies like Trondheim Energiverk, Nord-Trøndelag Elverk, Stavanger Energi, and Tromsø Kraftforsyning play a considerable role among medium-sized supply companies. In this group we also find Swedish companies like Malmö Energi, Graningeverken AB and Skellefteå Kraft. With the exception of Helsingfors Energi, those of the few Finnish companies among the 20 biggest in the Nordic market have traditionally been located in the lower-medium group.

Thus, there have traditionally been few Finnish companies among the large generators in the Nordic countries. The exceptions are IVO and PVO. Swedish companies have dominated the picture, both with respect to the absolute upper-and the upper-medium sized groups. The Norwegian companies, although ranked after Vattenfall, have been present in the upper-sized group, but are primarily characterised by their presence in the lower-medium group. Given that size is a considerable strategic factor in a Nordic market open to competition, the Swedish companies have structurally, through their historical legacy, been better prepared than their Norwegian and Finnish competitors.

Ownership networks

Structural differences in the Nordic electricity industry are reflected not only in ownership structure, but also in the underlying ownership network. These networks represent a considerable strategic potential – as a resource for potential co-ordination, but also as a possible barrier against strategic adaptation. As to company structure, ownership networks vary extensively across national boundaries well as between the production and distribution side.

The ownership network of Finnish electricity production has traditionally divided the industry into a state-owned and an industrially-owned group. The industrial owners include such major companies

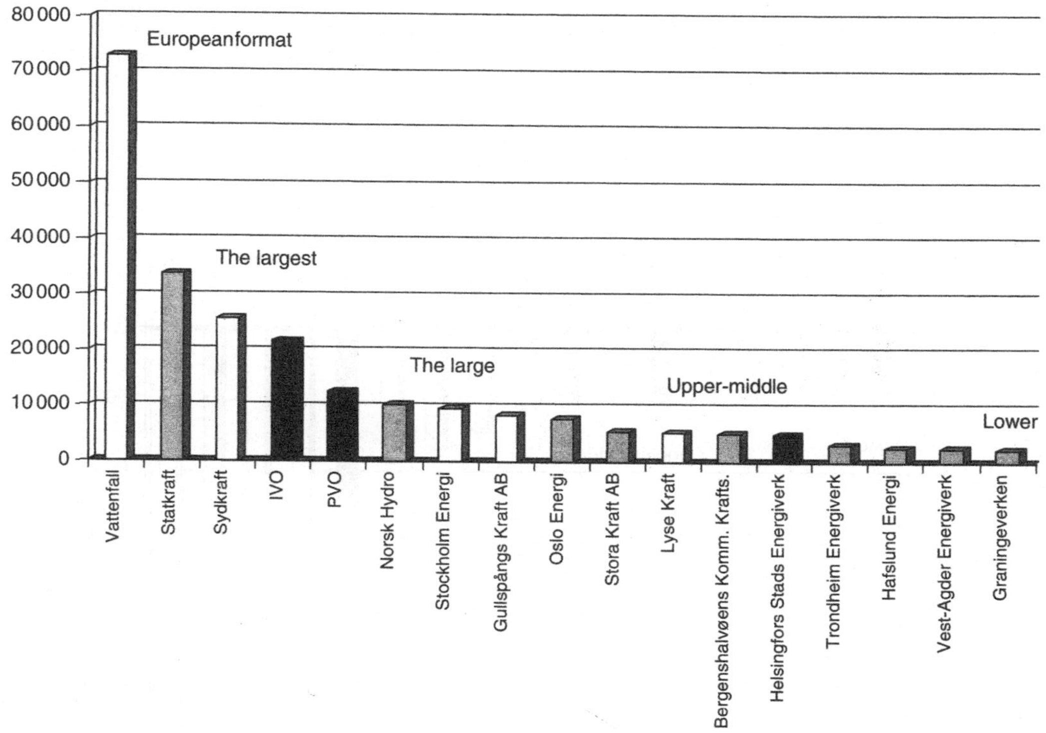

Figure 10.1 The 20 largest power generators in the Nordic countries, 1994
Source: Midttun and Handelande (1999) and *Annual Reports* for the 20 biggest producers in Finland, Norway and Sweden (1994).

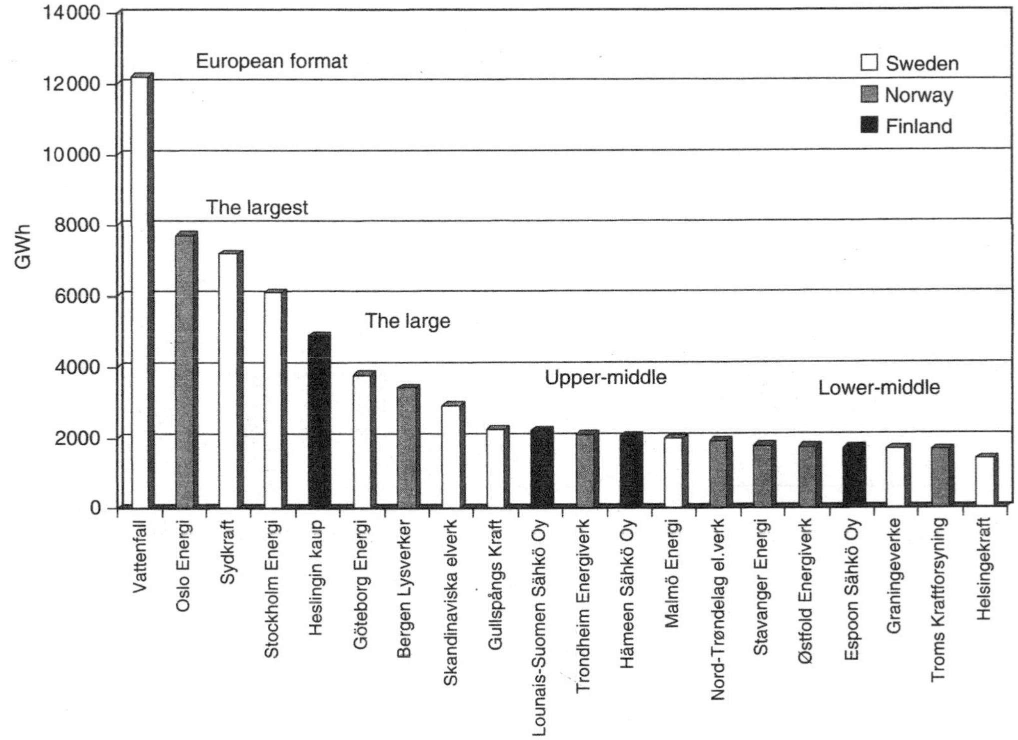

Figure 10.2 The 20 largest suppliers in the Nordic countries, 1994
Source: Midttun and Handelande (1999) and *Annual Reports* for the 20 biggest distributors in Finland, Norway and Sweden (1994).

within Finnish and European wood processing as Kymmene, United Paper Mills and Repola. In addition there is a considerably smaller group of municipal generators such as Helsingfors, Lahti, Oulun and Tammerfors.

The ownership network around the two co-ordinating companies TVO and PVO has served to integrate the industrially-owned part of the electricity supply effectively into a self-contained cluster with internal co-ordination and load sharing more or less cut off from the general market (Midttun and Handelande 1999).

This pattern has been strengthened as the Finnish system has moved towards a competitive market economy. When we turn to second-order ownership relations as well, we can note considerable integration between the two major groups in Finnish electricity supply. The state is the majority owner of large Finnish wood-processing companies such as Enzo Gutzeit and Veitsiluoto; it therefore has an indirect stake in the industry-controlled production as well. Furthermore, the Finnish state has also a 25 per cent ownership in the nuclear production of TVO, through its ownership in IVO.

Like Finland, the Swedish production side has traditionally been under governmental ownership. This is underlined by the fact that the totally state-owned company Vattenfall is in charge of more than half of all electricity production in Sweden. However, as already noted, a particular feature of the Swedish electricity production is the broad finance–capital network behind companies like Sydkraft, Gullspång, Båkab, MoDo, Korsnäs, Graningeverken, Stora Kraft and Nordkraft. These owners represent central parts of Swedish financial capital, such as the insurance companies SPP and ANF, Trygg-Hansa and the Folksam concern. In addition there are heavy Swedish industrial concerns such as AGA and Nobel industries. All and all, private Swedish ownership is wider and less industry-specific than the case in Finland. In addition, owners of electricity generation in Sweden comprise a range of municipally-owned facilities such as Skellefteå, Norrköpings Kraft, Lindköping, and others.

In Norway, the state has also traditionally been important on the generation side. However, with less than 30 per cent of total electricity generation, the role of the state is far less significant than in Sweden and Finland. In addition, contractual liabilities to deliver to the Norwegian energy-intensive industry have locked the state into a less dynamic role in the electricity market than it might otherwise have had with its large generation capacity. On the other hand, the state has also, through its 51 per cent majority ownership in Norsk Hydro,

Norway's second largest industry company, a considerable supplement to its state power works engagement in the electricity market.

Beyond that, Norwegian electricity generation has traditionally been owned by larger city and county utilities, which often have electricity generation to serve their own supply districts. As mentioned, there is in addition a considerable tradition of shared municipal ownership of electricity producers in Norway. Generators like Lyse Kraft, Bergenshalvøens Kommunale Kraftselskap, Skiensfjordens Kommunale Kraftselskap, Hedmark Energi and Vestfold Kraftselskap have been owned by municipalities in their region or by the utilities. These configurations have traditionally functioned as collective self-supply systems with a focus on local and regional electricity supply.

Despite this municipal bias, Norwegian electricity generation also contains some commercial elements, although commercial networks play a considerably smaller role than in Sweden and in Finland. Furthermore, in Norway commercial networks have traditionally concentrated around a few companies such as Hafslund, Aktieselskapet Tyssefaldene and Norwegian Hydro. In return, the ownership in Hafslund and Hydro (with the exception of the part owned by the state) is genuinely international. Compared to the situation in Finland and Sweden, Norwegian ownership network on the generation side appears rather fragmented. Despite certain finance–capital links between Norsk Hydro and Hafslund, and governmental ownership both in Statkraft and Norsk Hydro, the main impression is that of loosely coupled clusters with a municipal and county focus.

Traditionally, the ownership pattern on the supply side has differed considerably from the ownership network on the generation side. Municipal ownership has generally had a stronger position in electricity supply than in production. In Finland, for instance, this is reflected through a wide range of companies such as Helsingfors, Tammerfors, Turku and Lahti, who are all 100 per cent owned by their municipalities. Ownership networks in Finnish supply also include inter-municipal companies, such as Hämen Sähkö and Kymenlaakson. In addition, there are several companies with combined municipal–industrial ownership, such as Jyllinkosken and Etelä-Suomen Sähkö Oy.

On the other hand, Finland also has a tradition of commercial ownership through industrial–financial and private networks such as Luonais-Suomen Sähkö, and Paloheimo Oy. Thus, despite the dominant position of municipal ownership in Finland, there was already in the early 1990s a tradition of commercially-oriented ownership networks in supply. In addition to this, the Finnish state – mainly through IVO and Enzo Gutzeit – has been somewhat engaged in supply through Lounais-Suomen Sähkö and Pohjolan-Karjalan, respectively.

In Sweden, the state has traditionally been in a rather unique position in the Nordic market, with its dominance in Swedish supply. With 20 per cent of Swedish distribution capacity, Vattenfall was the largest Nordic supplier. As is the case in Finland, the Swedish supply side has been more marked by municipal ownership than the generation side; in 1991, individual municipal councils owned more than half of the 20 largest suppliers.

However, Swedish electricity industry has also traditionally included commercially-oriented networks on the supply side. Such networks existed around Sydkraft, Stora Kraft, Graningeverken and Gullspångs Kraft. In the Sydkraft case, the commercial networks occurred alongside a system of extensive municipal ownership. As these companies also are major producers, the commercial networks comprise the same clusters mentioned above on the electricity generation side. In addition to this, Swedish electricity supply also traditionally includes companies with a more narrow and direct industrial ownership, such as Båkab and Uddeholm Kraft, owned by the wood-processing concerns SCA and AGA AB, respectively.

Compared to Finnish and Swedish electricity industry, the Norwegian supply companies stand out with their purely municipal ownership. This pattern makes for a rather fragmented Norwegian industrial structure with fewer cross-company ownership ties than is the case in Sweden and Finland.

Patterns of strategic adaptation

The market reform in the early and mid-1990s has entailed a transfer for all of the Nordic countries from a planned economy to what we in Chapter 1 have called a 'competitive public economy', where the electricity industry has been competitively exposed, but where the old, dominant decentralised public ownership relations have been preserved (p. 8). In this respect, the Nordic market reforms differ from those of the UK which entailed liberalisation through privatisation while at the same time letting the industrial structure remain relatively centralised.

However, within the framework of a common competitive public economy there are considerable differences among the three Nordic countries studied here. On the one side we find Norway with the largest share of public ownership, but at the same time being most decentralised and, thus, structurally most open to competition. Finland, and Sweden in particular, are both significantly less decentralised and also exclusively publicly owned, although also here public ownership is important.

Finnish patterns

An analysis of strategic adaptation in Finnish electricity industry reveals two basic patterns (Figure 10.3). One is IVO's strategic configuration in Sweden, which will be discussed, in further detail on p. 221. The other is the consolidation of the industrial PVO group, which already prior to the Finnish reforms stood out as a central cluster in Finnish power industry (Midttun 1995). During 1995–6 a further consolidation of power resources from a number of the big industrial companies in the PVO Lämpövoima group took place. The trend seems to be for industrial companies to swap generation capacities for stakes in PVO with drawing rights on PVO's total capacity according to the self-cost principle. PVO now accounts for more than 20 per cent of Finland's generation and is in constant development, as the company is becoming a 'power co-ordinator' on behalf of its shareholders, and enters into bilateral agreements in the Nordic market. The consolidation of the industrial owned auto-production cluster must also be seen in the light of the parallel consolidation of the paper and pulp industry.

The PVO cluster is, however, not the sole supplier of electricity to Finnish industry. In addition to being a large wholesaler, IVO has in the past few years developed partnerships with a number of companies in Finland's heavy industry. The trend is for IVO to take over energy generation from the companies, carry out investments, and provide heavy industry with necessary energy supply. This allows heavy industry to focus on its core activities, usually paper and pulp manufacturing. Companies that have entered into such deals are Metsä-Serla, EnoCell, Ahlström, Outukumpu Zinc and Enso Laminating Papers AB.

On the supply side there have also been considerable changes in Finland (Figure 10.4). The pattern here is on the one hand a horizontal consolidation where suppliers form common purchasing companies. The most prominent example is Kymppivoima OY (Tiokraft), formed by 10 of the 20 largest Finnish distributors. The company's aim has been to negotiate lower prices and better conditions on behalf of its owners. Kymppivoima Oy represents about one-third of total Finnish supply (10 TWh) and covers approximately one-quarter of the country's customers. Kymppivoima may be seen as a new commercial challenge to IVO's historical monopoly on electricity supply, and an attempt to meet IVO's market power in electricity generation with market power on the supply side.

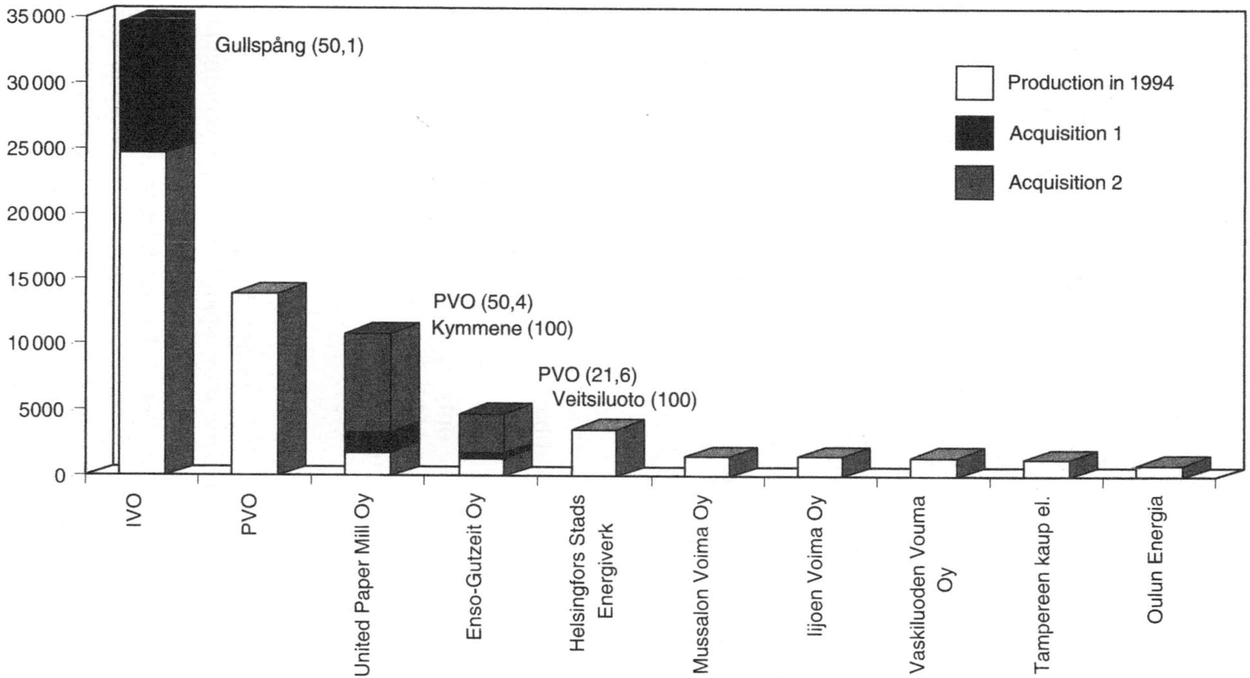

Figure 10.3 The largest Finnish generators in 1994, including acquisitions, 1994–6 (%)
Source: Midttun and Handelande (1999) and *Annual Reports* for the 20 biggest producers in Finland (1994); TDN Kraft; Reuters Business Briefing.

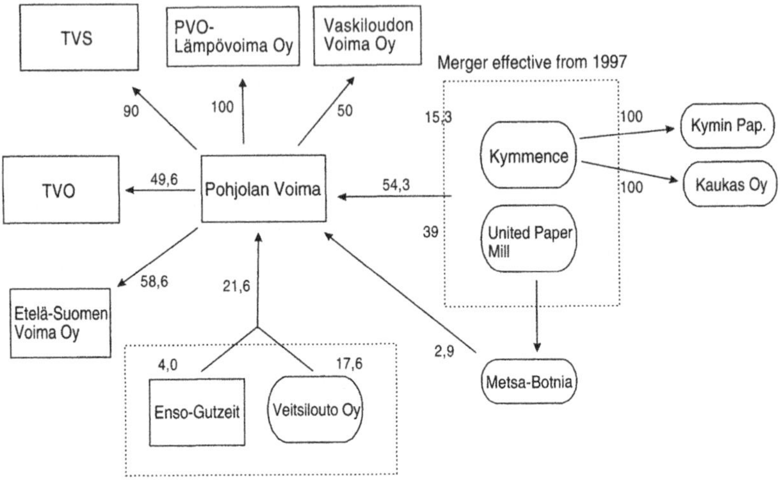

Figure 10.4 Strategic ownership integration in Finnish electricity industry, 1996 (%)
Source: Midttun (1997) and *Annual Reports* for the 20 largest Finnish companies.

On the other hand, Finnish electricity industry is also characterised by big generators' take-over of distributors. Examples here are Vattenfall's take-over of Hämeen Sähkö, IVO's take-over of Länsivoima, and the establishment of Uudenmaan (Figure 10.5). The tendency towards vertical consolidation seems to be only in its beginning. Vattenfall, IVO and several other large Swedish and European companies have focused their interest in Finnish supply, and several factors indicate that extensive take-overs are imminent.

Swedish patterns

Among the Nordic countries, the Swedish design of the competitive public ownership model seems the most open to strategic reconfiguration by commercial design. Swedish electricity industry is characterised by considerable vertical integration and consolidation of the major public and private companies. Sweden's international orientation and the tradition of large-scale industrial configuration seem, despite extensive public ownership, to have a bearing on the electricity industry.

The first half of the 1990s has seen a noticeable structural change in Swedish power industry (Figure 10.6). This has involved a consolidation of the larger companies such as Vattenfall, Sydkraft, Stockholm

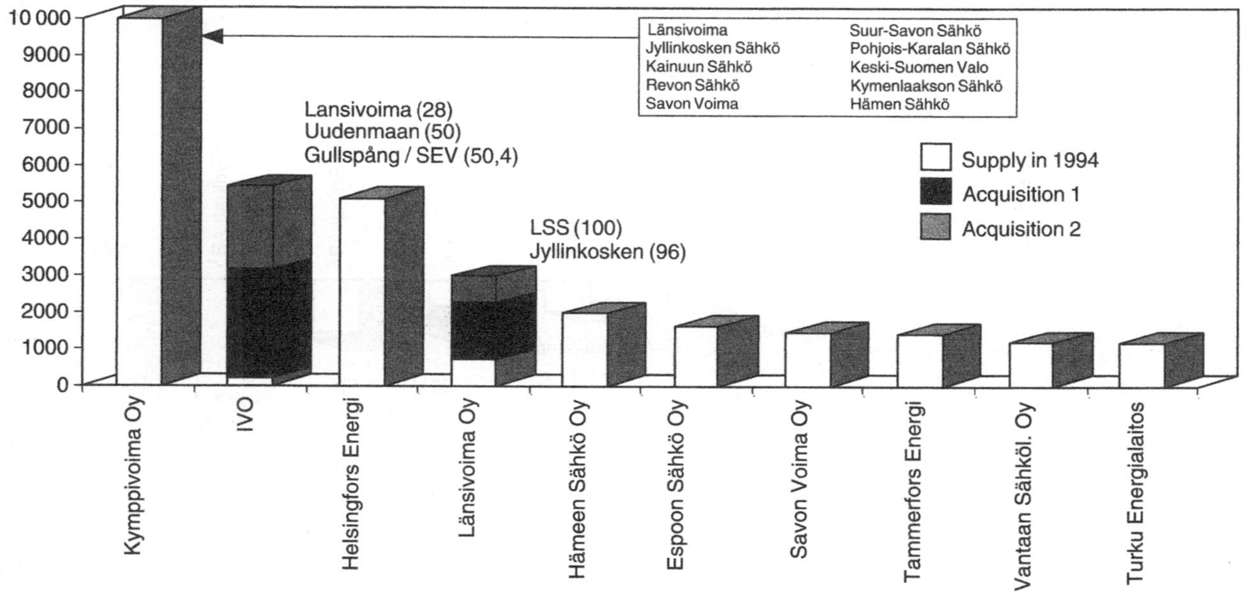

Figure 10.5 The largest Finnish suppliers, including acquisitions, 1991–6 (%)
Source: *Annual Reports* for the biggest suppliers in Finland (1994); TDN Kraft; Reuters Business Briefing.

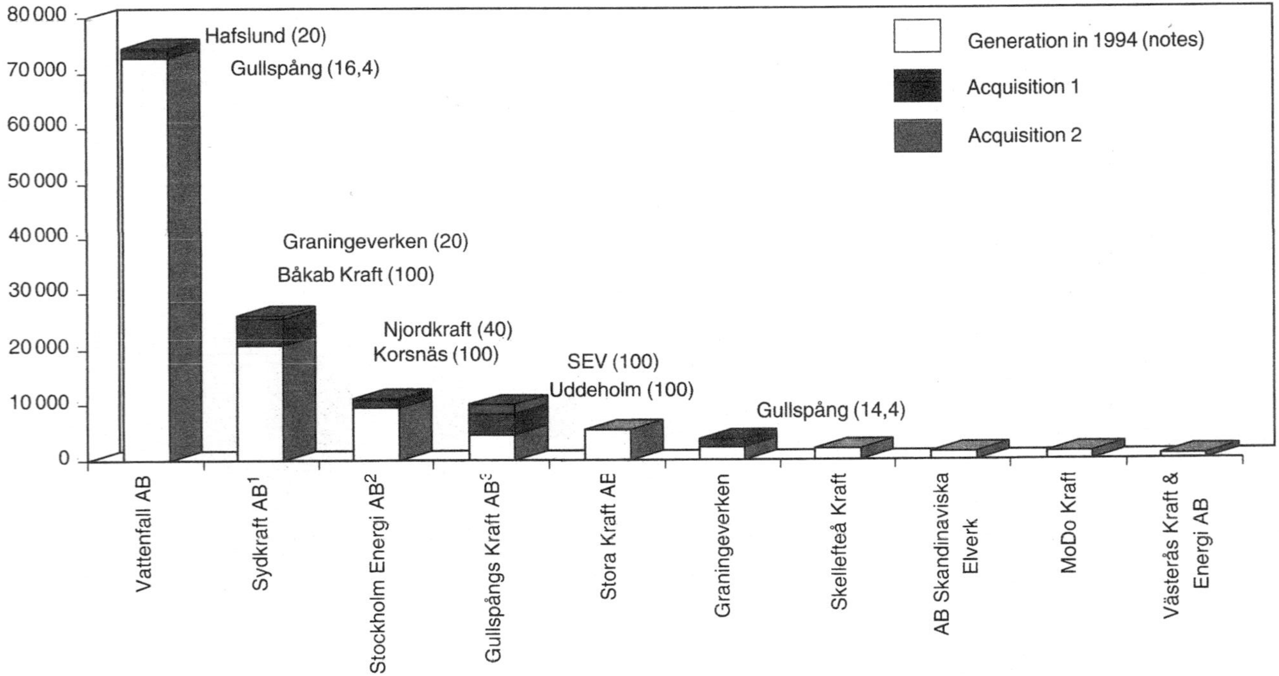

Figure 10.6 The largest Swedish generators in 1994, including acquisitions, 1992–6 (%)
Notes: 1, 3 Reference year is 1991, to be able to include important acquisitions in this period.
2 Reference year is 1992, to be able to include important acquisitions in this period.
Source: Midttun and Handelande (1999) and *Annual Reports* for the 20 biggest suppliers and generators in Finland, Norway and Sweden (1994); TDN Kraft; Reuters Business Briefing.

Energi, Gullspångs Kraft, Stora Kraft and Graningeverken, which have further consolidated their positions both horizontally as well as vertically. One important change in this period was the merger between the second largest generator, Sydkraft AB, and the fifth largest producer, Båkab AB. As of January 1993, Båkab is a fully owned subsidiary of the Sydkraft Group. In April 1996, Sydkraft also bought 20 per cent of the voting shares in Graningeverken AB, a company otherwise controlled by French state company EDF in collaboration with the Versteegh family. Sydkraft has thus far signalled that they wish to be a long-term owner in Graningeverken without decisive influence on its strategy.

As for Graningeverken, in April 1996 it bought 14.4 per cent of the votes in Gullspångs Kraft. In this purchase Graningeverken has signalled that it is primarily interested in a minority position and does not wish to enter into neither any power struggle over Gullspångs Kraft, nor any strategic alliance with the Finnish owners of Gullspångs Kraft.

Another noteworthy merger on the generation side took place in 1992 between the sixth largest producer, Gullspångs Kraft, and the seventh largest, Uddeholm. The new company, Gullspångs Kraft, doubled its production capacity to 8.3 TWh per year. Gullspångs Kraft further increased its volume in June 1996 when the Incentive Group sold its vertically integrated company Skandinaviska Elverk (SEV) to Gullspångs Kraft. SEV has a production capacity of approximately 2000 GWh. With its latest take-over, Gullspångs Kraft has become the third largest generator in Sweden, after Vattenfall and Sydkraft.

Stockholm Energi has also been very active in the Swedish transformation process. In 1993 the company bought electricity generation capacity including six hydropower plants in Dalaelven, and a stake in nuclear-power group Mellansvensk Kraftgrupp from the Korsnäs group. Furthermore, in 1994–5 Stockholm Energi bought a 40 per cent stake in the hydropower generator Njordkraft from the Dutch–Swedish company Akzo Nobel. At the time Njordkraft had an annual generation of about 1000 GWh which, when included, consolidates Stockholm Energi's role as the fourth biggest generator in Sweden.

As far as electricity supply to heavy industry is concerned, we have seen that Sweden has followed a path that differs somewhat from that of its Finnish neighbours. The Swedish path is characterised by two patterns. One pattern implies that power generation is separated from the energy-intensive industrial complex into a separate company but with the same institutional owners and with long-term supply agreements to its previous mother company based on self-cost. The other pattern implies that power generation is sold out to established power companies but very often with long-term supply agreements for the previous mother company at favourable prices. This industrial outsourcing has taken place amongst companies central in the paper and pulp industry like Stora Kraft, MoDo, Korsnäs and SCA (Svenska Cellulose AB). Buyers have often been the large power companies who have in this way further increased their market shares.

The Swedish electricity industry has also been characterised by considerable integration on the supply side. Besides its expansion on the generation side, Sydkraft AB has also been very active in acquiring new supply capacity. In 1992 the company bought Malmö Energi, the fifth largest supplier in Sweden, thereby consolidating its position as Sweden's second largest supplier next to Vattenfall. In addition to Sydkraft's purchase of Båkab AB and Graningeverken as noted above, Sydkraft also bought Örebro Energi from its municipal owners in December 1996. The intention behind this purchase was to strengthen Sydkraft in the expanding mid-Swedish market.

On the supply side Gullspångs Kraft has undergone a total readjustment as the result of two mergers. As of 1990 Gullspångs Kraft's supply activities amounted to only 300 GWh, whereas by 1994 supply had increased to 2.2 TWh. In addition to the acquisition of Uddeholm already mentioned, Gullspångs Kraft in 1992 bought the electricity supply part of paper and pulp company Stora Kraft, adding 1 TWh to its supply capacity. In 1996, Gullspångs Kraft bought the integrated company Skandinaviska Elverk, thereby increasing its supply from 2.2 to 4.5 TWh.

There have also been examples where Swedish industrial customers have engaged actively in electricity trading in strategic alliance with suppliers (Figure 10.7). In 1995 Telge Energi, in co-operation with three of their former customers (Ericsson, Scandia and Astra), formed the trade company Telge Kraft. Telge Kraft now buys its electricity from IVO, Sydkraft and Nord Pool ASA, serving both households and industrial end-users.

As in Norway, the establishment of trade companies plays an increasingly important role in Sweden. The trend lately has been for geographically bordering power companies to established separate units to co-operate on electricity sales and purchasing. Väner Energi is a good example, based on a co-operation between Gullspångs Kraft and Lindköping AB, where Lindköping transfers all of their customers to the new company, while Gullspångs Kraft transfers only customers in Lindköping region. Öresund Kraft, a co-operative venture between Helsingborg Energiverk and Høganses Energi, is another example.

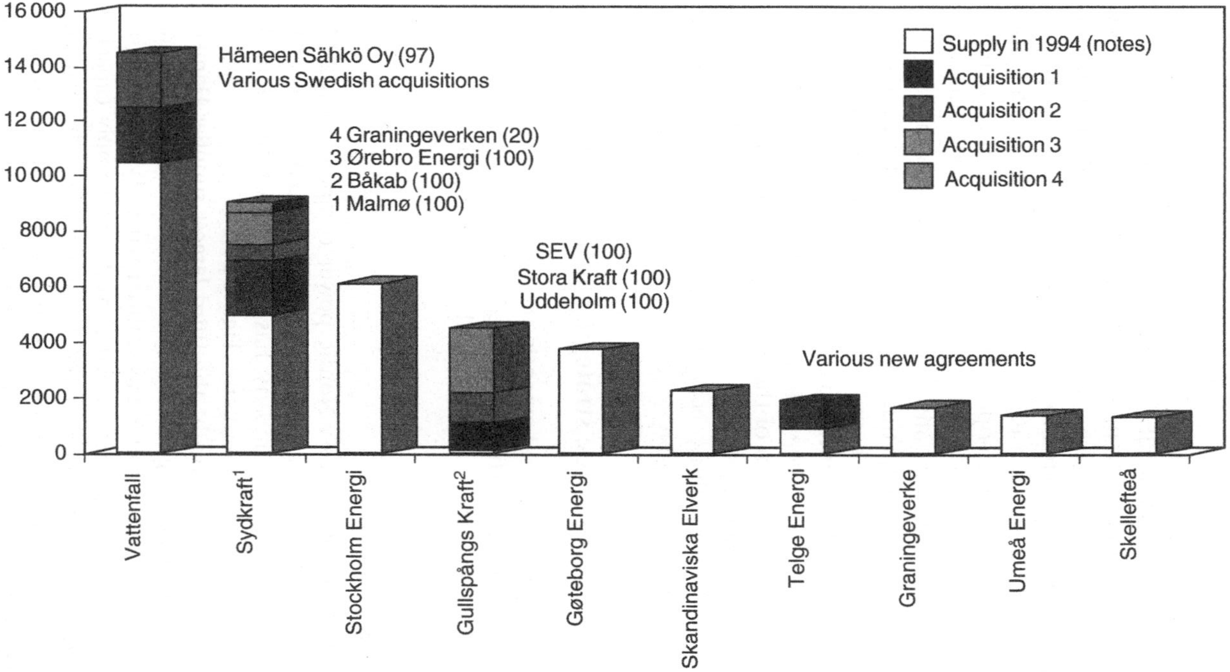

Figure 10.7 The largest Swedish suppliers, 1994, including acquisitions, 1991–6 (%)
Notes: 1 Reference year is 1991, to be able to include important acquisitions in this period.
2 Reference year is 1992, to be able to include important acquisitions in this period.
Source: Midttun and Handelande (1999) and *Annual Reports* for the Swedish companies; TDN Kraft; Reuters Business Briefing.

The Norwegian pattern

The Norwegian pattern has already been discussed in Chapter 2, so there is no need to go into detail here. Suffice it here to note that in Norway concession rules tend to preserve the structure the competitive public ownership model and have contributed to weaker take-over and consolidation activities compared to the other Nordic countries. In this institutional context it has been easier for the politically owned companies to integrate through co-operation rather then through take-overs. This situation is illustrated by the Sørkraft and later the Interkraft group. However, this 'non-capitalistic'-integration has been hard hit by a 'capitalistic'-oriented competition policy. The regulation and competition authorities in Norway have been quite reluctant to accept co-operation, and as a result the Interkraft group has, after a long process involving several rejections, been granted only a three-year exemption from co-operation. The problem of the Norwegian competition legislation is that it is designed according to international directions, and adapted to a private-capitalistic economy, which favours take-over strategies rather than co-operation.

The Nordic state companies: strategic configurations

Through their dominant size and extensive commercial freedom under a pragmatic state ownership, the state-owned Nordic power companies play an important strategic role in the liberalised Nordic electricity markets.

Vattenfall's configuration

As of the mid-1990's the biggest Nordic power company, Vattenfall, stands out as the most advanced in terms of the scale and scope of its strategic configuration. The company has ownership interests in all Nordic countries as well as in Germany (Figure 10.8).

In Finland Vattenfall has bought the third largest supplier Hämeen Sähkö Oy. This take-over has given Vattenfall access to Kymppivoima, the Finnish supplier alliance formed as counterpart to IVO. Through a series of take-overs Vattenfall has gained considerable supply capacity, and become the largest supplier in the Nordic region. This strategy has entailed Vattenfall over the last few years buying a dozen Swedish suppliers, such as Jämtkraft, Solna and Sundbyberg. Vattenfall has also bought up or entered into strategic alliances with several other Nordic companies. The result has been that Vattenfall, during the first half of

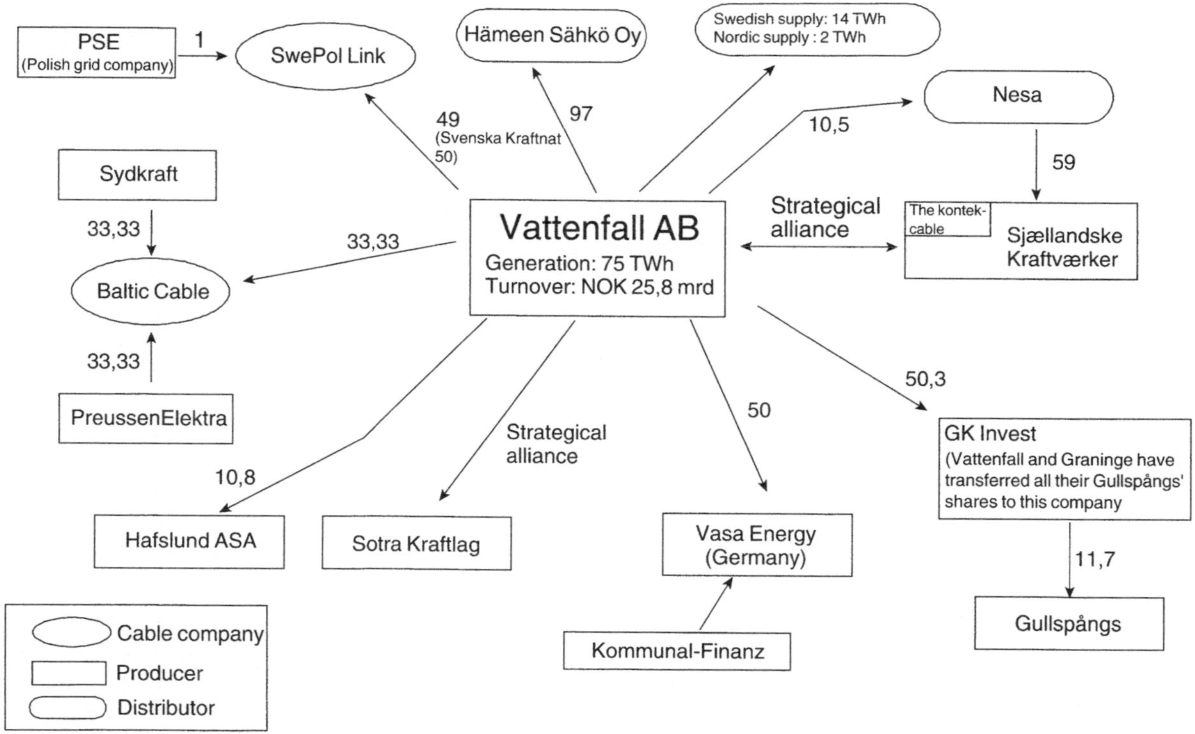

Figure 10.8 Vattenfall's strategic configuration (%)
Source: Midttun (1997) and *Annual Reports*; Reuters News Briefing; TDN Kraft.

the 1990s, managed to increase its vertical integration from 14.5 per cent to about 20 per cent. Further take-overs on the generation side in Sweden have not been politically possible, owing to Vattenfall's dominant position in the Swedish market. However, in light of the new Nordic market and also the emerging liberalisation of the European electricity market, the Swedish authorities seem more open to further integration in the future.

In Finland Vattenfall has bought the third largest supplier Hämeen Sähko Oy. This take-over has given Vattenfall access to Kymppivoima, the Finnish supplier alliance formed as a counterpart to IVO.

Vattenfall has also engaged itself strategically in Denmark through a combination of acquisitions and a strategic alliance with Sjællandske Kraftværker. A possible acquisition of the large East Danish company Nesa's stocks would leave Vattenfall with ownership control over the entire East Danish power system. However, new Danish legislation makes it less interesting for Nesa to sell, and thus effectively undermines Vattenfall's take-over strategy. The Danish alliance provides Vattenfall with the possibility of co-ordinating with Danish electricity generation, as well as providing transit access to Germany. For Sjællandske Kraftværker the alliance means direct access to the Nordic market through Swedish cables.

Norway has concession laws that limit take-over strategies. Therefore Vattenfall has not been able to undertake as ambitious integration strategies as in the Finnish and Swedish markets. Vattenfall's most ambitious acquisition in Norway is an acquisition of 50 per cent of Oslo Energi's supply, and of 20 per cent of Hafslund's shares. Hafslund and Vattenfall earlier worked closely together, among other things in an attempt to take over Skandinaviska Elverk. Besides the Oslo Energi and Hafslund engagements, Vattenfall has entered into a strategic alliance with Sotra Kraftlag, where Sotra, a small Norwegian distributor on the west coast, will work as a sales agent for Vattenfall. The latter is a pattern which Vattenfall wishes to develop further, and is not hindered by the restrictive Norwegian concession laws. Vattenfall was also a contender in the sales of Bergen Lysverker, which was eventually sold to Bergenshalvøens Kommunale Kraftselskap.

Besides the Nordic engagement, Vattenfall is an active participant in North European trading. In this trade, Vattenfall has signed trade agreements and cable co-operation deals with Polish PSE and Preussen-Elektra. As the only Nordic state company Vattenfall is further engaged in building a subsidiary outside the Nordic region. This is in Germany where Vattenfall in co-operation with Kommunal-Finanz has formed Vasa Energy.

Statkraft's configuration

The Norwegian state company Statkraft, until recently the second largest Nordic electricity company, lags far behind its Swedish counterpart, both in size and strategic scope. Until recently, Statkraft's strategic ventures have been of a purely trade-like character. The exception is the take-over of Finnmark Energi in 1993; however, this was intended primarily as a rescue operation to save the company from bankruptcy. Unlike Vattenfall, Statkraft has no supply capacity of its own (Figure 10.9).

Statkraft's major strategic engagement lies in international long-term trade agreements often involving construction of sea cables. Through this trade and the concomitant cable connections Statkraft hopes to establish itself as a North European load manager specialised in co-ordinated management of a Norwegian hydro-based system up against the thermal-based systems on the European continent. Statkraft's long-term trade agreements and cable connections today include recently renegotiated trade agreements with Elsam on Norwegian–Danish cables; trade agreements with PreussenElektra involving a Norwegian–German sea cable, the Viking Cable; and a trade agreement with the Dutch SEP together with other Norwegian parties involving the construction of a Norwegian–Dutch cable, the NorNed-Cable.

After a period of deficit owing to low market prices, tough regulation and hard taxation, Statkraft has recently improved its financial position. The company has now entered two strategic ventures and is pursuing a more dynamic investment policy, one being the acquisition of around 20 per cent of the shares in Swedish Sydkraft and the other a 20 per cent share-holding in Oslo Energi. In a short-term perspective these acquisitions are not sufficient for Statkraft to gain decisive control. Rather, they may serve as part of an information and learning process, where Statkraft gains insight into leading competitor's strategies. In the longer term these investments might be seen as part of the formation of strategic clusters. In this perspective, Statkraft's engagement in Sydkraft might indicate closer ties to PreussenElektra, with whom Statkraft is already committed to extensive trade.

The Oslo Energi involvement might also be part of a more powerful Norwegian alliance aimed at providing greater momentum in the Nordic market. Statkraft is, however, strategically hampered by politically enforced electricity contracts to heavy industry, which tie up approximately 50 per cent of Statkraft's generation. This gives the company a weaker strategic position than the total size of the company's generation would imply.

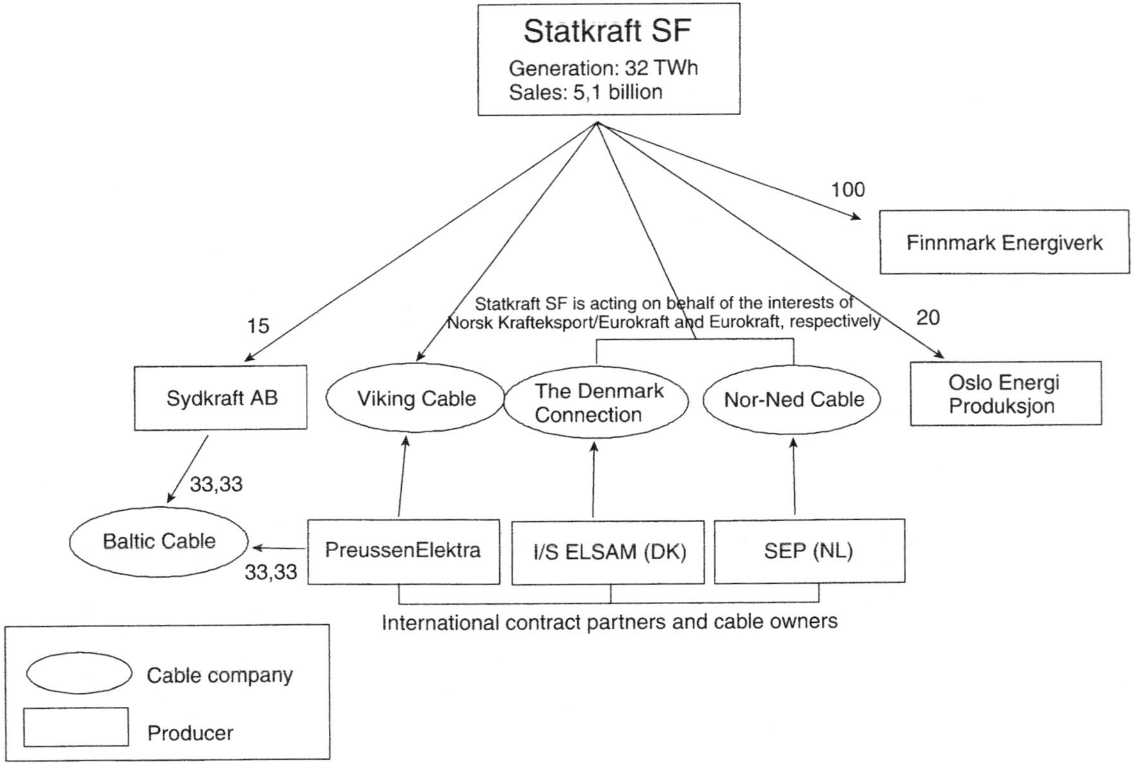

Figure 10.9 Statkraft's strategic configuration (%)
Source: Midttun and Handelande (1999) and *Annual Reports* for the companies; Reuters Business Briefing; TDN Kraft.

Imatran Voima's configuration

Imatran Voima Oy has until recently been the smallest of the Nordic state companies, but the company is now, as a consequence of its dynamic configuration, about to bypass Statkraft (Figure 10.10). In Finland, IVO has changed focus through a series of strategic arrangements, from being a pure wholesaler to becoming involved on the downstream side as well. The company has bought Finland's second largest distributor, Länsivoima Oy, and has also tendered bids for other major distribution companies.

IVO has not only aimed at full acquisitions but has also become involved in ownership alliances with other distributors. An example of this is the new supply company Uudenmaan, where IVO together with the industrial company Paloheimo has consolidated its total supply activities. Uudenmann has thereby become one of the biggest distributors in Finland. After this latest move IVO has become Finland's largest supplier, with a market share of 15 per cent. The motive behind this strong vertical focus seems both to counter Vattenfall's aggressive expansion in Finland, and to secure future outlets for IVO's production.

In the Nordic arena IVO has secured its stake in the Swedish electricity market through the purchase of a 90 per cent share in Gullspångs Kraft. The Gullspångs Kraft involvement has several strategic advantages. Productionwise, Gullspångs Kraft has significant ownership shares in the nuclear power plants Forsmark and Oscarshamn, both directly and indirectly through participation in three consortiums: Värmland Kraft OKG, Värmland Kraft FKG and Mellansvensk Kraftgrupp. Gullspångs Kraft is also the sole owner of Skandinaviska Elverk, which it purchased in fierce competition with Vattenfall/ Hafslund and other major electricity companies.

In addition to its main engagement through Gullspångs Kraft, IVO is also positioned in the Swedish market through its 50 per cent ownership of Birka Kraft, and through a strategic alliance with the other owner, Stockholm Energi (SE). The latter alliance has, together with IVO's ownership position in Gullspångs Kraft, given IVO considerable control over Mellansvensk Kraftgrupp, which in turn owns a significant part of the Forsmark Kraftgrupp AB. IVO has further developed its co-operation with SE in a new company Birka Norden, where Trondheim Energi of Norway is also a participant. Birka Norden will specialise in electricity sales and portfolio management of energy products to larger customers.

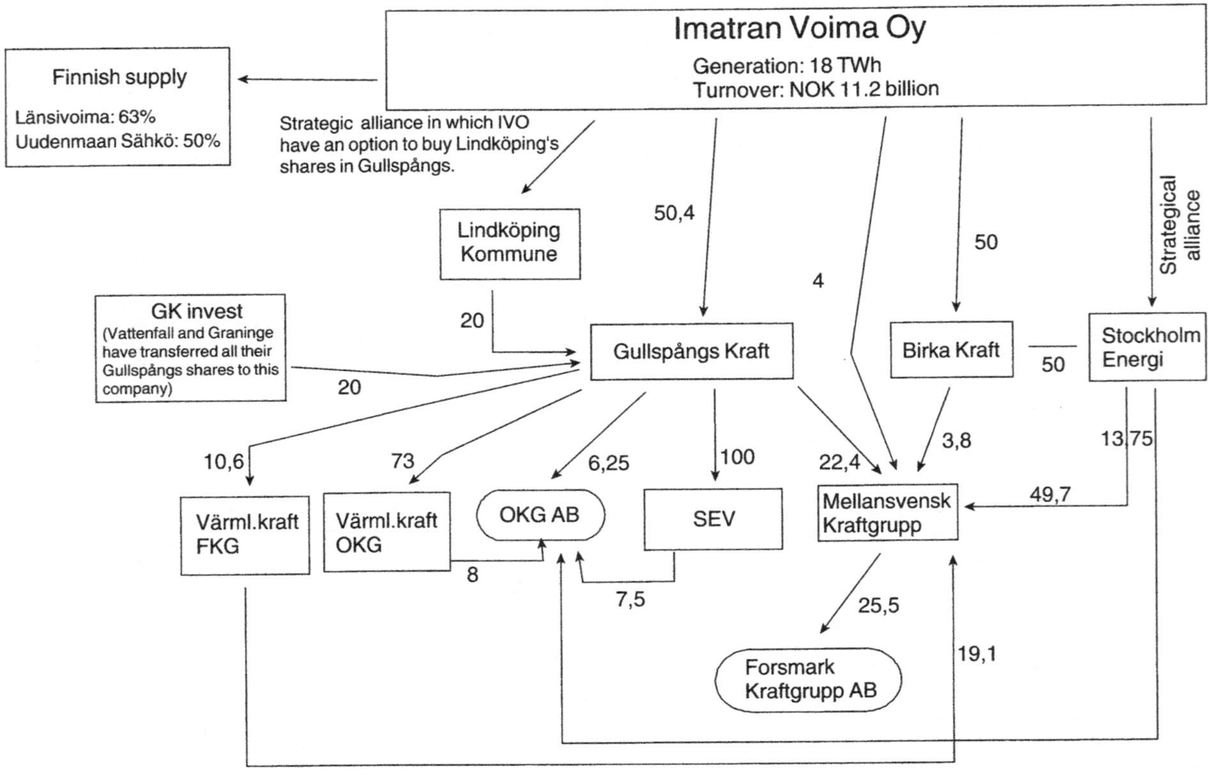

Figure 10.10 Imatran Voimas strategic configuration (%)
Source: Midttun and Handelande (1999) and *Annual Reports*; Reuters Business Briefing; and TDN Kraft.

Following several mergers, Gullspångs Kraft has acquired extensive supply capacity. This includes the take-over of Stora Kraft's supply activities, the previously mentioned take-over of Skandinaviska Elverk, the take-over of Uddeholm and the take-over of Hälsingekraft. This development has turned Gullspångs Kraft into one of Sweden's largest suppliers. Through its controlling position in Gullspångs Kraft, IVO has gained a considerable future sales channel and an important strategic position in the Swedish market.

After a lengthy process of deliberation in Finland, the government decided to merge IVO with state-owned petroleum giant Neste. The new energy company will be dominant in Finland, with a market share of over 50 per cent of the household electricity market and accounting for more than 80 per cent of all petrol and diesel fuel sold in Finland (TDN Kraft 1997). Total turnover for the new merged company will be approximately NOK 75 billion. Its petroleum activity and electricity-generation activity will both account for 37 per cent of the turnover, electricity activity being the more profitable of the two at present. The new company will thus become the second largest energy group in the Nordic countries, after Statoil of Norway.

New configurations in the light of old structural patterns

We have previously characterised the electricity industry of the Nordic countries as a competitive public economy, where state and municipal public ownership has been maintained while exposing the industry to competitive pressure. We have also accounted for structural patterns and historical traditions that, within the competitive public ownership model, make for considerable diversity among the three Nordic countries included in this study. In this concluding section, we shall discuss how the system of competitive public ownership has affected the industrial reconfiguration and how the divergence in Nordic industrial structures and institutional traditions has modulated this development into different strategic paths.

Schematically, the main features of strategic development can be described in the form of a two-dimensional matrix, where the relevant market arena or the geographical market reference is described on one axis, and company orientation is depicted on the other. The relevant market arena may range from local to global competition, with national and regional/North European arenas as intermediary positions. Company orientation may range from public service orientation, via static competitive orientation to dynamic configuration.

Traditionally the electricity sector has been organised and regulated within national and/or local market arenas and with a public service company orientation as described in the lower left-hand corner of Figure 10.11. The natural tendency for a mature international market economy is, however, to move towards the upper right-hand corner, with a global market reference and a company orientation focused on dynamic configuration. In an electricity context, limitations on transmission currently restrict trade to the North European market arena.

There is a tendency for the competitive public economy model to shape the reconfiguration as well as the operation of electricity companies in all three Nordic countries. Compared to the UK private capitalist model, the Nordic reform has been 'soft' on labour (Midttun and Thomas 1998), and mergers and acquisitions have been moderated by public ownership concerns. Most clearly in the Norwegian and Finnish cases, the decentralised municipal ownership still deeply marks the organisation of electricity production industry (Figure 10.12). Despite advanced reconfiguration by some of the major Norwegian and Finnish companies, a great many smaller companies, most of them municipally owned, constitute the main bulk of the power market.

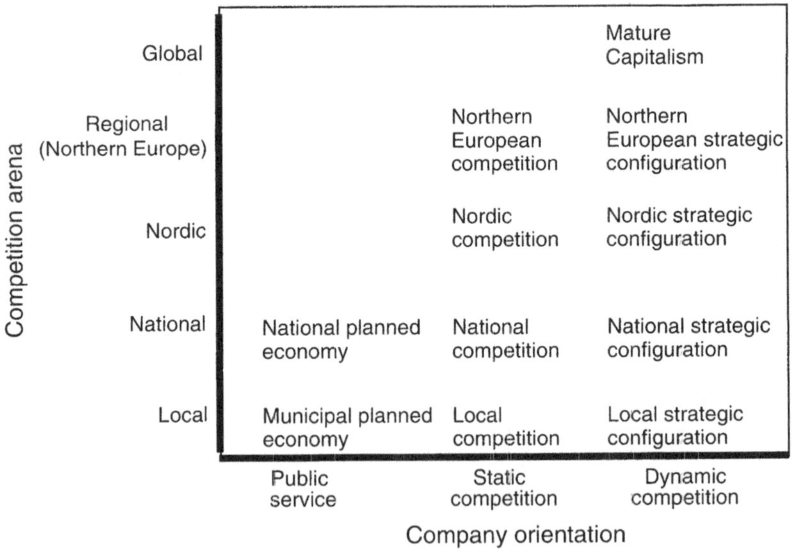

Figure 10.11 Outcome possibilities for challenges facing Nordic power companies
Source: Midttun (1997).

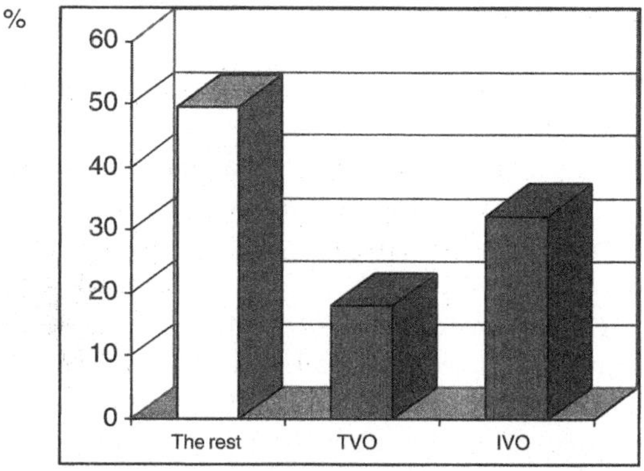

(a) Norway

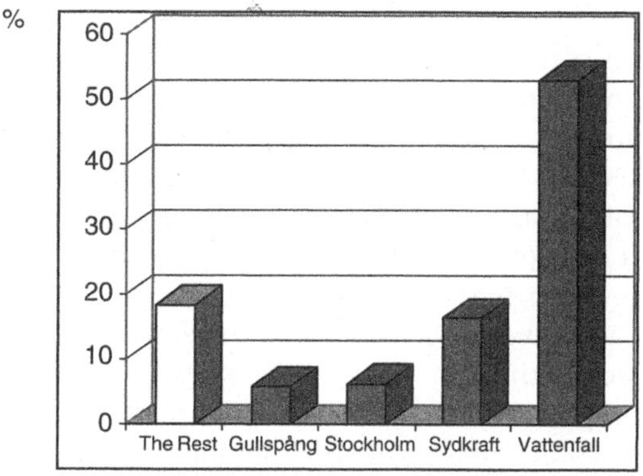

(b) Sweden

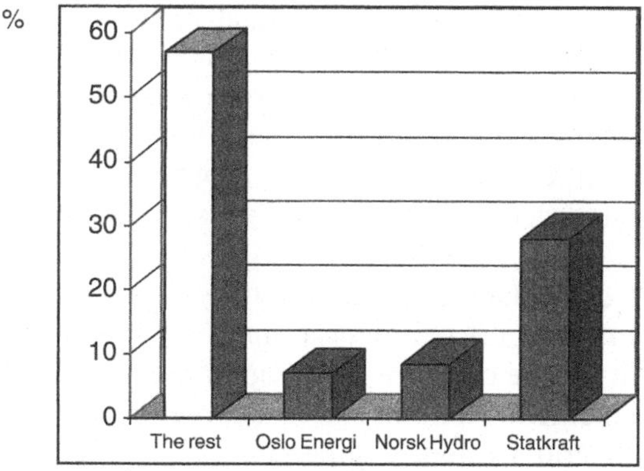

(c) Finland

Figure 10.12 Market shares for the biggest generators in Norway, Sweden and Finland
Source: Gundersen, Berggraf Jacobsen and Olsen (1995).

In the more centralised Swedish system, the share of smaller companies is considerably lower.

On the supply side the organisational pattern is even more dominated by municipal decentralisation. As for generation, this pattern is clearest in Norway and in Finland, but Swedish supply companies are also fairly decentralised.

In terms of the above scheme of strategic configuration, the Nordic market reforms would seem to lead to a *two-track solution*. On one side there are large companies with dynamic Nordic and partially North European strategies. On the other there is a layer of small-scale, locally-oriented 'followers'. There the focus is still largely orientated to public service; loyalty rests primarily with local customers; and strategic perspectives have a local focus.

Norwegian concession rules make the decentralised pattern particularly resistant to take-over strategies of producers and vertically integrated companies. However, in the other Nordic countries there also seems to be considerable inertia towards rapid sell-out of municipal or state companies, although the pressure from tight municipal budgets represents a considerable force working in the opposite direction.

As to the configuration strategies of the largest Nordic electricity companies, we have previously noted the extensive variation that may be traced back both to structural differences under the old regimes and to regulation practice under the process of market liberalisation.

As previously described, Vattenfall established extensive Nordic ownership networks, with ramifications into the central parts of both Danish and Finnish industry. Both before the market reform and relatively quickly after its implementation, Statkraft limited itself to trade expansions. Even though both Vattenfall and Statkraft are 100 per cent state-owned, Vattenfall has clearly been given a greater commercial scope, while the Norwegian version of the competitive public ownership model has been characterised both by more extreme competitive exposure and a stronger obligation to serve as an instrument of industrial policy.

Norway's deregulation was followed by a combination of dramatic falls in the market price, a radical annulment of Statkraft's sales contracts except for the contracts to energy-intensive industry, the maintenance of a planned economy based tax regime and the expropriation of Statkraft's grid without compensation. As a result of all this, the company faced an extensive deficit in the period 1992–4, and thus lacked sufficient capital to justify any offensive take-over strategy (Figure 10.13).

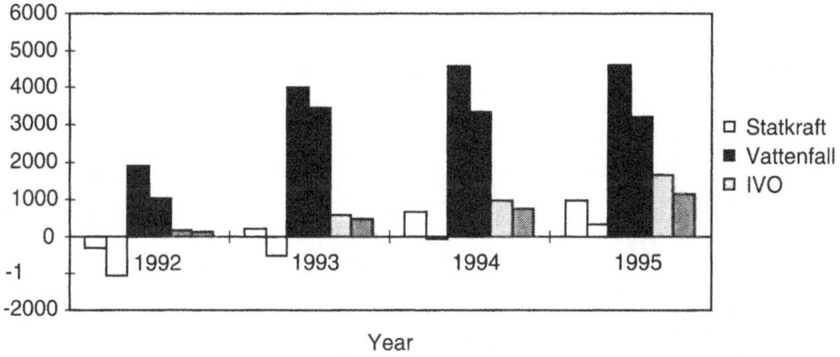

Figure 10.13 Result and taxation of state companies, 1992–5
Source: Midttun (1997) and the companies' *Annual Reports* for the years 1992–5.

Compared to Statkraft, conditions for Vattenfall and IVO were more favourable, and allowed them a more dynamic strategic position. When the Swedish market was liberalised five years after the Norwegian, Vattenfall never found itself exposed to market competition as Statkraft had been during the early Norwegian reform period, so it was able to avoid a low-price shock. Furthermore, the Swedish government did not annul Vattenfall's sales contracts, but allowed the contractual parties to enter into a gradual renegotiation process (Midttun and Summerton 1998). In addition, Sweden has practised more commercial fiscal regulations applying, as a starting point, real surplus rather than planned economy norms as the basis for taxation. The situation of IVO resembles that of Vattenfall. The Finnish authorities have practised a considerably milder form of competitive exposition by allowing IVO to maintain extensive control over electricity export and import through its international grid connection operations. IVO also profited from the sale of its grid company.

Large European companies in the Nordic market

Besides the Nordic companies that have already been discussed, the picture of large-scale configurations in the Nordic power market is characterised by the engagement of major European concerns and the beginnings of oil-company involvement in the Nordic electricity market (Figure 10.14).

Among the large non-Nordic companies, the German PreussenElektra, with the VEBA concern behind it, represents a combination of electricity

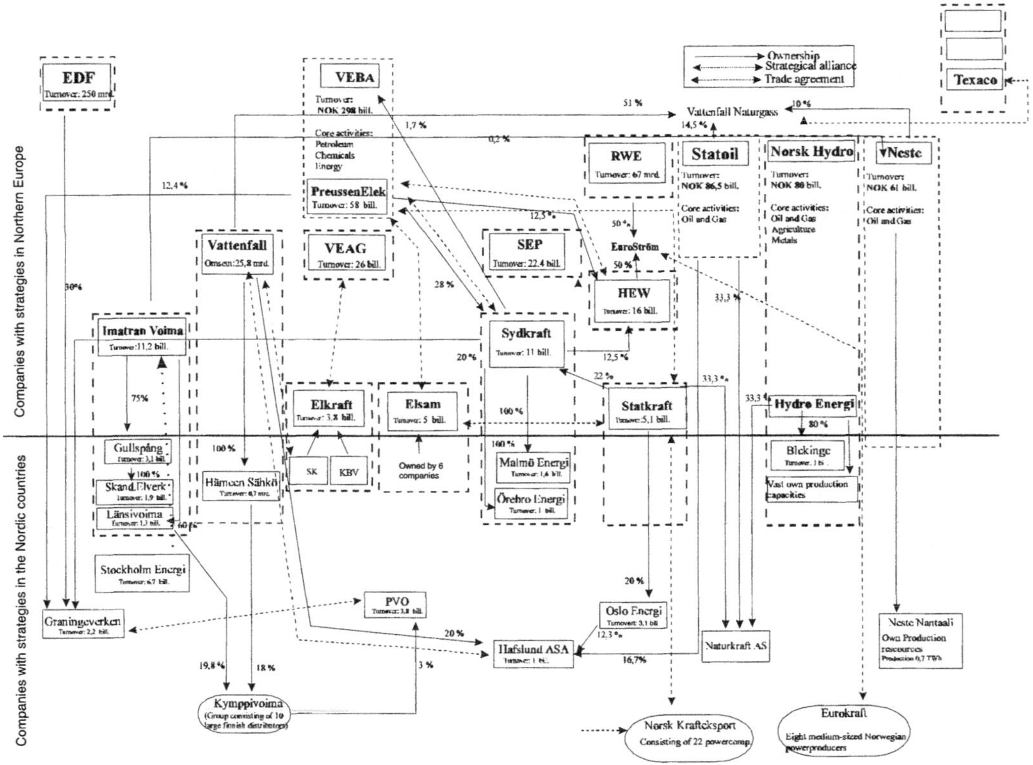

Figure 10.14 The configuration of power companies with a Nordic ambition
Source: Midttun (1997).

competence, complementary energy strategies and formidable resources that makes it a powerful and dynamic player in the North European market. The company already has strong linkages to the Nordic power market through mutual owner and trade engagements with Sydkraft, and through extensive long-term trade agreements with Statkraft and cable agreements with Statnett. With PreussenElektra's large ownership share (28 per cent) in Sydkraft and a similar ownership share of 1.7 per cent from Sydkraft in VEBA, the German concern is poised to integrate extensive German–Swedish energy resources in the North European energy market. This group also internalises considerable transport capacity and trade between the Nordic peninsula and continental Europe.

With 5 per cent ownership share in the Eurostrom cable together with Hamburgische Electricitäts-Werke (HEW) Germany's largest power producer *RWE Energie AG* is also directly involved in the Nordic power market. The Eurocable contract is clearly part of an active policy from RWE to gain access to the Nordic market. Here RWE's interests bring it in conflict with PreussenElektra, which wishes to monopolise Nordic power supply to the German market. Both PreussenElektra and RWE were rivals for shares in HEW when portions of the company were put up for sale. RWE here lost out to PreussenElectra and Sydkraft.

With its key role in central Europe, RWE also provides a link between the North European and the Central European markets and points towards an all-European strategy. The positioning within such a strategy is illustrated by the collaboration between EDF and RWE in their joint acquisition of 20 per cent of the shares of the Swiss holding company Motor Columbus, which in turn is a majority owner of the power company ATEL.

With its 29 per cent engagement in Graningeverken, where Electricité de France (EDF) controls the company in collaboration with the Versteegh family, EDF is also actively engaged in the Nordic power market. EDF's control of Graningeverken came about after rivalry with PreussenElektra, which has retained 12.4 per cent of the ownership engagement in Graningeverken. EDF's engagement in Graningeverken is still modest compared to PreussenElektra's Sydkraft engagement, but with EDF's total resources and central role in the European power market, considerable resources may be mobilised behind further expansion of this configuration, which may become the core of a French–Nordic cluster within the Nordic/North European power market. A strategic alliance between Graningeverken and PVO may indicate possibilities for a French–Swedish–Finnish cluster. If PVO changes character from industrial self-supply to a more dynamic Nordic market engagement, it can become an actor with considerable resources.

On the list of larger European actors involved in the Nordic power market we also find the Dutch SEP/*Dutch Electricity Board (SEP)*. This company now has a trade agreement with the Norwegian Power Export Consortium (Norsk Krafteksport) for start-up of power exchange in the year 2001. SEP, which is a collaborative alliance between the four Dutch regional production companies, is responsible for planning Dutch electricity production and co-ordinates production and transmission of electricity in the Netherlands. The Netherlands has been a pioneer on the continent in adapting to a liberal market economy. The Dutch authorities have for some time sought to build up the company to prepare for future European competition. The four production companies in the SEP alliance have, however had difficulties in reaching common agreement on this issue.

Oil companies in the electricity market

The Nordic and other oil companies are also poised for active involvement in the electricity market, on a Nordic and a European basis. This indicates that the actors expect significant synergy effects from a broader engagement in energy activities by building bridges over the traditionally separate markets for oil/gas and for electricity. The role as combined energy deliverers in flexible energy systems will, for instance, enable them to utilise the energy carriers which at any time are most advantageous, with the potential of economic gains.

Norsk Hydro ranks among the foremost strategic players in the Nordic power market. As a combined power generator, large-scale industrial power consumer and oil company, Hydro may optimise a combined multiple-carrier production and consumption/sales system. The company is among the most important oil and gas companies in Norway. It is also Norway's second largest power generator, as well as being a significant actor on the world market in fertilisers, light metals and oil refining products.

With a basis in the company's oil, gas and hydropower resources, it is natural for Norsk Hydro to work towards an integrated energy concept. Together with Texaco, Hydro Energy thus sells flexible heat services to large consumers, flexibly based on electricity or on oil, according to price. With its multiple energy-related engagements, Norsk Hydro is well placed with respect to harvesting scale and synergy advantages, and may work with several parallel energy strategies – with the resources to integrate them if necessary. Until now Norsk Hydro has not been expanding through acquisitions. Its most important Nordic investment has been the acquisition of 80 per cent of the municipal Swedish supply company Blekinge Energi AB. This venture was part of Norwegian Hydro's sales of power to industrial and household consumers in Sweden.

Statoil has recently become actively involved in the Nordic power market and now controls 16.7 per cent of the shares of Hafslund, a private Norwegian electricity producer, and one-third of the shares of Naturkraft, which together with Statkraft and Norsk Hydro has been planning to start utilising gas resources for electricity generation. The company also has experience from the electricity spot market, where they have bought electricity for their oil platforms. Statoil is now in the process of defining itself more as an energy company than as solely an oil and gas producer and, like Norsk Hydro, it is clearly aiming to become a total supplier of energy. Even if the company lacks Norsk Hydro's broad experience from the electricity sector, Statoil has the resources to become a powerful and dynamic actor in the energy markets of the Nordic countries and Northern Europe. These resources lie in the company's extensive surplus, their large gas resources and their broad presence in several European markets. Like Hydro, Statoil controls a sizeable gas network, which constitutes an alternative transport system to the electricity grid.

There is an evident complementarity between the oil and gas involvement and the hydropower activities undertaken by the Norwegian state through Statoil and Statkraft, respectively, with a considerable potential for a powerful positioning in the European market. However, an alliance between the two state companies would probably give rise to objections by market regulators. This means that Statoil can be expected to search for other acquisitions and strategic partnerships in order to develop its role in the North European power market.

Like the other oil and gas companies, *Neste Petroleum* is developing an integrated energy perspective, working with parallel electricity and gas strategies directed at the Nordic market. In January 1997, Neste bought up 10 per cent of Vattenfall's natural gas company Vattenfall Naturgass AB when Vattenfall sold 49 per cent of its shares. The other buyers were Ruhrgas (14.5 per cent), the Danish Oil and Gas Consortium (10 per cent) and Statoil (14.5 per cent). Neste saw this involvement as part of a strategy to develop an integrated gas market in the Nordic countries.

In addition to the Nordic oil and gas companies, the *big multinational oil companies* with headquarters outside of the Nordic countries may also engage in the Nordic electricity market. Royal Dutch Shell has several times stated that it intends to become involved in electricity markets. Shell has already considerable competence in electricity from its activities in developing countries. Also Esso/Exxon is into electricity in Asia, but does not seem to have wider ambitions to engage more globally in electricity. As of today, Exxon controls about 7500 MW thermal-based electricity generation capacity. In line with the other oil companies, Texaco has shown interest in the electricity sector and is, together with Norsk Hydro, combining electricity and oil as a basis for its services in the heating market. What characterises all the multinational oil companies are their huge resources, both financially and in terms of competence. A decision to engage in the North European electricity market from their side might therefore lead to very forceful action.

Concluding comments

The broad international participation in the Nordic electricity market indicates that dynamic configurations with wide-ranging multinational aims are about to become a strategic reality. Here the competitive public ownership model has clear advantages and disadvantages. The advantages, seen from the side of society, are that it enables a 'softer' transition than under private capitalist governance. Employees especially, but also society at large, will probably be better served by this, as the transformation costs to a larger extent are integrated within the sector. Public ownership may also represent a strength as a guarantee against hostile take-overs and short-sighted profit orientation without ability to develop long-term industrial strategies. The disadvantage of this model, in a business strategy perspective, is that the public ownership may create unclear mandates as to when to take political and when to take commercial concerns into account. Public ownership may also hinder necessary organisational adaptation to international competition, and thus limit the dynamic scope of the companies.

While the competitive public economy probably is a useful construction, as seen from the perspective of closed and static competition, it is far more debatable from an open and dynamic point of view, particularly when it is as strongly locally anchored as in the Nordic countries. The participation of multinational actors and the competitive pressure across national boundaries points to a more integrated European competitive arena. As national regulatory regimes themselves become part of this competition, they are likely to come under pressure for standardisation. Confronted with international dynamic competition, the Nordic tradition of 'societal' management may have to be anchored in new ways if the competitive position of Nordic electricity industry is to be maintained. This applies to Norway in particular, as it is here that the political ties locking industry into a given structure are the strongest.

Bibliography

Andersen, P.C. and Høisveen, P.H. (1995), *Energiloven, med forskrifter og kommentarer,* 2 edition, Oslo: Høisveen and Andersen.

Averch, H. and Johnson, L.L. (1962), 'Behavior of the firm under regulatory constraint', *American Economic Review,* 52, pp. 1053–69.

Brown, L., Einhorn, M. and Volgelsang, I. (1989), *Incentive Regulation: A research report,* 89–3: Federal Energy Regulatory Commission, November.

Bråten, J. (1996), *To metoder for effektivitetsmåling i eldistribusjon,* ECON-Report 48/96, Commissioned by the Norwegian Research Council and the Norwegian Electricity Federation.

Buchanan, J.M., Tullison, R.D. and Tullock, G. (eds) (1980), *Towards a Theory of Rent-Seeking Society,* College Station: Texas A&M University Press.

Charnes, A. and Cooper, W.W. (1985), 'Preface to Topics in Data Envelopment Analysis', *Annals of Operation Research,* 2, pp. 59–94.

Davis, M. and Magnus, E. (1998), *An International Review of Institutional Reform in the Electricity Sector,* Commissioned by the Government of the Republic of Namibia, Ministry of Mines and Energy, submitted by SADELEC (Southern African Development through Electricity), Johannesburg.

ECON (1994), *Virkning av langsiktige utvekslingsavtaler med kontinentet (Impact of long-term export–import contracts).* Report 325/94. Commissioned by the Norwegian Research Council.

ECON (1995a), *Effektiv Distribusjon.* Report 313/95. Commissioned by the Norwegian Electricity Federation.

ECON (1995b), *Regulering av utenlandskhandelen med kraft* (Regulation of international electricity trade). Report 302/95. Commissioned by the Norwegian Research Council and the Norwegian Electricity Federation.

Energidata (1995), *NM-95 for nettvirksomhet, Distribusjonsnett,* Energiforsyningens Fellesorganisasjon, Lysaker.

Farrell, M.J. (1957), 'The Measurement of Productive Efficiency', *Journal of the Royal Statistical Society,* 120, pp. 449–60.

Fredriksen, O. (1994), *Analyse av effektiviteten i regionalnett – hovedprosjekt,* ED 94-286, Energidata, Trondheim.

Gröner, H. (1980), 'Regulation and efficiency in the electric utility industry', *Zeitschrift für die gesamte Staatwissenschaft,* 136, pp. 556–75.

Gundersen, E., Berggraf Jacobsen, O.M. and Olsen, P.I. (1996), *Markedsmakt i et deregulert nordisk kraftmarked,* Research Report, 2/1996, Norwegian School of Management, Sandvika.

Halseth, A. (1998), 'Market Power in the Nordic electricity market', *Utilities Policy* 7, pp. 259–68.

Hirschmann, A.O. (1970), *Exit, Voice and Loyalty Responses to Decline in Firms, Organisations and States,* Cambridge, MA: Harvard University Press.

Hope, E., Magnus, E. and Matland, R. (1983), 'Economic Incentives and Public Firm Behavior', *Scandinavian Journal of Economics,* 85 (3), pp. 339–457.

Hope, E. and Strøm, S. (eds) (1992), *Energy Markets and Environmental Issues: a European Perspective*, Oslo: Scandinavian University Press.

Iulo, W. (1961), *Electric Utilities – Cost and Performance*, Pullman: Washington State University Press.

Laffont, J. and Tirole, J. (1993), *A Theory of Incentives in Procurement and Regulation*, Cambridge, MA: MIT Press.

Magnus, E. (1994), *Konkurransenøytrale og effektive monopoler*, ECON Report 313/94. Commissioned by the Research Council of Norway and the Norwegian Electricity Federation, Oslo.

Magnus, E. and Bråten, J. (1996a), *Incentiver til effektivisering i norske everk*, ECON Report 18/96. Commissioned by the Research Council of Norway and the Norwegian Electricity Federation, Oslo.

Magnus, E. and Bråten, J. (1996b), *Om kostnadseffektivitet og reguleringsprinsipper for monopoler innen distribusjon av kraft*, ECON Report 17/96. Commissioned by the Research Council of Norway and the Norwegian Electricity Federation, Oslo.

Magnus, E. and Bråten, J. (1996c), *Mål og beslutningsstrukturer i norske distribusjonsverk*, ECON Report 36/96. Commissioned by the Norwegian Water and Energy Resources Administration, Norway.

Magnus, E. and Davis, M. (1999), 'Managing Social and Environmental Obligations in Liberalised Markets', in *The New Power Markets: Corporate Strategies for Risk and Reward*, London: Risk Books.

Midttun, A. (1995), *Forhandlingsbasert omstilling fra plan til marked: Det store hamskiftet i norsk kraftindustri, Sosiologi i dag*, 4, Novus Forlag.

Midttun, A. (1996), 'Electricity Liberalisation Policies in Norway and Sweden', *Energy Policy*.

Midttun, A. (1997a), 'Strategisk tilpasning under offentlig konkurranseøkonomi', Report 3, *Centre for Electricity Studies, Norwegian School of Management*.

Midttun, A. (1997b), 'Strategic Challenges and Institutional Patterns: Nordic Heavy Industry's Adaptation to Marketoriented Electricity Reform', *Scandinavian Economic History Review*.

Midttun, A. (ed.) (1997), *European Electricity Systems in Transition*, London: Elsevier Science.

Midttun, A., Garsjø, P.O. and Joa, T. (1993), 'Norsk Kraftforsyning mellom Marked, Hierarki og Nettverk II: Et institusjonelt søkelys på markedsreformens politiske økonomi': BI *Working Paper*, Sandvika.

Midttun, A. and Handelande, J. (1999), 'The Nordic Public Ownership Model under Transition to Market Economy: The Case of Electricity', Report 2 from the Norwegian School of Management, Centre for Energy and Environment.

Midttun, A. and Køber, M. (1994), 'Market Structure and Price Structure' (in Norwegian), *Working Paper 38*, Norwegian School of Management.

Midttun, A., Svindland, E. and Andreassen, E. (1997), *Strategic Aspects of Power Trade under Institutional Pluralism*, Report 4/1997, Centre for Electricity Studies, Norwegian School of Management.

Midttun, A. and Summerton, J. (1998), 'Loyalty or Competition? A Comparative Analysis of Norwegian and Swedish Electricity Distributors' Adaptation to Market Reform, *Energy Policy*, February.

Midttun, A. and Thomas, S. (1998), 'Theoretical Ambiguity and the Weight of Historical Heritage': A Comparative study of the British and Norwegian Liberalisation, *Energy Policy.*

Nordel (1996), Statistics, Finland.

Nord Pool (1997), 'Historical prices; Norway and Sweden', Internet at ⟨http://www.nordpool.no⟩

NOU (1985), 9 *Energy Law Issues*, Oslo.

NVE (1997), Retningslinjer for inntektsrammen for overføringstariffene, Oslo.

NVE (1990), Korttidsstatistikken (Shortterm statistics), Oslo.

Olsen, P. (1994), 'Tacit Collusion in the Deregulated Norwegian Electricity Market', Masters thesis, Norwegian School of Management (BI), Sandvika, February.

Pollitt, M.G. (1995), *Ownership and Performance in Electric Utilities*: The International Evidence on Privatization and Efficiency, Oxford: Oxford University Press.

Reuters Business Briefing, On-Line Database.

Rotemberg, J.J. and Saloner, G. (1989), 'The Cyclical Behaviour of Strategic Inventories', *Quarterly Journal of Economics*, 104, February, pp. 73–91.

Sandmo, A. and Hagen, K.P. (1992), *Offentlig politikk og private incitamenter*, Bergen: Tano AS.

Schmalensee, R. and Willig, R. (1989), *Handbook of industrial organisation*, II, Amsterdam: North Holland.

Shleifer, A. (1985), 'A Theory of Yardstick Competition', *RAND Journal of Economics*, 16, pp. 319–27.

Staiger, R.W. and Wolak, F.A. (1992), 'Collusive Pricing with Capacity Constraints in the Presence of Demand Uncertainty', *RAND Journal of Economics*, 23, Summer, pp. 203–20.

Statistiska Centralbyrån (1991), Översikt över elförsörjningen, Stockholm.

Statnett Marked (1996), 'Spot prices 1985–96', Oslo: Statnett Publications.

Sørgaard, L. (1993), *Produsentsamarbeide i kraftsektoren*, SNF, Report to Konkurransetilsynet.

TDN Kraft (1997), On-Line Database and Newsservice, 1995–98.

Thue, Lars (1995), 'Electricity Rules: The Formation and Development of the Nordic Electricity Regimes', in Arne Kaijser and Marika Hedin (eds), *Nordic Energy Systems: Historical Perspectives and Current Issues*, Canton, MA: Science History Publications.

Norwegian Parliamentary Documents

The Ministry of Oil and Energy (1985) *Energy Law Issues*, NOU No. 9. The State Printing Office, Oslo.

The Ministry of Oil and Energy (1988–9) *The Energy Law*, Government Bill, Ot prp. No. 73.

The Energy and Industry Committee (1988–9) *Withdrawal of the Energy Law*, Parliamentary Treatment of Government Bill, Innst O, No. 93.

The Energy and Industry Committee (1989–90) *The Energy Law*, Parliamentary Treatment of Government Bill, Innst O, No. 67.

Index

The manufacturer's authorised representative in the EU is Springer Nature Customer Service Centre GmbH, Europaplatz 3, 69115 Heidelberg, Germany. If you have any concerns regarding our products, please contact ProductSafety@springernature.com

Printed and bound by CPI Group (UK) Ltd, Croydon, CR0 4YY

14/10/2026

02233150-0009